DIVINE FOREKNOWLEDGE

Four Views

WITH CONTRIBUTIONS BY
Gregory A. Boyd, David Hunt,
William Lane Craig, Paul Helm

EDITED BY
JAMES K. BEILBY
& PAUL R. EDDY

InterVarsity Press
Downers Grove, Illinois

InterVarsity Press
P.O. Box 1400, Downers Grove, IL 60515-1426
World Wide Web: www.ivpress.com
E-mail: mail@ivpress.com

InterVarsity Press® is the book-publishing division of InterVarsity Christian Fellowship/USA®, a student movement active on campus at hundreds of universities, colleges and schools of nursing in the United States of America, and a member movement of the International Fellowship of Evangelical Students. For information about local and regional activities, write Public Relations Dept., InterVarsity Christian Fellowship/USA, 6400 Schroeder Rd., P.O. Box 7895, Madison, WI 53707-7895, or visit the IVCF website at <www.ivcf.org>.

Scripture quotations, unless otherwise noted, are from the New Revised Standard Version of the Bible, copyright 1989 by the Division of Christian Education of the National Council of the Churches of Christ in the USA. Used by permission. All rights reserved.

Cover illustration: Tatsuhiko Shimada/Photonica

ISBN 0-8308-2652-1

Printed in the United States of America ∞

Library of Congress Cataloging-in-Publication Data

Divine foreknowledge: four views/edited by James K. Beilby & Paul R. Eddy; with contributions by William Lane Craig . . . [et al].
    p. cm.
    Includes bibliographical references.
    ISBN 0-8308-2652-1 (paper: alk. paper)
    1. God—Omniscience. 2. Free will and determinism. I. Beilby, James K. II. Eddy, Paul
R. III. Craig, William Lane.
    BT131.D575 2001
    231'.4—dc21   2001039355

20	19	18	17	16	15	14	13	12	11	10	9	8	7	6	5	4	3	2	1
17	16	15	14	13	12	11	10	09	08	07	06	05	04	03	02	01			

Dedicated to our wives,
Michelle Beilby and Kelly Eddy

CONTENTS

Introduction _____ 9

1 THE OPEN-THEISM VIEW   *Gregory A. Boyd* _____ 13

   A Simple-Foreknowledge Response _____ 48

   A Middle-Knowledge Response_____ 55

   An Augustinian-Calvinist Response_____ 61

2 THE SIMPLE-FOREKNOWLEDGE VIEW   *David Hunt* _____ 65

   An Open-Theism Response _____ 104

   A Middle-Knowledge Response_____ 109

   An Augustinian-Calvinist Response_____ 114

3 THE MIDDLE-KNOWLEDGE VIEW   *William Lane Craig* _____ 119

   An Open-Theism Response _____ 144

   A Simple-Foreknowledge Response _____ 149

   An Augustinian-Calvinist Response_____ 155

4 THE AUGUSTINIAN-CALVINIST VIEW   *Paul Helm* _____ 161

   An Open-Theism Response _____ 190

   A Simple-Foreknowledge Response _____ 195

   A Middle-Knowledge Response_____ 202

Glossary _____ 207

Subject Index_____ 215

Scripture Index _____ 219

Introduction

Throughout the history of the church, Christians have discussed the nature and content of God's foreknowledge. For instance, one finds Augustine wrestling with this question in part three of his famous work *Freedom of the Will*. In recent years, the debate over the foreknowledge of God has come to be one of the most controversial theological issues disputed among evangelicals. Indeed, some claim it is the most heated controversy to hit evangelicalism since the inerrancy debate of the 1970s. One distinctive aspect of this contemporary debate is that it is taking place not only in elite theological circles, but also in churches, on campuses, at denominational conferences and in popular Christian magazines.

To understand why this debate has assumed the proportions it has within contemporary evangelicalism, one must realize that the question is not simply about the nature of divine foreknowledge. Rather, for many this issue has become a theological lightning rod, largely due to the implications this question has for other areas of theology. At least three fundamental theological areas are involved in this debate. First, and most immediately, there is the question of the nature and mode of God's foreknowledge. Second, in the eyes of many, there are important implications for the question of the nature of divine sovereignty (i.e., whether God's sovereignty operates in a general or in a particular and meticulous fashion). Finally, there are direct implications for the question of the nature of human freedom (i.e., whether humans possess compatibilistic or libertarian freedom). Further, each of these theological questions plays an essential role in the articulation of a stance on the "problem of evil."

The primary catalyst for the contemporary discussion has been the recent debate concerning what has come to be called *open theism*. According to its adherents, God knows the future partly as a realm of possibilities, not exclusively as settled facts. Much of the contemporary foreknowledge debate remains centered on the openness controversy, but this controversy has also fueled the debate that has existed for centuries among more traditional Christian theologians. Though many laypersons remain unaware of this fact, Christian theologians throughout church history have entertained a diversity of opinions on the nature and content of God's foreknowledge. This book has been written to bring clarity to the contemporary discussion by presenting the four major views that scholars in the evangelical community embrace. These four views are the open view, the simple-foreknowledge view, the middle-knowledge view and the Augustinian-Calvinist view.

Gregory Boyd begins by defending the open view. This view has been relatively rare in church history, but it is gaining popularity today in certain sectors of evangelicalism. Unlike the other three views represented in this book, the open view holds that the future is partly open to God, for God cannot foreknow the decisions that free agents shall make. God is omniscient, this view insists, for he perfectly knows all reality. But the reality God perfectly knows is partly composed of possibilities, "maybes." Hence, while God knows much of the future as settled—for he can sovereignly decide to settle whatever he wishes—he knows some of the future as a "maybe." Boyd argues that only this view can make good sense out of passages in the Bible in which God changes his mind, regrets decisions he makes, speaks of the future in conditional terms, expresses surprise or disappointment over what transpires, or tests people's hearts "to know" what they shall do.

The second essay is by David Hunt, who defends the simple-foreknowledge view. Scholars debate how traditional or nontraditional the simple-foreknowledge view is, but unquestionably it has a number of learned advocates today. Those who believe in simple foreknowledge maintain that God "simply" knows what is going to come to pass. Unlike the open view, the simple-foreknowledge view rejects the notion that any aspect of the future is open from God's perspective. Unlike the middle-knowledge view, this view does not hold that God chose which future to bring about based on his knowledge of how free agents would act in any "possible world." And unlike the Augustinian-Calvinist view, this view doesn't hold that God knows the future because he preordains it. God simply knows what free agents shall do, not what they would do in different circumstances or what he ordains them to do. According to Hunt, this view is consistent with what Scripture says about God's foreknowledge and is the most philosophically defensible position to hold.

The third essay is by William Lane Craig, who defends the middle-knowledge, or Molinist, view. Scholars debate the extent to which this view was presupposed by various theologians in church history (some interesting current research suggests that Jacobus Arminius held a position similar to Molinism), but the view was first formalized by Luis de Molina in the sixteenth century, hence the name Molinism. In the middle-knowledge view, God knows not only what shall come to pass, he knows what would have come to pass if he had chosen to create any other world—this is his "middle" knowledge. Indeed, God chose to create the world he did because he foresaw that this exact world best attained his objectives for creation while preserving the freedom of creatures. Unlike the open view, therefore, this view allows no open-ended possibilities. Unlike the simple-foreknowledge view, this view maintains that God knows counterfactuals of creaturely freedom (namely, what agents would do in other circumstances). And unlike the Augustinian-Calvinist view, this view does not hold that God knows what agents do because he preordains their behavior. He simply has an innate eternal knowledge of how free agents would behave in all possible circumstances. Craig believes that this perspective has scriptural warrant and is able to incorporate both the insights about God's sovereignty held by Calvinists and insights about human freedom and responsibility held by Arminians.

The final essay, by Paul Helm, defends the Augustinian-Calvinist, or Reformed, view. Though this view is commonly traced back to Calvin, most scholars believe it was closely anticipated by Augustine, Thomas Aquinas and other noteworthy theologians. In this view, God knows all that shall come to pass because he preordains all that shall come to pass. Unlike the other three views presented in this book, this view denies that agents possess self-determining (or libertarian) freedom. Agents are free to do as they want and are morally responsible for the choices they make. But all their choices nevertheless fall within the sovereign plan of God, which governs all things. Helm argues that those who want to hold to God's exhaustive foreknowledge while embracing libertarian freedom (e.g., Hunt and Craig) are logically inconsistent. Moreover, Helm argues that only the Reformed view squares with passages in Scripture which assert God's meticulous sovereign control of the world and that only this view is consistent with the Christian understanding that salvation is exclusively by God's grace.

We have sought to make this book accessible to educated laypeople and college students who have had a first course in theology or philosophy. That being said, some of the issues raised in this book are quite technical. This is simply unavoidable; questions about divine foreknowledge are by their nature very complex. Wherever possible, the contributors have tried to use technical terminology sparingly and provide examples to explain complex arguments. We have also included a glossary that provides definitions of the technical terms used in this book. As a whole, however, we think that one does not need a specialist's level of knowledge to follow the central arguments in this book.

This book is structured as follows: Each contributor presents an essay that serves to articulate his view. This essay is then followed by a series of three responses from the other contributors. Whatever understanding of divine foreknowledge one adopts in this present controversy, it is vital that we in the Christian community understand what other Christians believe and why they believe it. Our hope and prayer is that this book will help us to understand and learn from one another, and serve to facilitate healthy dialogue on this controversial topic within the evangelical community and beyond.

We would like to express our appreciation to our four contributors to this project—Gregory Boyd, William Lane Craig, Paul Helm and David Hunt. Working with them has been as enjoyable as it has been fruitful. We also want to express our gratitude to our InterVarsity Press editor, Dan Reid, for his ongoing support of this project. A special word of thanks is offered to Chelsea DeArmond for her invaluable assistance in preparing the manuscript and to Michael Kukuska for compiling the index. Finally, we want to thank our wives— Michelle Beilby and Kelly Eddy—for their unwavering love and support throughout our various ventures, academic and otherwise. It is to them that we dedicate this book.

James K. Beilby
Bethel College

Paul R. Eddy
Bethel College

1

THE OPEN-THEISM VIEW

Gregory A. Boyd

*T*he debate over the nature of God's foreknowledge is not primarily a
debate about the scope or perfection of God's knowledge. All Christians agree
that God is omniscient and therefore knows all of reality perfectly. The debate
over God's foreknowledge is rather a debate over the *content of reality* that
God perfectly knows. It has more to do with the doctrine of creation than it
does with the doctrine of God.

Although the other three views of divine foreknowledge represented in this
work disagree with one another on many points, they agree that the content of
reality, and therefore the content of God's infallible knowledge, is *exhaustively
settled*. These views agree that every detail of what shall transpire in creation
has been settled from all eternity. Hence God has always been as certain about
the future as he is about the past. In these views God knows possibilities only
as what *might have been,* never as what *might be.* He knows possibilities only
as having been forever *excluded* from reality, never as having been *included*
within reality. In other words, God eternally knows reality as one settled story

line in contrast to all other forever-excluded story lines. This perspective may be called "the classical understanding of divine foreknowledge," though, as I've suggested, it would be technically more accurate to refer to it as the "classical understanding of creation."

The view I shall defend agrees unequivocally with the classical view that God is omniscient, but it embraces a different understanding of creation. It holds that the reality that God perfectly knows not only excludes some possibilities as what might have been, but also includes other possibilities as what might be. Reality, in other words, is composed of both settled and open aspects. Since God knows all of reality perfectly, this view holds that he knows the possible aspects as possible and knows the settled aspects as settled. In this view, the sovereign Creator settles whatever he wants to settle about the future, and hence he perfectly foreknows the future as settled *to this extent*. He leaves open whatever he wants to leave open, and hence he perfectly foreknows the future as possible *to this extent*. This view has recently been labeled the "openness view of God," though, as with the classical view, it would be technically more correct to refer to it as the "openness view of creation."

Since exegesis should always drive our philosophy, instead of the other way around, and since this essay must be restricted in terms of its length, my defense of the openness view shall be almost exclusively along exegetical lines.[1] In part one, I shall demonstrate that while the Bible certainly celebrates God's foreknowledge and control of the future, it does not warrant the conclusion that the future is *exhaustively* controlled or foreknown as settled by God. In part two, I shall discuss the biblical basis of the openness view of the future by outlining six aspects of an important scriptural motif that depicts the future as partly open and as known by God as such. And in part three, I shall defend this view against five common objections.

Part One: The Biblical Foundation of the Classical Position
The Bible unequivocally celebrates God's foreknowledge and control of the future. The theme is found most strongly in Isaiah. At a time when many Jews were tempted to trust in pagan idols, the Lord demonstrated that he alone was the sovereign Lord of history by declaring his ability to foretell the future:

> for I am God, and there is no other;
> I am God, and there is no one like me,

---

[1] I develop both the exegetical and philosophical defenses of the openness view more fully in *The God of the Possible: A Biblical Introduction to the Open View of God* (Grand Rapids, Mich.: Baker, 2000).

declaring the end from the beginning
and from ancient times things not yet done. . . .
I have spoken, and I will bring it to pass
I have planned, and I will do it. (Is 46:9-11)

Two chapters later we read an even more emphatic proclamation.

The former things I declared long ago,
they went out from my mouth and I made them known;
then suddenly I did them and they came to pass.
Because I know that you are obstinate,
and your neck is an iron sinew
and your forehead brass,
I declared them to you from long ago,
before they came to pass I announced them to you,
so that you would not say, "My idol did them,
my carved image and my cast image commanded them." (Is 48:3-5)

The Lord's ability to declare "from ancient times things not yet done" (Is 46:11) is demonstrated throughout Scripture. For example, the Lord predicted that the Israelites would be in captivity in Egypt for four hundred years (Gen 15:13-15). He occasionally foretold the future destruction of nations and cities, such as the city of Tyre (Ezek 26:7-21). Even more impressively, the Lord actually named several individuals before they were born and foretold some of their accomplishments (1 Kings 13:1-2; Is 45:1). Moreover, God foreknew that Christ would be crucified by wicked people (Acts 2:23; 4:27-28; 1 Pet 1:20). He also seems to have foretold a number of specific details about Christ's death: that his side would be pierced (Jn 19:34-37) and he would be served vinegar (Jn 19:28-29), for example. Indeed, Jesus himself knew that Judas would betray him and that Peter would deny him three times (Mt 26:34; Jn 6:64, 70-71; 13:18-19; cf. Jn 17:12).

These passages clearly exalt God as the sovereign Lord of history. This scriptural motif reassures believers that however out of control the world may seem, the Lord is steering history toward his desired end. His overall purposes for creation cannot fail, and his eternal purpose for our lives is secure (e.g., Job 42:2; Is 14:27; Rom 8:28; Eph 1:11). This motif clearly entails that much of the future is settled ahead of time and is therefore known by God as such. Indeed, it clearly demonstrates that God can settle whatever he wants to settle about the future: "The former things I declared long ago; . . . then suddenly I did them and they came to pass" (Is 48:3).

But does this motif entail that the future is *exhaustively* settled and known by God as such? I would answer yes to this question if this motif constituted everything relevant to God's relationship to the future in Scripture. But as we shall see in part two, this motif hardly exhausts the relevant biblical material. In order to account for other biblical material that depicts the future as partly open, I will now show that the above biblical evidence, cited in support of the classical position, does not require the conclusion that the future is exhaustively settled.[2]

Declaring the end from the beginning.

Isaiah 46:9-11. One could argue that Isaiah 46:9-11 comes closest to suggesting that the future is exhaustively settled. God describes himself as "declaring the end from the beginning and from ancient times things not yet done" (v. 10). Yet does this passage teach or imply that everything about the future is settled in God's mind? Two observations suggest that it does not.

First, neither this nor any other passage in Scripture says that God foreknows or declares *everything* that is going to occur. This passage specifies that God declares "*the end* from the beginning" and "from ancient times *things* not yet done."[3] God declares the conclusion of certain processes from their inception, and God declares certain things not yet done before they occur. But the passage doesn't teach or logically imply that everything leading up to the conclusion is declared, or foreknown, nor does it imply that God declares all things "from ancient times."

Second, it's important to notice how the context of the passage qualifies its claims. Immediately after telling us that he declares "from ancient times things not yet done," the Lord adds, "*My purpose* shall stand, and *I will fulfill* my intention" (v. 10). This implies that the Lord is not simply declaring information about the future that he happens to possess. He knows "the end" of the process at "the beginning" and can declare aspects of the future "from ancient times" because he has predetermined this much of the future. He knows *his own purpose and intention* to steer history in this fashion.

This point is emphasized when the Lord goes on to say, "I have spoken, and I will bring it to pass; I have planned, and I will do it" (v. 11). Verse 10 specifies "the end" and the "things" that the Lord declares ahead of time. It teaches us that the future is settled *to the extent* that the Lord has decided to settle it. But the verse does not teach or imply that the Lord will bring *everything* about the future to pass and, thus, that the Lord foreknows all that will come to pass. Indeed, if

---

[2]For a more complete argument, see chapter one of Boyd, *God of the Possible*.
[3]All quotations are from the NRSV. All italics in scriptural quotations are added.

everything came to pass according to the Lord's will, it seems odd that he would need to overcome the Israelites' obstinacy with these assertions about particular things in the future he intends to bring about. If the Lord controlled everything, the stubbornness of the Israelites itself would be the Lord's doing.

Isaiah 48:3-5. The same observation applies to Isaiah 48:3-5. The Lord says, "The former things I declared long ago; . . . then suddenly *I did them*" (v. 3). The Lord does this because he did not want Israelites saying, "My idol did them" (v. 5). In other words, Yahweh proclaimed and then demonstrated *his sovereign ability* to bring about events as a supernatural means of confronting the lie that idols have the power to bring about events. Again, this is not simply a matter of the Lord's possessing information about what is going to take place. It is, rather, a matter of the Lord's *determining* what is going to take place and telling his people ahead of time. The passage does not teach or imply that the Lord determines and thus foreknows every event that shall come to pass.

Foreknown details and the openness of creation. Given the particular examples where the Lord decrees that certain things shall come to pass, must one conclude that the future is exhaustively settled in God's mind? I shall briefly consider three examples to illustrate why I believe the answer to this question is no.

The coherence of a partially open future. The Lord prophesied that Israel would be in captivity to Egypt for four centuries long before this captivity became a fact (Gen 15:13). This is a spectacular demonstration of the Lord's sovereign control of the future. But is it evidence that the future is exhaustively settled? Not at all. It only implies that *some* of the future is settled. People tend to assume that if some of the future is settled, all of it must be settled. The idea of a partially settled future strikes them as implausible, if not incoherent. This is one reason they tend to misinterpret biblical evidence of a partly settled future as evidence of an exhaustively settled future. A closer examination, however, reveals that the notion of a partly settled future perspective is both coherent and plausible.

First, the coherence of the view that the future is partly open and partly settled is demonstrated whenever we deliberate about a decision, for in every act of deliberation we presuppose that the future is partly up to us to decide and partly decided for us.[4] For example, suppose I am deliberating about whether or not to purchase a new edition of Kant's *Critique of Pure Reason* tomorrow.

---

[4]The argument for a partially open future on the basis of the nature of deliberation is developed further in my book *Satan and the Problem of Evil: Developing a Warfare Theodicy* (Downers Grove, Ill.: InterVarsity Press, 2001), chap. 2.

My act of deliberation presupposes that it lies within my power either to purchase this book or to not. It illustrates my conviction that at least this much of my future is up to me to decide. But my deliberation also presupposes that much of the future is not up to me to decide. I couldn't deliberate about this particular purchase if it were up to me to decide whether, say, the bookstore would exist or whether money would have any value tomorrow.

In other words, to deliberate about any *particular* matter, we must be freed from deliberating about *every* matter. Our sense of freedom presupposes that much of the future is already settled. Our freedom must always take place within the parameters of things we do not choose. We have no choice but to live as though some things are up to us to resolve and some things are not. In short, we live *as though* the future is partly settled and partly open. The openness view of the future simply roots this "as though" in reality and renders it intelligible. Of the four views considered in this book, it is the only view that can claim this.

Second, this view of reality is being explored and confirmed in many branches of contemporary science, a fact that further confirms the coherence and plausibility of the openness view. For example, contemporary physics has demonstrated that we can accurately predict the general behavior of a group of quantum particles but that we cannot in principle predict the exact behavior of any individual particle. Indeed, the regularity of the phenomenological world—despite quantum indeterminacy—is the manifestation of this statistical regularity. The phenomenological world is settled, though the world of quantum particles is somewhat open.

Similarly, chaos theory has recently demonstrated that all predictable aspects of reality incorporate unpredictable aspects and vice versa.[5] Moreover,

---

[5]Chaos theory is deterministic but nevertheless supports the coherence of the openness view of the future insofar as it demonstrates that predictability and unpredictability are complementary, not antagonistic, principles. The way in which branches of contemporary science (especially quantum theory, chaos theory and complex-systems theory) support the openness view of the future is developed further in Boyd, *Satan and the Problem of Evil*, chaps. 4-6. For an overview of how the concept of time as a real, unidirectional reality is increasingly being explored and applied in science, see P. Coveney and R. Highfield, *The Arrow of Time* (New York: Basic-Books, 1990). For more detailed discussions, see also P. Coveney, "The Second Law of Thermodynamics: Entropy, Irreversibility and Dynamics," *Nature* 333 (1988): 409-15; I. Prigogine, *From Being to Becoming* (San Francisco: W. H. Freeman, 1980); I. Prigogine and I. Stengers, *Order Out of Chaos: Man's New Dialogue with Nature* (New York: Bantam, 1984); "Time, Dynamics and Chaos: Integrating Poincaré's 'Non-Integratable Systems,' " in *Chaos: The New Science: Nobel Conference XXVI*, ed. J. Holte (Landham, Md.: University Press of America, 1993), pp. 55-88; "Irreversibility and Space-Time Structure," in *Physics and the Ultimate Significance of Time*, ed. David Ray Griffen (Albany: SUNY Press, 1986), pp. 232-49; H. Hollinger and M. Zenzen, *The Nature of Irreversibility* (Dordrecht, Holland: Reidel, 1985); and P. Horwich, *Asymmetries in Time* (Cambridge, Mass.: MIT Press, 1989).

social scientists, anthropologists and biologists have demonstrated that the behavior of groups of humans, animals and even insects is much more predictable than the behavior of the individuals. A colony of ants behaves in remarkably predictable ways, for example, even though the behavior of any particular ant is much more difficult to predict.

Our own experience and recent scientific developments demonstrate that the view of creation as partly settled and partly open is both coherent and plausible. Hence, there should be no difficulty conceiving how God could determine and foreknow that a particular event was going to take place (e.g., the Egyptian captivity) without determining or foreknowing every detail surrounding this event (e.g., every future individual decision). The classical jump from evidence for *some* of the future being settled to the conclusion that *all* of the future must be settled is unwarranted.

Prophecies against cities. Many of the fulfilled prophecies against nations or cities in Scripture can be explained this way. God can decree that a nation or city shall be judged without his ordaining or eternally foreknowing every future decision throughout all of history.[6] Indeed, Scripture makes it clear that the sovereign Lord is always involved in setting the scope and duration of nations (Acts 17:26). But it doesn't teach that God determines or foreknows as settled all the decisions of all the individuals within these nations. Indeed, Paul tells us that God establishes these national parameters with the hope "that they [the nations] would search for God and perhaps grope for him and find him" (Acts 17:27). Within the parameters settled by God, there is an unsettled future, a "perhaps." God determines whatever he sees fit and leaves as much of the future open as he sees fit.[7]

Foreknown individuals and the openness of the future.

The names and activity of Josiah and Cyrus. As a sign to his people, God named Josiah ("the LORD strengthens") and Cyrus and declared some of their accomplishments before they were born (1 Kings 13:1-2; Is 45:1). These decrees obviously established parameters around the parents' freedom to nam-

---

[6]In the light of Jer 18:1-10 (to be discussed below), many prophecies against nations or cities may be conditional. That is, if the nations or cities had repented, God would have canceled his judgment. Still, openness theists must explain how God could ensure that such and such future events would take place if the nation or city did not repent. This, I am now arguing, would not be difficult for God to do.

[7]This is not to suggest that God is the only variable to be considered in assessing the parameters within which freedom occurs. Many of the parameters that condition an individual's freedom are established by the decisions of other agents. A more nuanced and developed presentation is in Boyd, *Satan and the Problem of Evil,* chaps. 5-7.

ing these individuals (cf. Lk 1:18-22, 59-64) and also restricted the scope of freedom these individuals could exercise regarding *particular foreordained activities*. But in other respects these two individuals and their parents remained self-determining agents. To conclude from these two examples that God has settled the names and activities of *all* people from eternity is unwarranted. These examples certainly show that Yahweh is the sovereign Lord of history and can predetermine and thus foreknow whatever he pleases. But they do not justify the conclusion that he desires to predetermine or foreknow the whole of the future.

Peter's denial. Future actions might also be settled not only because the Lord has decided them beforehand, but also because a person's character settles them. As we all know, character becomes more predictable over time. The longer we persist in a chosen path, the more that path becomes part of who we are. Hence, generally speaking, the range of viable options we are capable of diminishes over time.[8] Our omniscient Creator is able to predict our behavior far more extensively than we could predict it ourselves because he knows us far better than we know ourselves (Ps 44:21; 139:1-6). This does not mean that our every move is predictable, for our present character doesn't exhaustively determine our future behavior. But it does mean that our future behavior is predictable to the extent that our present character is solidified.

A familiar example of this is when the Lord tells Peter he will deny him three times before morning (Mt 26:34). We don't need to suppose that the future is exhaustively settled in God's mind to explain this prediction. We only need to believe that God the Father knew and revealed to Jesus one solidified aspect of Peter's character that was predictable in the immediate future. Anyone who knew Peter's character perfectly could have predicted that under certain highly pressured circumstances (which God could easily orchestrate, if he needed to), Peter would act the way he did.[9]

One of the central points of this divinely orchestrated lesson was exposing the superficiality of Peter's characteristic boldness. Peter had just made the (typically) proud claim to Jesus, "I will never desert you. . . . Even though I must die with you, I will not deny you" (Mt 26:33, 35). Jesus told him of his denial at this point in order to help Peter eventually realize just how deluded

---

[8]This insight is developed and defended in ibid., chap. 6.

[9]It is possible to interpret Jesus' prediction of Peter's betrayal as a conditional prophecy: Jesus was warning Peter, hoping he wouldn't deny him (cf. John Sanders, *The God Who Risks: A Theology of Providence* [Downers Grove, Ill.: InterVarsity Press, 1998], pp. 135-37). However, this interpretation doesn't adequately explain why the Lord specified that Peter would deny him three times.

he was about his own character as well as about the character of the Messiah.

Like most Jews of his time, Peter believed that the Messiah would be a military leader who would not suffer but rather would vanquish his enemies. This explains why Peter opposed Jesus' teaching about the need for his sacrificial suffering (e.g., Mt 16:21-23). It also explains why Peter *appeared* so courageous when Jesus was performing miracles but became cowardly after Jesus' arrest. His false expectations of what Jesus was going to accomplish were shattered.

God of course saw through Peter's misplaced boldness and knew the effect Jesus' arrest would have on him. God used his knowledge to teach Peter—who would become a pillar of the church—an invaluable lesson about love and servant leadership. We do not know how much, if any, supernatural intervention was behind the events of that evening. But the outcome was just as God anticipated. Three times Peter's true character was squeezed out of him so that, after the resurrection, Christ could squeeze his character into him three times. It is no coincidence that *three times* the resurrected Jesus asked Peter, "Do you love me?" After each of these three refrains Jesus told Peter to feed his sheep and concluded with a prophecy that Peter would die a martyr's death, just as he had (Jn 21:15-19). Peter would never again identify leadership with military victory. For in the kingdom of God, leadership is about laying down one's life and feeding the Lord's sheep, about knowing the meaning of love (Lk 22:24-27; cf. Eph 5:25-27). It was a lesson Peter had to learn and live if he was to become everything God wanted him to be in the church and for the world.

In any event, we are clearly going beyond the evidence if we conclude that the future is exhaustively settled from all eternity on the grounds that Jesus predicted what Peter would do in the next twelve hours. The only conclusions justified by this episode are that *God possesses perfect knowledge of the past and present* and that some of the future is settled, either by present circumstances (Peter's character) or by God's sovereign design.

Judas's betrayal. Scripture says that Jesus knew "from the first" that Judas would betray him (Jn 6:64). This phrase *(ex archē)* does not imply that Jesus knew who would betray him from a time *before* the person decided, in his heart, to betray him (let alone that he knew from all eternity, as the classical view of foreknowledge requires). It can more plausibly be taken to mean that Jesus knew who would betray him *early on* (cf. Phil 4:15), either from the moment this person resolved it in his heart to betray him or from the time Jesus chose him to be a disciple.

Jesus tells us that Judas fulfilled Scripture, not that Judas was the individual who *had* to fulfill Scripture. Judas could have and should have chosen a different path for his life than the one he chose. But, as a free moral agent, Judas tragically chose a path of self-interest and ultimately self-destruction (Jn 17:12).[10] If his choices had been more godly, he would not have been a candidate for fulfilling the prophecy of the Lord's betrayal. In this case the Lord would have found someone else to fill this role.

In my view, this is how we should understand the wicked activity of all the individuals who played foreordained roles in the death of Jesus: for example, the rulers who had Jesus crucified (Acts 2:23; 4:27-28), the soldier who pierced his side (Jn 19:34-37) and the soldier who gave Jesus vinegar (Jn 19:28-29).[11] As seen in its references to Judas, Scripture never suggests that these specific individuals were destined or foreknown to carry out these wicked deeds. It only teaches that these specific deeds were destined and foreknown to take place. Saying that someone carried out a predestined or foreknown wicked event is much different from saying that someone was predestined or foreknown to carry out a wicked event. Scripture affirms the former but not the latter. These passages only require us to believe that, when he so chooses, God can narrow the parameters within which certain people act out their freely chosen character.

Again, we are outrunning the evidence if we conclude that everything about creation is eternally and exhaustively settled based on these examples. We

---

[10]Some assume that when Jesus referred to Judas as one who was "destined to be lost," he meant that Judas was damned from the beginning of time (Jn 17:12). However, the verse doesn't imply this. The Greek translated as "destined to be lost" literally says "son of perdition" with no indication as to when Judas had become this. We only know that by the time Jesus said this, Judas had, of his own free will, become a person fit for destruction. Scripture elsewhere suggests that God may discern that it is useless to strive with a particular individual or a group of people any longer. At this point he withdraws his Spirit from these people, hardens their hearts and thus seals their destinies (e.g., Gen 6:3; Rom 1:24-27). When this occurs the only remaining issue from God's perspective is how he might strategically weave the wicked character of these "sons of perdition" into his divine plan (see, e.g., Prov 16:4; Rom 9:22). Thus God wove Judas's self-chosen wickedness into his providential scheme by having him "fulfill" the Scripture about the Messiah's being betrayed.

[11]Many Bible scholars maintain that at least some messianic prophecies are illustrative, not predictive. In this view, New Testament authors cite certain Old Testament passages to show that Jesus' life and death illustrate what the passages are about, not to show that Jesus' life had to unfold in a particular manner. For example, when Matthew notes that Jesus' family fled to Egypt to fulfill the prophecy, "Out of Egypt I have called my son" (Mt 2:15), he wasn't thereby claiming that Hos 11:1 originally referred to Jesus. He was, in this view, simply saying that Jesus' life illustrates the same motif as the one found when God called Israel out of Egypt. If this view is accepted, one could argue that no one had to betray Jesus. But given the fact that by the time of the Last Supper it was certain Judas was going to betray Jesus, Psalm 41:9, which describes David's betrayal by a close friend a thousand years earlier, could now be cited as an inspired anticipation of what the Messiah would endure. See J. Sawyer, *Prophecy and Biblical Prophets,* rev. ed. (Oxford: Oxford University Press, 1993), and Sanders, *God Who Risks,* pp. 135ff.

might be justified in going beyond the evidence in this fashion if this were all the evidence we had. If we did not have any scriptural evidence of the future's being open at least in part, then we could perhaps justifiably argue that the above evidence—which suggests that some of the future is settled—supports the conclusion that the future is exhaustively settled. As we shall now see, however, this is not at all the case.

Part Two: Scripture and the Openness of Creation
Alongside the scriptural motif that celebrates God's control and knowledge of the settled aspects of creation is another, rarely appreciated motif that celebrates God's creative flexibility in responding to open aspects of his creation. In this motif, God asks questions about the future, speaks of the future in conditional terms, regrets the outcome of decisions he has made, changes his mind in response to changing situations, and so on. I call this "the motif of future openness," and it pervades Scripture at least as thoroughly as the first motif, as I shall briefly demonstrate.

The classical view assumes that the first motif tells the whole story about God's relationship to the world. Since this view holds that the future is exhaustively settled, it often minimizes or dismisses as nonliteral the second motif, which teaches that some of the future is not settled. These texts, it is argued, do not describe God as he *really* is; rather, these texts describe him only as he *appears* (phenomenologically) or describe him using nonliteral figures of speech (anthropomorphically).[12]

The critical difference between the openness view and all versions of the classical view is that the openness view rejects this reinterpretation of this biblical motif. Generally speaking, it interprets the second motif the same as it does the first. It believes that both motifs can and should be interpreted as describing what God and creation are really like. Thus it arrives at the balanced conclusion that the future is settled to the extent that Scripture suggests

---

[12]There is, of course, a sense in which all language about God is analogical. When we say God loves, judges or foreknows aspects of the future, for example, we are saying that he does things like what we do when we love, judge or know things ahead of time—but he does so without any attendant imperfections. Still, the classical tradition holds that language about, say, God's changing his mind was nonliteral in a way that, say, language about God's foreknowing the future was not. The latter describes God as he really is; the former does not. My argument is simply that the second motif describes God as he really is just as much as the first motif does. God really does love, judge and foreknow aspects of the future. In this sense we should take Scriptures that depict God as loving, judging and foreknowing "literally." God really does change his mind, regret decisions and anticipate open possibilities in the future. We should take these Scriptures just as "literally" as we take those supporting the first motif.

it is settled and open to the extent that Scripture suggests it is open. I shall now review six groups of passages that compose this latter motif and address objections to this view.

God confronts the unexpected. Passages that describe God's response to unexpected behavior suggest that while the Lord can never be caught off guard—for he anticipates all possibilities—he is nevertheless occasionally surprised at the improbable behavior of people.

Unexpected wild grapes. For example, in Isaiah 5 the Lord describes Israel as his vineyard and himself as its loving owner. He explains that as the owner of the vineyard, he "*expected* it to yield grapes, but it yielded wild grapes" (v. 2). He then asks, in verse 4:

> What more was there to do for my vineyard
> > that I have not done in it?
> When I *expected* it to yield grapes,
> > why did it yield wild grapes?

Because the vineyard unexpectedly failed to yield grapes, the Lord sadly concludes, "I will remove its hedge and it shall be devoured" (v. 5). How can the Lord say that he "expected" one thing to occur, only to discover something else occurred instead, if he is eternally certain of all that shall ever occur? Can a person expect something he is certain will never happen? Taking the passage at face value, does it not imply that God was not certain of the future of Israel, the "vineyard," until the Israelites settled it by choosing to yield "wild grapes" instead of the grapes God expected?

Similarly, three times in Jeremiah the Lord expresses his surprise at Israel's behavior by saying his children were doing things "which I did not command or decree, *nor did it enter my mind*" (Jer 19:5; cf. 7:31; 32:35). However we interpret the difficult phrase "nor did it enter my mind," it seems to preclude the possibility that the Israelites' idolatrous behavior was *eternally certain in God's mind.* If the classical view is correct, however, we have to grant that God could say, "I have been eternally certain that the Israelites would engage in this behavior, but it never entered my mind that they'd actually engage in this behavior." If this doesn't constitute a contradiction, what does?

"I thought, . . . but you . . ." Several other examples of the Lord's confronting unexpected behavior are found in Jeremiah. Beholding Israel's remarkable obstinacy, the Lord says, "*And I thought,* 'After she has done all this she will return to me'; but she did not return" (Jer 3:6-7). He repeats his dismay to Israel several verses later:

I *thought*

> how I would set you among my children. . . .

And I *thought* you would call me, My Father,

> and would not turn from following me.

Instead, as a faithless wife leaves her husband,

> so you have been faithless to me. (Jer 3:19-20)

How is it possible for the Lord to tell us he *thought* something was going to happen that did not happen if he is eternally certain of all that shall ever happen? If we take these passages at face value, do they not demonstrate that the Lord faced a future in which Israel *might* or *might not* respond to him? He expected that Israel would respond, but it does not. This is not possible unless the future is partially open.

Does the fact that the Lord's expectations are sometimes not met imply that he can be mistaken? Only if one assumes that the future is settled from all eternity. In this case, given the information (i.e., Israel's future behavior), one could judge God's expectations as mistaken. But we should, rather, allow the biblical teaching—that God's knowledge is perfect—drive our understanding of what is real, not vice versa. If God wasn't certain how Israel would behave, this must mean that this information didn't yet exist; for if it did exist, God would certainly have known it. The information that did exist was that it was probable (but not inevitable) that Israel would return to God. Hence the omniscient God perfectly expected (but was not certain) that Israel would turn to him.

The classical view assumes that the future is settled and that therefore God knows it; thus proponents of this view reinterpret these passages figuratively. That is, passages describing unmet expectations—one in which God says he "thought" something would happen, yet it doesn't—are not to be taken as literally as are passages in which God says, "The former things I declared long ago" (Is 48:3). This preference for certain texts seems to be motivated by a philosophical preconception of what is and is not worthy of God (viz., God is "above" disappointment), and as such it is unwarranted and arbitrary. It also fails to adequately explain passages like Jeremiah 3. As we shall argue more fully in part three, nonliteral figures of speech must reflect reality at some point if they communicate anything meaningfully. So we must ask, what reality is reflected by passages like Jeremiah 3:6-7, 19-20?

More specifically, the question is, if in fact God never thinks an event that doesn't happen was going to happen, what truth is communicated in the Scripture when he *says* he thought an event that didn't happen was likely to happen? There is no adequate answer to this question—certainly none that is rooted in a straightforward reading of these texts.

God experiences regret. God sometimes expresses in Scripture disappointment with the results of decisions *he himself made*. This is difficult to square with the view that God knows the future as exhaustively settled for an eternity prior to any decision he makes.

Regret for making humans. For example, when the Bible recounts humanity's depravity prior to the flood, it says, "The Lord *was sorry* that he made humankind on the earth, and it grieved him to his heart" (Gen 6:6). How can God feel this regret if he knew, even before he created them, that humans would degenerate to this exact condition? If God truly wished he had never made humans—to the point of his wanting to destroy them and start over—shouldn't we conclude that the extent of their depravity *wasn't* a foregone conclusion at the time he created them? Shouldn't we conclude that God *hoped* (but was not certain) things would not have turned out the way they did? And doesn't this imply that the future was not exhaustively settled in God's mind when he created humanity?

Regret for making Saul king. Another fascinating example of the Lord's regret concerns his decision to make Saul king of Israel. While having a human king rule over Israel was not God's first choice, God knew Saul could be a good king. Indeed, God genuinely intended to bless him and his household for many generations (1 Sam 13:13). Unfortunately, Saul chose to forsake God's ways and to pursue his own agenda. When Saul's heart changed, God's plan for him changed. Instead of blessing him, God removed him from his appointed office and allowed his sin to take its course. Saul had become so wicked that the Lord said, "I *regret* that I made Saul king, for he has turned back from following me" (1 Sam 15:10). This point is reiterated for emphasis several verses later (1 Sam 15:35).

The Lord says that he regretted making Saul king because Saul "turned back from following [him]." But if he was eternally certain that Saul would "turn back" when he made him king, how can God regret making him king because he "turned back"? Don't God's regret and sorrow over his decision suggest that at the time he appointed Saul he *truly hoped* Saul would *not* turn back from following him? Moreover, doesn't Samuel's inspired declaration that the Lord "would have established [Saul's] kingdom over Israel for ever" had he not sinned mean that God *genuinely intended* to bless Saul prior to his turning back (1 Sam 13:13)? Doesn't all of this imply that at the time of Saul's appointment it was at least *possible* that he would not fall and that God hoped this possibility would be actualized?

Does regret show a lack of wisdom? Some argue that we cannot interpret passages like this literally because if God were to regret his own decisions, he could not be perfectly wise. However, if God never does regret decisions he's made, the "nonliteral" meaning communicated when Scripture explicitly tells us he does regret some decisions is not clear. We should allow Scripture to reveal the nature of divine wisdom rather than assume we know what divine wisdom entails and then dismiss passages that suggest otherwise as not depicting what God is "really" like. If Scripture says God regretted a decision and if it also says that God is perfectly wise, then we should simply conclude that regretting a decision apparently does not mean that one is not perfectly wise. Even if this is a mystery to us, allowing the mystery is better than presuming that we know what God's wisdom is like and thus concluding that Scripture can't mean what it clearly says.

Actually, there isn't much mystery involved in reconciling God's perfect wisdom with his occasional regret over previous decisions. Once we understand that the future is partly open and that humans are genuinely free, the paradox of how God genuinely regrets a decision disappears. God made a wise decision because his decision had the greatest *possibility* of yielding the best results. But God's decision wasn't the only variable in the matter of Saul's kingship: Saul's will was also a variable. Saul freely strayed from God's plan, but that is not God's fault. Nor does it make God's decision unwise. If God was certain how Saul would behave once he made him king and certain that he'd regret his decision to make him king—and then went ahead and made him king anyway—*that* would not only be unwise, it would be incoherent.

This scriptural truth has some helpful pastoral implications, though we can't discuss them at length now.[13] Suffice it to say that Christians often sense God's leading about a decision they should make, only to have the decision turn out disastrously. Suppose God gives a young woman the "green light" on a marriage proposal. Then, two years into the marriage, her husband becomes persistently unfaithful and abusive. In the classical view either this woman failed to discern God's will or the pain of having an unfaithful and abusive husband was God's plan for her all along. The openness view offers a third alternative: God's decision to lead these two to marry was perfectly wise, for it was likely to become a God-honoring marriage. But like Saul, the husband made sinful choices and ruined God's good plan. And God now regrets allowing this woman to marry him just as he regretted making Saul king. This is not the woman's fault: she discerned God's will correctly. Nor is it God's fault: he led her wisely. The fault rests squarely on the man who chose to become unfaithful and abusive.

---

[13]For a fuller discussion, see Boyd, *God of the Possible,* chap. 4.

In the openness view we aren't forced to conclude either that this woman was spiritually deaf or that God set her up for the pain she experienced. Whenever we go through painful circumstances, we can know that God is graciously at work to bring good out of them (Rom 8:28). When a Saul "turns back" from following God, there is a David waiting in the wings (1 Sam 16:18-23). The sovereign and creative God revealed in the Bible is never without options. He knows no limits.

God expresses frustration. In the Bible we find many occasions when God expresses frustration toward people who stubbornly resist his plans for their lives. These passages are difficult to reconcile with the view that the future is exhaustively settled and known as such by God from all eternity. How can the Lord become frustrated trying to achieve things he is certain will never come to pass?

Searching for an intercessor. For example, at one point in Israel's rebellious history the Lord declared, "I *sought* for anyone among them who would repair the wall and stand in the breach before me on behalf of the land, so that I would not destroy it; but I found no one. Therefore I have poured out my indignation upon them" (Ezek 22:30-31). This passage is a powerful testimony to the urgency and power of prayer. It teaches us that if God had found *anyone* to pray, his judgment on the nation of Israel would have been averted. But even though God earnestly sought for someone to "stand in the breach," he found no one. This episode stands in stark contrast to the many other times in Israel's history when God's plan to bring judgment *was* reversed through the power of prayer.[14]

It is difficult to understand how God could have sincerely "sought for" someone to intercede if he had been certain all along that there would be no one, as the classical view of foreknowledge must contend. Could someone genuinely search his house trying to find, say, a pair of shoes he knew he didn't own? And even if someone did do this, would one consider him supremely wise for doing so? Of course not. Yet the classical view would have us believe that the all-wise God sought for an intercessor he eternally knew would not be found. Given that God *tried* to raise up an intercessor, is it not more reasonable to conclude that it was *possible* an intercessor would have responded to God? Yet to do so would mean admitting that the future is composed partly of possibilities, not exclusively of settled realities.

Creating damned people. We also see God's frustration when we consider

---

[14]See, e.g., Ex 32:14; Num 11:1-2; 14:12-20; 16:20-35, 41-48; Deut 9:13-14, 18-20, 25; Judg 10:13-15; 2 Sam 24:17-25; 1 Kings 21:27-29; 2 Kings 13:3-5; 20:1-7; 2 Chron 12:5-8.

that not everyone he creates accepts his invitation to eternal life. Peter tells us that the Lord delays his return because he doesn't want "any to perish, but all to come to repentance" (2 Pet 3:9). The God whose essence is love wants everyone he's created to turn to him (Ezek 18:23, 32; 33:11; Jn 3:16; 1 Tim 2:3-4; 4:10). Paul teaches that the Creator steers world history in hopes that all people "would search for [him] and perhaps grope for him and find him" (Acts 17:27), for "he commands all people everywhere to repent" (Acts 17:30). God's Spirit continually strives with people to bring them to the place where they put their trust in him, and he is genuinely grieved when they refuse to yield to his influence (e.g., Is 63:10; cf. Eph 4:30; see also Acts 7:51; Heb 3:8, 15; 4:7).

Why would God strive to the point of frustration to get people to do what he was certain they would never do before they were even born: namely, believe in him? Doesn't God's sincere effort to get all people to believe in him imply that it is not a foregone conclusion to God that certain people would *not* believe in him when he created them? Indeed, doesn't the fact that the Lord *delays* his return imply that neither the date of his return nor the identities of who will and will not believe are settled in God's mind ahead of time? God delays his return in hope of saving more people, whoever would believe (Jn 3:16-18). If this isn't what 2 Peter 3:9 explicitly teaches, what does it teach?

If it is difficult for the classical view to explain why God strives with people he is certain will not be saved, it is even more difficult to explain why God would create these people in the first place. We can understand why God would sorrowfully allow people to choose hell *once he has created them*. To revoke this freedom *once it has been given* on the grounds that it is being used wrongly would mean that their freedom was disingenuous. The risk of self-damnation is inherent in creating free beings. But it is very difficult to understand why a God who loves all people and who wants no one to perish would give freedom to people he is certain are going to use it to damn themselves to hell. If it is better to never have been born than to suffer in hell, as Jesus suggests (Mt 26:24), and if God always does what is best, why would he create condemned people?[15]

In the openness view, when God creates people, he knows the possibility (but not the certainty) that they will become citizens of the eternal kingdom. He genuinely strives to win them because he hopes that they will surrender to him. When they refuse, he is genuinely grieved, for he knows that their loss

---

[15]The simple-foreknowledge position avoids this particular difficulty but ends up placing God in the unfortunate position of eternally foreknowing the damnation of people he regretfully is going to create.

was not inevitable. They could have, should have and would have been his children if only they had said yes to him.

God speaks in conditional terms. If everything were settled in God's mind from all eternity, as the classical view holds, we would expect God to speak of the future in terms of what *will* and *will not* happen. Remarkably, however, throughout Scripture God often speaks of the future in terms of what *might* or *might not* happen.

They may believe. For example, when God tries to convince Moses to be his representative to the Israelite elders who are in bondage to Pharaoh, he initially tells Moses that the elders will heed his voice (Ex 3:18). Moses apparently doesn't hold to the classical view of divine foreknowledge, however, for he immediately asks, "But suppose they do not believe me or listen to me?" (Ex 4:1).

God's response suggests that God doesn't hold to this view of foreknowledge either. He first demonstrates a miracle "so that they may believe that the LORD . . . has appeared" to Moses (Ex 4:5). Moses remains unconvinced, so the Lord performs a second miracle and comments, "*If* they will not believe you or heed the first sign, they *may* believe the second sign" (Ex 4:8). How can the Lord say, "they *may* believe"? Isn't the future behavior of the elders a matter of certainty for the Lord? Apparently not. Indeed, the Lord offers Moses a third sign in case the second sign didn't work (Ex 4:9).

If the future is exhaustively settled, God would have known exactly how many miracles, if any, it would take to get the elders to believe Moses; and this means that the meaning of the words he chose *(may* and *if)* could not be sincere. If, however, God is speaking straightforwardly here, it seems he did not foreknow exactly how many miracles it would take to get the elders of Israel to believe Moses.

This passage demonstrates that God is perfectly confident in his ability to achieve his desired results (viz., getting the elders of Israel to listen to Moses) even though he works with free agents who are, to some extent, unpredictable. He is able to declare to Moses the conclusion of his plan from the time he first announces it (cf. Is 46:10, "the *end* from the *beginning*") without controlling every variable in between. *That* the Israelites will get out of Egypt is certain; *how many miracles* it will take to pull this off depends on the free choices of some key people. This is a picture of a God who is as creative and resourceful as he is wise and powerful.

What may or may not happen. While the Lord often expresses his future plans as certainties (e.g., Christ's return, ultimate victory over Satan), there are also times in Scripture where God expresses his desires for the future as possibilities. For example, the Lord instructed Ezekiel to symbolically enact Israel's exile as a warning, telling him, "*Perhaps* they will understand, though they are a rebellious house" (Ezek 12:3). As it turns out, Israel did not "understand." So if God was certain all along that Israel would not understand, then he must have lied to Ezekiel when he assured him that they *might* understand. Yet if we agree that God cannot lie (Heb 6:18), then his statement to Ezekiel must reflect reality. That is, when God gave Ezekiel his instructions, God must have hoped (without certainty) that the Israelites might understand. Their response, therefore, could not have been known by God beforehand.

Along the same lines, the Lord commanded Jeremiah to stand in the court and preach to the Judeans, promising him that "it *may be* that they will listen, . . . that I may change my mind about the disaster I intend to bring" (Jer 26:3). God's use of the subjective as well as his willingness to change his declared intention is difficult to reconcile with the view that God eternally knows the future as exhaustively settled.

Similarly, Scripture states that God did not lead the children of Israel near the Philistines because "God thought, 'If the people face war, they *may* change their minds and return to Egypt'" (Ex 13:17). In this passage God actually reveals his inner thoughts and motives—things we would never know if he didn't tell us. And we find that to some extent God *thinks about the future in terms of possibilities.* Since God is the only one in a position to know the nature of the future perfectly, we would do well to take his thoughts about it as the surest indication of what the future is actually like. It is, in fact, partly composed of possibilities!

One final example of the Lord's speaking or thinking about the future in open terms will have to suffice. In the garden of Gethsemane, Jesus "threw himself on the ground and prayed, 'My Father, *if it is possible,* let this cup pass from me'" (Mt 26:39). Now, if any event was settled in the mind of God from the creation of the world, it was that the Son of God was going to be killed (Acts 2:23; 4:27-28; Rev 13:8). Indeed, Jesus himself taught this very truth to his disciples (Mt 12:40; 16:21; Jn 2:19). Yet here Jesus made one last attempt to change his Father's plan, saying, "If it is possible . . ."

This prayer is unintelligible if Jesus believed that the entire future was eternally settled in the Father's mind. Jesus must have believed there was at least a chance another course of action could be taken at the eleventh hour. Jesus' prayer illustrates the truth that to God the future is at least partly open, even if in this instance Jesus' own fate was not.

God tests people "to know" their character. God often tests his covenant partners to discover whether or not they will choose to follow him.

Throughout the Bible, this testing lies at the heart of God's call to keep covenant with him. For example, when Abraham successfully passed God's test by being willing to sacrifice his son, Isaac, the Lord declared, "*Now* I know that you fear God, *since* you have not withheld your son" (Gen 22:12). The verse clearly says that it was *because* Abraham did what he did that the Lord *now* knew he was a faithful covenant partner. What do the terms *now* and *because* mean if God had been certain from all eternity that Abraham would remain faithful? Similarly, the Bible says that God tested Hezekiah "*to know* what was in his heart" (2 Chron 32:31). Again, if God eternally knew how Hezekiah would respond to him, God couldn't have *really* been testing him in order to gain this knowledge. Unfortunately for the classical view, however, *this is exactly what the text says.*

Many of the "testing" passages of Scripture concern the behavior of Israel as a whole. For example, Moses tells the Israelites, "The LORD your God has led you these forty years in the wilderness in order to humble you, testing you *to know* what was in your heart, whether or not you would keep his commandments" (Deut 8:2). Later he tells the Israelites that the Lord allowed false prophets to be correct sometimes because the Lord "is testing you, *to know* whether you indeed love the LORD your God with all your heart and soul" (Deut 13:1-3). And in another instance God leaves Israel's opponents alone "for the testing of Israel, *to know* whether Israel would obey the commandments of the LORD" (Judg 3:4).

Note carefully that these verses do not say, as defenders of the classical view usually contend, that the purpose of the testing was for *covenant partners* to know *their own* hearts. Rather, these inspired passages specify that the tests were *so God could know.* How are these passages to be reconciled with the classical assumption that God never "really" comes to know anything, for supposedly his knowledge is eternally settled? These verses can only be accepted straightforwardly if we accept that God and humans face a partly open future.

Some have attempted to resist this conclusion by arguing that if God truly tests people "to know what is in their heart," he cannot know all present realities. Since Scripture clearly reveals that God knows all present realities, they argue, we must interpret these "testing" passages figuratively.[16] We must wonder if "God tests people to know what is in their heart" does not reveal that God truly tests people to know what is in their heart, what *do* they truly reveal? The standard claim that God tests people so that *they* will know what is in their

---

[16]See, e.g., Bruce Ware, "An Evangelical Reformulation of the Doctrine of the Immutability of God," *Journal of the Evangelical Theological Society* 29 (1986).

heart does not explain these passages, it flatly contradicts them.

An examination of the context of each of these passages reveals a much easier way of reconciling them with the truth that God knows all present realities. The context interprets "in their heart." In each episode God elicits a *decision* from the people he tests. God wants to know whether Abraham will choose to obey him or not, for example. So too he tests the Israelites "to know what was in [their] hearts, *whether or not* [they] *would keep his commands*" (Deut 8:21). If read in context, there is no difficulty reconciling the testing passages with God's knowledge of all present realities; future decisions are *not* present realities.

God changes his mind. Scripture contains many examples of God's changing his mind in response to events that transpire in history. By definition, one cannot change what is permanently fixed. Hence, every time the Bible describes God's change of mind, it suggests that God's knowledge and intentions are not eternally settled.

Scripture clearly depicts God as willing and able to change his mind. One of the best illustrations of this is found in Jeremiah 18. The Lord has revealed his plan to bring judgment on Israel, but he wants Jeremiah and the Israelites to know that he is willing to change his plans if they will change their wicked ways. So the Lord directs Jeremiah to go observe a potter at work.

> The vessel he was making of clay was spoiled in the potter's hand, and he reworked it into another vessel, as seemed good to him.
>
> Then the word of the LORD came to me: Can I not do with you, O house of Israel, just as this potter has done? says the LORD. Just like the clay in the potter's hand, so are you in my hand, O house of Israel. At one moment I may declare concerning a nation or a kingdom, that I will pluck up and break down and destroy it, but if that nation, concerning which I have spoken, turns from its evil, I will *change my mind* about the disaster that I intended to bring on it. And at another moment I may declare concerning a nation or a kingdom that I will build and plant it, but if it does evil in my sight, not listening to my voice, then I will *change my mind* about the good that I had intended to do to it. (vv. 4-10)

The Lord then applies this teaching to Israel, saying, "Look, I am a potter shaping evil against you and devising a plan against you. Turn now, all of you from your evil way, and amend your ways and your doings" (v. 11).

Though Calvinists frequently cite the potter-clay analogy in support of an omnicontrolling model of divine sovereignty, the only passage that develops the analogy at length makes the opposite point. This passage celebrates the fact that God is *not* a unilaterally controlling deity who decrees an unalterable future. Instead, this passage teaches that even after God has devised and announced a certain course of action, he (like a flexible potter) is willing and able to revise his plan if the people (like the clay) will change.

If the future is eternally and exhaustively settled in God's mind, then it is not clear what this passage is intended to communicate. If God knows from all eternity that a certain nation will repent, how can he genuinely "devise a plan" against it in case it doesn't repent? Can God sincerely plan a course of action he knows with certainty he will never carry out? And how can God honestly "change his mind" if he eternally knew he would never embark on the course of action he is now supposedly deciding against? These are serious difficulties for the classical position, for the *point of this passage* is to encourage people to believe that God is willing and able to change his mind. If we, following the classical tradition, insist that God never "really" devises a plan against a nation and then changes his mind, we are not simply reinterpreting the passage—we are contradicting it.

The Lord emphasizes his virtuous flexibility again in Jeremiah 26:2-3. As we saw earlier, the Lord here tells Jeremiah to prophesy to Judah that they should repent, saying, "I may change my mind about the disaster that I intend to bring on [Judah] because of their evil doings." When the priests and officials of Judah hear Jeremiah's prophecy, they want to kill him because they are angry about the judgment he has pronounced (Jer 26:7-11). But Jeremiah responds, "Amend your ways and your doings, and obey the voice of the LORD your God, and the LORD will change his mind about the disaster that he has pronounced against you" (Jer 26:13). Some of the elders come to Jeremiah's defense and remind the priests and officials of another instance in Judah's history when, because of the repentance of King Hezekiah and the people of Judah, God changed his mind about the judgment the prophet Micah had prophesied against them (Jer 26:16-19; cf. Micah). This passage encourages believers *to trust in God's wise flexibility.* Scripture celebrates this as one of God's attributes of greatness (Joel 2:12-13; Jon 4:2).

If we refuse to believe that God is capable of changing his mind—insisting instead that God is "above" such change and that the future is exhaustively settled in his mind—aren't we disobeying the explicit teaching of Jeremiah 26? If we don't contradict this passage when we say that God *doesn't* change his mind, what would a contradiction of this passage say? Similarly, if this text does not teach that God may really change his mind, what would a text that *did* teach this say? Suppose, for the sake of argument, that God in fact wanted to tell us, "I may change my mind." How could he do so more clearly and convincingly than he did here? If his saying "I may change my mind" in Scripture isn't enough to convince us that God may in fact change his mind, then nothing would be. Despite the fact that critics accuse openness theists of being influenced by philosophical presuppositions, I submit that it is the classical view's *denial* of God's ability to change his mind—not the openness view's *affirmation* of this capacity—that is driven by philosophical presuppositions. It seems that what Scripture is and is not allowed to say has been decided beforehand. One of the things it is not allowed to say is that "the LORD will change his mind," even if this is exactly what the text says (e.g., Jer 26:13). Ironically, among some evangelicals today, those who *do* accept that "the Lord may change his mind" are actually judged to be unbiblical and even heretical for doing so![17]

Other passages showing divine flexibility. Many other passages reinforce the teaching that God may change his mind. Space allows us to sample only a few. In 1 Chronicles 21:15, for example, the author tells us that the Lord sent "an angel to Jerusalem *to destroy it*." However, "when he was about to destroy it, the LORD . . . *relented* concerning the calamity." We must wonder whether the Lord genuinely intended "to destroy" Jerusalem—to the point of actually dispatching an angel to accomplish the task—if he was certain from all eternity that he

---

[17]Thomas Oden referred to the openness view of the future as "a heresy that must be rejected on scriptural grounds" in "The Real Reformers and the Traditionalists," *Christianity Today,* February 9, 1998, p. 46. Robert Strimple also labeled the openness view "heretical" and associated it with Socinianism in "What Does God Know?" in *The Coming Evangelical Crisis,* ed. J. H. Armstrong (Chicago: Moody Press, 1996). While the openness view is rarely found in church history, it has never been pronounced heretical when held by orthodox Christians. To date, little research has been done on the presence of this view among orthodox Christians throughout history, but we know it was explicitly held by Calcidius, a fifth-century theologian. It was also held and frequently debated among nineteenth-century Methodists, such as Lorenzo McCabe, the chancellor of Ohio Wesleyan University, and the popular circuit preacher Billy Hibbard. Nineteenth-century theologians such as G. T. Fechner, Otto Pfeiderer and Jules Lequier as well as the great Bible commentator Adam Clarke also held this view. Finally, according to some African American theologians, the openness view is commonly assumed within the African American Christian tradition. On the views of Calcidius, see J. Den Boeft, *Calcidius on Fate: His Doctrine and Sources* (New York: E. J. Brill, 1997); Calcidius, *Timaeus a Calcidio translatus Commentarioque instructus,* ed. J. H. Waszink, 2nd ed., vol. 4 of Plato Latinus (Leiden: E. J. Brill, 1975); G. Verbeke, *The Presence of Stoicism in Medieval Thought* (Washington, D.C.: Catholic University Press of America, 1983), pp. 82-83. Lorenzo D. McCabe's writings are *Divine Nescience of Future Contingencies a Necessity* (New York: Philips & Hunt, 1882) and *The Foreknowledge of God* (Cincinnati: Cranston & Stowe, 1887). Billy Hibbard's remarkably insightful views can be found in his *Memoirs of the Life and Travels of B. Hibbard,* 2nd ed. (New York: Piercy & Reed, 1843), pp. 372-414. On the openness of the future within the African American Christian tradition, see Major Jones, *The Color of God: The Concept of God in Afro-American Thought* (Macon, Ga.: Mercer, 1987), p. 95. The most fundamental question is this: How much should the presence or absence of a view in history count for or against it? For Protestants who affirm *sola scriptura,* the validity of theological views must be assessed strictly by their compatibility with Scripture. Tradition is only authoritative insofar as it illuminates Scripture.

wouldn't destroy the city? If God always knew he wouldn't destroy Jerusalem, isn't Scripture simply wrong in claiming that God sent the angel "to destroy it"?

Similarly, the Lord told King Hezekiah he would not recover from his sickness (2 Kings 20:1). Hezekiah pleaded with him, however, and as a result the Lord reversed his stated intention, even saying, "I will add fifteen years to your life" (2 Kings 20:6). Now, if the Lord was certain all along that Hezekiah wouldn't die, wasn't he being duplicitous when he told Hezekiah he would not recover? And if God's plan all along was for Hezekiah to live another fifteen years, isn't Scripture misleading when it says God *added* fifteen years to his life?

One of the most familiar examples of the Lord's changing his mind involved Moses as an intercessor. Because of Moses' intercessory prayer, the Bible says, "The LORD *changed his mind* about the disaster that *he planned* to bring on his people" (Ex 32:14). David later recounts this episode when he writes:

> Therefore he [the Lord] said he would destroy them—
> had not Moses, his chosen one,
> stood in the breach before him,
> to turn away his wrath from destroying them. (Ps 106:23)

If God was certain from all eternity that he wouldn't bring disaster on his people, isn't Scripture wrong when it explicitly states that God *planned on doing just this?*

Other examples that further illustrate this point include the following:

☐ At one point, the Bible says, "the LORD *intended* to destroy [the Israelites]" (Deut 9:25; cf. 9:14) and was even "ready to destroy [Aaron]" (9:20), but Moses' forty-day intercession altered God's intention (9:25-29).

☐ God promised Eli he would allow his family to minister before him forever, but God then reversed his decision when Eli scorned God's sacrifices (1 Sam 2:27-31).

☐ God announced his plan to "bring disaster on [Ahab]" but then changed his mind when Ahab "humbled himself" (1 Kings 21:21-29).

☐ Because of Rehoboam's rebellion the Lord announced his plan to allow Shishak to conquer the Israelites but then reversed his decision when they repented (2 Chron 12:5-8).

☐ When Ezekiel found a request of the Lord to be offensive, the Lord modified his request (Ezek 4:9-15).

☐ The Lord gave Amos several visions of future judgments he was planning; God then changed his mind in the light of Amos's intercessory prayer (Amos 7:1-6).

☐ The people of Nineveh repented and believed that "God may relent and change his mind" (Jon 3:9). Consequently, "God changed his mind about the calamity that he had said he would bring on them" (Jon 3:10).

☐ Several times the Lord threatens to "blot out" the names of people he has written in his book of life (Rev 3:5; 22:18-19; cf. Ex 32:32; Ps 69:28), demonstrating a change in God's heart and intentions toward people.

Scripture explicitly teaches and frequently illustrates that God changes his mind. Together with the other passages that compose the motif of future openness, they form a compelling biblical case for the partial openness of the future. If we accept what these texts clearly say, we must conclude that, despite the classical view's conclusion, the first motif does not tell the whole story of God's relationship to the future. The motif that celebrates God's control and foreknowledge of a partially settled future is complemented by an equally strong motif that celebrates God's wise and creative responsiveness to a partly open future.

Part Three: Five Objections

We have discussed the biblical foundation of the classical view and have concluded that it does not warrant the conclusion that the future is exhaustively settled. We then outlined the biblical case for the openness view of creation and have concluded that it warrants the conclusion that the future is partly open. Our final task shall be to defend this view against five of its most common objections.

The passages used to support the openness view are anthropomorphic and phenomenological. The most frequent objection to the openness view of creation is that it takes the Bible too literally. Defenders of the classical view argue that every passage openness theists cite to support a partly open future is either anthropomorphic or phenomenological. If we speak of God as he *really* is, the argument goes, God is "above" the sort of change these verses ascribe to him.[18] I will offer five responses to this objection.

---

[18]See, e.g., John Calvin, *Commentaries on the First Book of Moses*, trans. J. King (Grand Rapids, Mich.: Eerdmans, 1948), 1:248-49. For several contemporary restatements of this position, see Ware, "Evangelical Reformulation," p. 442; N. Geisler, *Creating God in the Image of Man? NeoTheism's Dangerous Drift* (Minneapolis: Bethany House, 1997), pp. 90, 108. This interpretation originates with ancient Greek philosophers who sought to demythologize popular stories about the gods. So far as I've been able to discover, Philo was the first within the Jewish tradition to apply it to the Bible. From him it crept into the Christian tradition through Clement of Alexandria and Origen. On this, see J. C. McLelland, *God the Anonymous*, Patristic Monograph Series (Cambridge, Mass.: The Philadelphia Patristic Foundation, 1976), 4:37-40, 122-23, and passim. On the use of this interpretative strategy among the ancient Greeks, see W. Jaeger, *The Theology of the Early Greek Philosophers* (reprint, Oxford: Clarendon, 1948).

First, nothing in any of these passages suggests that they are either anthropomorphic or phenomenological. They don't say that it is *as though* God changes his mind, regrets previous decisions, is surprised or disappointed and so on. They rather teach these things in a very straightforward manner (cf. Jer 26:3). As we have argued earlier, if God can't convince us by explicitly saying he can and does change his mind, experience regret and so on, *how could he convince us if he wanted to?*

Second, the arguments used to justify treating this entire motif as anthropomorphic are weak and sometimes self-refuting. Consider, for example, John Calvin's treatment of passages which teach that God may change his mind. Calvin argues that Scripture depicts God as changing his mind "because our weakness does not attain to his exalted state." Hence, "the description of him that is given to us must be accommodated to our capacity so that we may understand it." This "mode of accommodation is for him to represent himself to us not as he is in himself, but as he seems to us." Therefore, although God seems to change his mind, in truth "neither God's plan nor his will is reversed, nor his volition altered."[19]

Calvin's argument is inconsistent, however. He apparently believes that *his* "weakness" does not preclude *him* from "attaining to" God's "exalted state." In other words, Calvin exempts himself from his explanation of why God must use anthropomorphic language (viz., that our weakness cannot attain to God's exalted state). And from this exempt position he then represents God to us *as he truly is* as opposed to the way *God represents himself* in Scripture (viz., "according to our weakness" and as he "seems to us").

Not only is this line of reasoning inconsistent, it is presumptuous and arbitrary. It could be used to defend any philosophical presupposition. To illustrate, suppose my philosophical presupposition is that God is really "above love." Following Calvin, I could argue that when Scripture says God loves us, it is describing God as he appears to us and in language we can understand, not God as he really is. God accommodates himself to us in this way because our weakness cannot attain to his "exalted state." Fortunately, I am exempt from this weakness and can therefore see past this accommodation and understand God in his "exalted state." Indeed, I now reveal to you what God had difficulty revealing in a literal fashion: namely, that in truth neither God's nature nor his will is really loving. Don't be deceived by God's accommodation. Follow my theology and think of God as he truly is. For people who adhere to the princi-

---

[19]John Calvin, *Institutes of the Christian Religion,* ed. J. T. McNeill, trans. F. L. Battles (Philadelphia: Westminster Press, n.d.), 1.17.13, p. 227.

ple of *sola scriptura,* the presumptuousness of this approach should be cause for concern.

Third, the texts that constitute the second motif do not readily lend themselves to the classical interpretation. Like all figures of speech, anthropomorphisms must reflect reality at some level if they communicate anything truthful. Expressions like "the right hand of God" or "the eyes of the Lord," for example, communicate something true of God's strength and knowledge. But what does the concept of God's changing his mind communicate, for example, if indeed it is an anthropomorphism? If God in fact never changes his mind, saying he does so doesn't communicate anything truthful: it is simply inaccurate.[20] This observation is especially important when we recall that several passages expressly encourage us to think about God as being capable of changing his mind (Jer 18:1-10; 26:2-3, 13) and depict God's willingness to change as one of his praiseworthy attributes (Joel 2:13-14; Jon 4:2).

Nor do these passages easily lend themselves to phenomenological interpretations. Most of them concern material that doesn't *appear* to us at all. When Scripture reports that the Lord's expectations or plans did not come to pass, for example, it is revealing something we wouldn't otherwise know. We are given access to God's subjective states—what he thinks, plans and feels. For example, "God thought, 'If the people face war, they *may* change their minds'" (Ex 13:17). There is nothing *apparent* about the material of these passages; hence they can't be explained away phenomenologically.

Fourth, as we saw in the passages that depict God as changing his mind, these passages cannot be dismissed as anthropomorphisms without undermining the integrity of Scripture. For example, Scripture says that because of Moses' intercession, "the LORD changed his mind about the disaster that *he planned* to bring on his people" (Ex 32:14; cf. Deut 9:13-14, 18-20, 25; Ps 106:23). If the Lord didn't really change his mind, then neither did he really plan to bring disaster on his people. Scripture thus misleads us when it explicitly tells us the Lord planned this before he changed his mind. While other expressions such as "the right hand of God" are rightly considered anthropomorphisms to preserve the integrity of Scripture, considering the portrayals of God's changing his mind in this fashion has the opposite effect. Out of fidelity to Scripture we ought to abandon this classical interpretation.

Finally, it can be argued that the classical view of God as "above" time, change, disappointment, suffering, empathy, vulnerability and so on is itself

---

[20]See Sanders's similar argument in *God Who Risks,* pp. 69-70. His discussion on "divine repentance" (pp. 66-75) is illuminating.

anthropomorphic.[21] This philosophical presupposition is not based on theological reflections of Jesus Christ as the definitive revelation of God (Jn 1:18) or on acceptance of the plain meaning of Scripture. Ancient Greek philosophers advocated essentially this view of God without the aid of the revelation of Jesus Christ or the biblical narrative. This view of God is arrived at rather as a result of people's relying on natural reason, thus making God in their own image, according to their own expectations of what God is "supposed" to be like. The truly nonanthropomorphic God does not conform to our natural expectations. He reveals his unchanging character of love by his willingness to change in response to us (Jer 18:1-10). He reveals his unchanging omnipotence by his willingness to become a human being who is crucified. He reveals his unsurpassable sovereignty by his willingness to move with us in history, to experience disappointment and frustration and to become vulnerable to those he loves.

The openness view contradicts Scripture. Another objection frequently raised to the openness view of the future in general, and the notion that God changes his mind in particular, is that it seems to contradict several passages of Scripture. In 1 Samuel 15:29, the prophet Samuel tells Saul that "the Glory of Israel will not recant or change his mind; for he is not a mortal, that he should change his mind." Numbers 23:19 declares that "God is not a human being, that he should lie, or a mortal, that he should change his mind." Defenders of the classical view of foreknowledge argue that these two passages contradict those passages that describe God as changing his mind. Unlike all those verses, however, these two verses specify that they are speaking about God in nonanthropomorphic ways (e.g., God is not a human being). Hence, it is concluded, these passages describe God as he *really* is, not in human terms or in terms of how he appears.

A closer examination of both passages reveals that they do not contradict the teaching that God changes his mind and do not warrant being taken more literally than passages which teach that God changes his mind.

1 Samuel 15:29. First, the teaching that God changed his mind about Saul's kingship is not based on one or two incidental phrases in this chapter, but rather it is central to the broader narrative. Scripture tells us that God originally intended to have Saul's family reign and to bless him (1 Sam 13:13-14). In good faith God made him king over Israel. After Saul's fall, however, God revoked

---

[21]Dietrich Bonhoeffer argued along these lines: "The abstract concept of God is fundamentally much more anthropomorphic, just because it is not intended to be anthropomorphic, than childlike anthropomorphism" (*Creation and Fall* [London: SCM Press, 1959], p. 43).

his blessing and replaced his kingship with David's. The two statements in 1 Samuel 15 reveal the motive behind this change in divine plans: God regretted his decision to make Saul king. The point is that this portion of the narrative is *structured* around God's regret concerning Saul's kingship. We cannot dismiss these two statements as anthropomorphisms without calling into question the integrity of the history which this portion of the narrative reports.

Second, Samuel prayed all night *trying to change the Lord's mind* regarding Saul's dethronement (1 Sam 15:11). Apparently Samuel believed that God could *in principle* change his mind about things. After crying out to the Lord all night, however, Samuel concluded that in this case God *wouldn't* change his mind. There is a big difference between *couldn't* and *wouldn't*. The classical view of divine foreknowledge teaches the former, but Scripture teaches the latter—and only in certain instances. We find several examples of God's declaring, essentially, "I *will not* change my mind" (Ezek 24:14; Zech 8:14). At one point the Lord actually declares, "I am weary of relenting" (Jer 15:6). Sometimes the Lord resolves to change his mind no more. But the exceptions prove the rule. It is only meaningful for God to say he *will not* change his mind if it is also true that God *can* and *does* change his mind when he wants to.

If Saul had genuinely repented of his sin instead of begging *Samuel* to change things with a purely selfish motive (1 Sam 15:24-25, 30), God may have reversed his decision once again for all we know. Unfortunately, Saul gave God no reason to forgive him or restore him. And, unlike fallible and fickle humans, God can't be cajoled into altering his plans for any reasons other than what are consistent with his unchanging holy character. In this sense he "is not a mortal, that he should change his mind."

Numbers 23:19. In Numbers 23:19, Balak attempted to get Balaam (a "prophet for hire") to prophesy what he wanted to hear (cf. Num 22:38—23:17). The Lord informed Balak that he, the true God, is not like a human being who can lie when it's profitable or a mortal who will change his mind when it's convenient. False prophets like Balaam commonly portrayed fickle false gods when it suited the prophets' cause. But for the first time in his life, Balak (and Balaam!) had confronted the real God. This God is not like a mortal who would change his mind for the carnal reasons Balak gave.

There is no contradiction between this teaching (i.e., God is not a mortal) and the pervasive teaching that God's intentions can and do change. There is, therefore, no reason to interpret less literally than these passages the numerous passages which teach that God sometimes changes his mind. Both sets of passages should be affirmed as accurately depicting God *as he really is.* God's mind is unchanging in every way in which it is virtuous to be unchanging, but it is open to change in every way in which it is virtuous to be open to change.

The openness view undermines God's omniscience. The openness view of the future is often accused of undermining God's omniscience. Indeed, sometimes it is referred to as the "limited omniscience" position.[22] As noted in the introduction, the disagreement between the openness and classical views is not over the scope or perfection of God's knowledge; it is rather over the content of reality that (we all agree) God exhaustively knows. More specifically, it is over whether or not reality includes, or merely excludes, possibilities. God's omniscience is the presupposition, not the subject matter, of this debate.

To illustrate, suppose two people disagree about the number of hairs on someone's head. They both believe that because God is omniscient, God perfectly knows the number of hairs on this person's head (Mt 10:30). While they may disagree over the number of hairs on this person's head, they are not disagreeing about the perfection of God's knowledge. It would be ludicrous for one party to accuse the other of limiting God's knowledge on the grounds that in their view God knows a smaller number of hairs. Accusing openness theists of limiting God's knowledge is no less ludicrous, however. Openness theists could just as easily accuse a defender of the classical view of limiting God's knowledge because they *deny* that God knows possibilities as genuine possibilities.

Christians have historically agreed that God cannot do the logically impossible. God cannot create a rock so heavy he cannot lift it, for example, because the concept of such a rock is meaningless. We would not be ascribing anything positive to God by insisting that he *could* create such a rock because he is omnipotent and can therefore "do anything." For the same reason, we would not be ascribing anything positive to God by insisting that he could know the weight of this unliftable rock because he is omniscient and thus "knows everything."

Now, theologians sometimes disagree about whether or not something is a logical contradiction and thus about whether or not God can perform it. But that doesn't mean they question whether or not God is omnipotent. For example, some Calvinists claim that God is able to determine all events while nevertheless preserving the morally responsible freedom of agents. Arminians argue that God is not able to do this because it constitutes a logical contradiction. But they are not, on this account, disagreeing about whether or not God is omnipotent. So too, the classical view affirms that God can eternally foreknow the

---

[22]For example, F. Beckwith, "Limited Omniscience and the Test for a Prophet: A Brief Philosophical Analysis," *Journal of the Evangelical Theological Society* 36, no. 3 (1993): 357-62.

future with exhaustive settledness while nevertheless preserving the morally responsible freedom of agents. Openness theists argue that God is not able to do this because it constitutes a logical contradiction. He can't know future free actions before they are resolved for the same reason he can't know the weight of a rock he cannot lift. But this doesn't mean openness theists question God's omniscience. This frequent criticism of openness theism is a caricature that only serves to install unnecessary fear in people's minds toward this view. It hinders the discussion from moving forward in a healthy, Christian manner.

The openness view undermines God's sovereignty.

Sovereignty and control. Another common objection to the openness view of creation is that it undermines God's sovereignty. The extent to which the future is open-ended, it is argued, is the extent to which God is not in control. For some critics, this is tantamount to denying that God is God.[23]

The openness view does emphasize the role of free agents in influencing what transpires in world history. It also agrees with classical Arminianism that not everything happens according to God's will. This explains why the world is full of suffering and evil even though it was created by an all-holy and all-loving Creator. As in classical Arminianism, the openness view holds that humans and fallen angels can and do thwart God's will for their own lives and interfere with God's will for others.

This does not compromise God's sovereignty over the world, however. In contrast to what is called "process thought," openness theism and classical Arminianism hold that God *chose* to create this world and give agents power to resist him. Only in this way could God create a world that was capable of love, for love must be chosen. In making this decision, God temporarily *limited his*

---

[23]For example, R. C. Sproul argues, "If there is any part of creation outside of God's sovereignty [viz., control], then God is simply not sovereign. If God is not sovereign, then God is not God." Hence, he concludes, "If we reject divine sovereignty then we must embrace atheism" (*Chosen by God* [Wheaton, Ill.: Tyndale House, 1986], pp. 26, 27). In other words, God must control everything to exist as God. If any element of chance existed in the universe, Sproul argues, "it would destroy God's sovereignty. . . . If God is, chance is not. The two cannot coexist by reason of the impossibility of the contrary." God's control must extend to every molecule. Sproul's argument continues: "If there is one single molecule in this universe running around loose, . . . then we have no guarantee that a single promise of God will ever be fulfilled. Perhaps that one maverick molecule will lay waste all the grand and glorious plans that God has made and promised to us. . . . Maybe that one molecule will be the thing that prevents Christ from returning" (*Not a Chance: The Myth of Chance in Modern Science and Cosmology* [Grand Rapids, Mich.: Baker, 1994], p. 3). There is, I submit, no conceivably weaker view of divine sovereignty than one that is threatened by a single maverick molecule.

own ability to unilaterally get his way. But, as Scripture clearly shows, God has not given away more power to creatures than he can handle. That would obviously be an unwise decision, and thus an all-wise God would not make it.

Far from diminishing his sovereignty, this understanding of God's relation to the world most exalts it. Some Christians use the word *sovereignty* as though it is synonymous with *control*. Hence any view (including classical Arminianism) that does not portray God as controlling everything by definition undermines God's sovereignty. But can't we conceive of a more praiseworthy way that God might choose to be sovereign over his creation? If we take our model of divine sovereignty from the biblical narrative, centered on the crucified Son of God, we discover that God's sovereignty is a *sovereignty of love* rather than control. Fallen humans tend to make God after our own image by projecting our own lust for control onto him. But, I submit, such a portrait of God is not reflected in Scripture or revealed in the character of Christ.

God demonstrates his sovereignty by empowering others to enter into a loving relationship with him. He demonstrates his sovereignty when, out of love, he puts himself in a position where his heart might be grieved and frustrated because of the adultery of his beloved (Hos 3). And, most importantly, he demonstrates his incomprehensible sovereign power when he himself comes to earth and allows himself to be crucified for sinners. *This* is what it is for God to have all power and authority, and *this* ought to be the model by which we exercise power within the body of Christ (Lk 22:24-27; Eph 5:25-27; Phil 2:5-8).

It takes a truly sovereign God to make himself vulnerable like this. It takes a God who is truly in control to be willing to give away some of his control, knowing that doing so might cause him incredible pain. It takes a truly wise and creative God to guarantee victory without having to control every detail of history. By contrast, to simply control others so that you always get your way is a sure sign of insecurity and weakness.

The praiseworthy chess master. At this juncture an analogy might help demonstrate this point. Which of the following three chess masters would you admire most? The first chess master is confident of victory in a given match because she is playing a computer that she personally programmed. She foreknows every move her "opponent" will make because she programmed its moves. The second chess master is confident of victory because she too is playing a computer. While she didn't personally program this computer, she possesses a manual with exhaustive information of exactly how the computer will respond during this match. A third chess master is confident of victory even though she is playing a real person, not a computer. Though she cannot be certain of how her opponent will move, for her opponent is a free agent, she is certain she can wisely out-maneuver him. This chess master does not foreknow exactly what moves her opponent *will* make, but she perfectly anticipates all the moves her opponent *might* make. And on the basis of this superior intelligence, she is confident of victory.

Acknowledging that all analogies break down somewhere, I believe the scenario of the first chess master corresponds to the Calvinist view, in which God foreknows everything as settled because he predestines everything. The second corresponds to the Arminian view, in which God foreknows everything as settled though he has not predestined everything. The third corresponds to the openness view, in which God neither predestines nor foreknows everything as settled but is nevertheless certain of victory because of his divine wisdom. It is the only model in which God wins by virtue of his wisdom, creativity and problem-solving intelligence, because it is the only model in which God has to genuinely think, plan and respond to other personal agents. To simply control or possess information about the future requires no virtuous attributes.

Despite the various claims made by some today that we must protect "the sovereignty of God" by emphasizing his absolute control over creation and by denouncing the openness view, I submit that we ought to denounce the view that God exercises total control over everything, for a truly sovereign God is powerful enough to share power and face a partly open future.

The openness view is discomforting. A final objection is that the openness view of creation has pastoral disadvantages. If God doesn't foreknow all that shall come to pass, he doesn't specifically choose to allow all that comes to pass. Hence, in the openness view, there is no assurance that all the events in our life fit into God's plan. Our suffering may be meaningless. As a pastor I am sensitive to this charge, and I shall offer four responses to it.

First, it is important that we distinguish between objective and personal preferences. In our postmodern age people tend to decide what they will and will not believe on the basis of what they like and don't like. But does truth always conform to our preferences? We don't think so when the truth is a doctor's report on our health. So too, some may find it comforting to believe that everything that happens was specifically pre-ordained or at least pre-allowed by God. But this sense of comfort doesn't at all count in favor of the truth of these beliefs or against the view that denies these beliefs.

Second, while the belief that there is a specific purpose behind every event is sometimes comforting, at other times it is horrifying. Every year several thousand children disappear. Suppose this year your daughter becomes one of them. In one nightmarish moment, your life changes forever. You now live in the tormented reality of wondering what is being done to your little girl, if she is still alive. How does the belief that God always knew this would happen and intentionally allowed (or ordained) it for a higher purpose help you cope with this nightmare? Would it not make God a co-conspirator with the kidnapper?

I do not mean to suggest that the openness view by itself adequately resolves the problem of evil. But I believe it is an important piece of a comprehensive approach that does adequately resolve this problem. We can understand why God must allow free agents to exercise their freedom *once he has given it,* for to revoke freedom because it is being misused would mean that it was never genuinely given in the first place.[24] But how are we to understand God's giving freedom to creatures whom he is certain ahead of time (let alone has predestined ahead of time) will use it to commit atrocious acts on innocent people and eternally damn themselves to hell? The answer that he has a "good sovereign reason" wears thin, especially when you are the parent of a kidnapped child.

Third, as I have argued elsewhere, the assumption that there is a divine reason behind every event in history is contradicted by Scripture.[25] True, God sometimes ordains or at least allows hardships to occur to individuals or nations in order to punish them, to refine their character or to achieve some other purpose. But nothing warrants the assumption that this truth should be universalized to cover all hardships. For example, without exception, Jesus treated disease as ultimately coming from Satan, not God (Acts 10:38). He demonstrated God's will by defeating the devil and eliminating these things.[26]

Fourth, while the openness view can't assure people that all the events in their lives fit into God's plan (if this should be called an "assurance"), it can offer people the same comfort the New Testament offers. The New Testament never guarantees people protection from harm. Instead, it promises them eternal life in the coming kingdom of God, and this makes hardships in this life worth enduring (Rom 8:18). Jesus taught us to pray that the Father's will would be done "on earth as it is in heaven" (Mt 6:10)—which implicitly assumes that his will is not uniformly being done on earth *now.* In the meantime, we find assurance in the New Testament that nothing can separate us from the love of God in Christ (Rom 8:35-39). It promises that God is with us in the midst of our suffering (Mt 28:20; Rom 8:17) and that he gives us a peace that passes understanding (Phil 4:7-9). And it promises that whatever happens, God will work to

---

[24]I develop this "principle of irrevocability" further in chapter six of *Satan and the Problem of Evil.*

[25]Gregory Boyd, *God at War: The Bible and Spiritual Conflict* (Downers Grove, Ill.: InterVarsity Press, 1996).

[26]According to 1 Jn 3:8, this was the primary reason the Son of God was revealed. On Jesus' healing, deliverance and teaching ministry as warfare against the devil, see ibid., chaps. 6-8.

bring good out of it (Rom 8:28). Because God is infinitely wise and sovereign, no event remains meaningless for those who love God and work with his sovereign purposes (cf. Eph 1:11). This, I suggest, is a much better—and more biblical—consolation than the belief that every nightmarish thing about our world is specifically allowed or ordained for a divine reason.

Conclusion

Proponents of the classical view mistakenly interpret the scriptural evidence that *some* of the future is settled as evidence that *all* the future is settled. This required them to dismiss the entire motif of future openness as anthropomorphic or phenomenological. Though opponents of the openness view frequently allege that it is unbiblical and principally motivated by philosophical considerations, I submit that in fact the classical view is unbiblical and overly motivated by philosophical considerations. Though I would argue that sound philosophy also supports the openness view, the motivating force behind the openness view is a desire to be faithful to the witness of Scripture. The openness view does not interpret the motif of future openness any less literally than it does the motif that celebrates God's control over and foreknowledge of the future.

The openness view not only makes better sense out of the whole of Scripture than alternative views, but has a number of theological and practical advantages as well. For example, it offers an answer to the question of why God creates people who end up inflicting horrifying suffering on others and damning themselves. The openness view of creation is most consistent with the understanding of reality that is being developed in contemporary science. It renders intelligible and motivates believers to assume an aggressive stance in combating evil in the world. It most effectively renders the power and urgency of prayer intelligible. Prayer not only changes us; it may change God's mind as well as the course of history. And the openness view provides a model of sovereignty that is most consistent with the revelation of God in Christ and that is therefore most exalted.[27]

I concede that traditional concepts should not be revised without a lengthy and prayerful process of discernment. Yet Protestantism is fundamentally rooted in the conviction that if there are sufficient scriptural reasons to do so, traditional doctrines can and should be revised. This essay has argued that the classical understanding of God's foreknowledge is a case in point. I have argued that in the light of Scripture it should be modified and expanded to include possibilities rather than limiting God's foreknowledge to settled facts.

---

[27]All these issues are covered in Boyd, *God of the Possible.*

A SIMPLE-FOREKNOWLEDGE RESPONSE

David Hunt

*G*regory Boyd's case for the open view is richly grounded in Scripture, and my response must therefore take this into account. But I want to begin where Boyd himself begins—with his attempt to recast the debate in this book as one over *creation* rather than *foreknowledge.*

The Nature of the Dispute

Boyd claims that he "agrees unequivocally with the classical view that God is omniscient" (p. 14). Yet he also denies that God has exhaustive knowledge of the future. Isn't this a contradiction? Not necessarily. An omniscient being must know all truths; but where there are no truths, there is nothing for an omniscient being to know.

This is where the doctrine of creation is supposed to come in. God had the power to create a world in which *everything* is exhaustively settled in advance, and he had the power to create a world in which (at least) *some* things are *not* exhaustively settled in advance. If God created the first world, there *would* be a complete set of truths about the future, and God (being omniscient) would know them; but if he created the second world, there would be gaps in the set of future truths and correspondent gaps in God's foreknowledge. In both worlds God is omniscient; but because of differences in *what* he created, there are consequent differences in what he can know.

Interestingly, Boyd and Helm both think that divine foreknowledge some-how depends on the kind of world we live in—and both appeal to science in support of their opposite conclusions! Helm cites universal causal determinism as essential to scientific explanation, while Boyd appeals to quantum indeter-minacy and chaos theory. But in my view such appeals are irrelevant. Consider a phenomenon favorable to Boyd's open view: the random decay of a radioac-tive particle as registered by a Geiger counter. Suppose the following *past-tense* sentence expresses a true proposition:

(p) This Geiger counter *emitted* a click at time *T*.

But if (p) is now true, then *prior* to *T* the following *future-tense* sentence would have expressed a true proposition:

(f) This Geiger counter *will* emit a click at time *T*.

And how could (f) be true *before* the click occurs? The question itself is con-fused: that's just what it is for a statement to be about the *future!* A past-tense statement is about what has *already* happened; a future-tense statement is about what has *not yet* happened. Of course the random character of the click means that the scientist monitoring the Geiger counter could not have *pre-dicted* (f). But this fact about the cognitive limitations of finite knowers is irrel-evant to (f)'s *truth*. For (f) to be true, it is enough that the Geiger counter emits a click at *T;* if it does, then (f) was true. And because (f) was true, a being who failed to know (f) would not be omniscient.

I suspect that Boyd's rendering of the dispute rests on an equivocation. There's a sense in which someone might "settle" or "determine" what happens by *making* it happen; there's also a sense in which someone might "settle" or "determine" what happens by *finding out* about it. With respect to a crime, for example, the criminal does the former whereas the detective does the latter. It's in this latter sense that exhaustive foreknowledge settles or determines the future—God simply *finds out* about it in advance. This does not entail that God *or anyone* has already settled or determined the future in the first sense.

Boyd and I in fact *agree* that God created a world in which at least some of the future has been left causally open, undetermined by the past and present. But we *disagree* about the conditions under which a future-tense sentence may express a true proposition. I think he's wrong, for the reasons just given. But this is a difference in the logical or metaphysical theories to which we subscribe, not a difference over the kind of world God created.

The Biblical Evidence

Boyd's first move, following the introductory clarification of his position, is to review the scriptural case for the classic "exhaustive foreknowledge" position and note that the texts do not absolutely *require* this position. This is correct, though not much follows from it. The case for the classic position is partly exegetical (Boyd himself allows that the scriptural evidence provides prima facie support for the classic view [p. 23]), but it's *only partly* exegetical. Though Boyd proposes that "exegesis should always drive our philosophy, instead of the other way around" (p. 14), his own procedure shows this to be an oversimplification. After all, there are no proof-texts to demonstrate beyond a shadow of a doubt that God knows the *past* or *present* in exhaustive detail; yet Boyd is comfortable asserting that "God possesses perfect knowledge of the past and present" (p. 21). Why? My guess is that Boyd probably subscribes (as do the rest of us) to some version of Helm's principle *A,* which inclines us to maximize the scope of divine omniscience wherever possible. Good for him! We disagree about divine foreknowledge not because some of us resist while others succumb to the temptations of a philosophically driven exegesis, but because we make different inferences from a philosophical presupposition (itself grounded in but not entailed by Scripture) that we all share.

Since there is a prima facie exegetical/philosophical case in favor of exhaustive foreknowledge, the important question is whether there is an even stronger case against it. This brings us to the heart of Boyd's argument. Since I cannot possibly respond to the full variety of texts Boyd deploys, let me look just at the first set and, more briefly, the last.

"God confronts the unexpected." In Isaiah 5:4 the Lord is said to have expected (domesticated) grapes from a vineyard that instead yielded wild grapes. Boyd asks (p. 24):

> Can a person expect something he is certain will never happen? Taking the passage at face value, does it not imply that God was not certain of the future of Israel, the "vineyard," until the Israelites settled it by choosing to yield "wild grapes" instead of the grapes God expected?

But there *is* no single "face value" reading of this passage. The statement "I expect that things will go this way" can express my *belief* about what will happen or it can announce my *standards* for future behavior ("these are my expectations"). The latter reading is no less natural than the former, and it implies nothing whatsoever about divine foreknowledge. "I expect you to be on your best behavior," I tell the five boys at my third-grade son's sleepover party, knowing full well that they will fall short of this standard during the course of the evening. Read this way, there is no problem seeing how God could expect one thing while knowing something else.

Boyd then refers to Jeremiah 19:5, where the Lord is surprised that Israel would do things "which I did not command or decree, nor did it enter my mind." Boyd adds, "However we interpret the difficult phrase 'nor did it enter my mind,' it seems to preclude the possibility that the Israelites' idolatrous behavior was *eternally certain in God's mind*" (p. 24). I don't believe it does preclude this. Learning that my best philosophy student has plagiarized his term paper, I exclaim, "I can't believe it!" This "can't believe" must be distinguished from the *ignorance* I was in before the facts came out; it's a disbelief that's possible even when I know the truth. I'm simply dumbfounded that someone with such ability, who did not need to plagiarize in order to write an "A" paper, would stoop to cheating. God must be similarly frustrated that his chosen people, on whom he lavished so much attention, would betray him. "It would never cross my mind that someone with all your advantages would do such a thing," he might say; and he might say it even though he knew from all eternity what they would do.

Not only are there perfectly natural alternatives to the readings that Boyd offers, but his own readings can be turned against him, since they implicate God in various *mistaken beliefs:* the belief that the vineyard would yield grapes, the belief that Israel would return to him (the "I thought" passages in Jeremiah 3) and so on. Boyd is understandably anxious to deflect this criticism. He therefore argues that the thoughts and expectations in question were really perfect and inerrant *probability estimates* based on the information then available to God (p. 15). In other words, the Jeremiah 3 passages are really attributing to God a belief something like this:

> (i) The probability that Israel will return to me, given how matters now stand, is greater than 0.5.

But Boyd denies that the passage attributes *this* belief to God:

> (ii) Israel will return to me.

This is both thoroughly implausible *and* fatal to Boyd's argument.

It is implausible because the passages speak simply of God's *expecting* or *thinking* that something will happen; there is nothing whatsoever to suggest probability estimates. This reading is clearly driven not by the text, but by the need to avoid at all cost attributing any mistake to God. (Ironically, the very next paragraph [p. 25] finds Boyd chiding proponents of the classical view for interpreting such passages figuratively, resisting the literal meaning of the text and allowing their exegesis to be "motivated by a philosophical preconception of what is and is not worthy of God"!)

It is also fatal to his argument because these passages are supposed to provide evidence that God sometimes does not know what is going to happen, and (i) provides no such evidence. Suppose (i) is true and the passages simply convey God's recognition of this fact, without suggesting in any way that God also believes (ii). Then how is this a proof-text for limited foreknowledge? Only if these passages are asserting (ii) as well as (i) do they conflict with exhaustive foreknowledge; but Boyd's own "philosophical preconception of what is and is not worthy of God" rightly rules this out of bounds.

"God changes his mind." Boyd illustrates this final motif with Jeremiah 18:4-10, whose key passage is this: "At one moment I may declare concerning a nation or a kingdom, that I will pluck up and break down and destroy it, but if that nation, concerning which I have spoken, turns from its evil, I will *change my mind* about the disaster that I intended to bring on it." Boyd comments, "The *point of this passage* is to encourage people to believe that God is willing and able to change his mind" (p. 34). But why is that encouraging? We wouldn't be much encouraged to discover that God changes his mind *arbitrarily!* The point presumably is that God might change his mind *in response* to what we do. This, however, is perfectly consistent with exhaustive foreknowledge and even with Boethian timeless omniscience, both of which allow that God's knowledge (and the intentions based on it) may *depend* on what we do.

But while the *point* of the passage does not require that God's knowledge be incomplete, the temporal *language* of the passage seems to do so. A defender of exhaustive foreknowledge therefore has no choice but to appeal to an "accommodationist" hermeneutics. But what's wrong with that? If this hermeneutic can be abused (and it certainly can), the moral is not to abuse it.

Here's one reading that I think is nonabusive. God's intentions (like ours) are sensitive to the beliefs he holds, and his total intention reflects his total body of beliefs—which in God's case includes exhaustive knowledge of the future. But it's also possible to consider just part of a body of beliefs, in abstraction from the rest, and to consider the partial intention corresponding to this partial set of beliefs. Sometimes it's even useful. When deliberating about my plagiarizing student, I might reason like this: "Considering just the fact that he cheated, I'm inclined to give him an F; but considering the quality of his other work, I'm inclined to be more lenient." Likewise, when God considers just a nation's current wickedness, the appropriate response might be to punish it; and this partial intention (reflecting only part of the information available to God) is the relevant one to make known to that nation if it is to mend its ways. God "changes his mind," then, in the sense that his beliefs and intentions, while not themselves undergoing change, are nevertheless responsive *in advance* to the changing conditions that obtain at different moments of time.

Boyd and Open Theism

I understand the excitement over Molinism; I don't understand the excitement over open theism. The idea that God becomes aware of contingent events only as they happen, just like we do, is supposed to make God's failure to prevent horrendous evils somehow more comprehensible. But how? The open theist's God, despite his precognitive impairment, has perfect knowledge of what is going on *now;* in the case of Boyd's kidnapped child, he has sufficient knowledge (and power) to stop a crime in progress, to rescue the victim and so on. Why doesn't he? I just don't see how Boyd's answer would differ from the "he has a 'good sovereign reason' " answer that Boyd thinks is so unsatisfactory when it comes from a classical theist. (Boyd does suggest that God refrains from intervening *out of respect for the kidnapper's free will,* but this strikes me as much more disturbing than the "good sovereign reason" answer.)[1]

The open view of the future is also supposed to be liberating; but it's liberation from an illusory enslavement. Given exhaustive foreknowledge, it follows that the future is *epistemically* settled in the divine mind; but it does *not* follow that the future is *causally* settled in any way that conflicts with human freedom. Boyd's acceptance of this fallacious inference, and his consequent rejection of exhaustive foreknowledge in the interests of human freedom, has the ironic result that he finds *less* free agency in the Bible than I do; for every time the Scriptures are unambiguously clear that someone's actions are divinely foreknown, Boyd must deny the person's freedom. With respect to Josiah and Cyrus, God's foreknowledge "obviously established parameters around the parents' freedom to naming these individuals . . . and also restricted the scope of freedom these individuals could exercise regarding *particular foreordained activities*" (p. 20). As for Christ's prediction that Peter would thrice betray him, Boyd must postulate divine manipulation of Peter's circumstances

---

[1]This paragraph responds to pp. 45-46.

so that "three times Peter's true character was squeezed out of him" (p. 21). There is in this respect a striking convergence between Boyd and Helm, the opposite ends of the spectrum of opinion represented in this volume.

Of the two, my preference is for Helm, for at least a couple of reasons: (1) I am more troubled by the proof-texts that Helm could cite (but doesn't), like Romans 9:15-21, than I am by Boyd's proof-texts. (2) God is the ultimate explanation for *all reality:* for everything *X,* if there were no God, there would be no *X.* Think about that. Now ask yourself, how could such a being be revealed to us *except* by anthropomorphizing him?

Despite disagreeing with Boyd on the merits of his position, I think it's important to put this disagreement in perspective. Both sides agree that God (sometimes) speaks about himself *as though* he changes his mind. If it were religiously important that we believe that God *never* changes his mind—important in the sense that, if we believed otherwise, we might fall into grievous error, perhaps even jeopardizing our salvation—it would be absolutely inexplicable why God would present himself *as though* he changes his mind. So while I disagree with Boyd on whether God changes his mind and on the best way to interpret Scripture, I can't get too exercised over our differences. No one's salvation hangs on this dispute.

A MIDDLE-KNOWLEDGE RESPONSE

William Lane Craig

*T*he debate over the nature of God's foreknowledge *is* primarily a debate about the scope or perfection of God's knowledge. Despite his protestations to the contrary, Gregory Boyd espouses a view that threatens to undermine divine omniscience. First, as I explain in my essay, both the standard definition of omniscience (O) and the revisionist's own (inadequate) definition (O") require that if future contingent propositions or counterfactuals of creaturely freedom (CCFs) are true, then they must be known by God. Since Boyd affirms divine omniscience and yet denies that God knows future contingents, he must hold that such propositions are not true. If such propositions are true, then Boyd's view undermines divine omniscience.

Second, (O) also requires that God hold no false beliefs. But on Boyd's account God does appear to hold many false beliefs, since God believes and expects that certain things will happen and is sometimes disappointed and even regretful about how things turn out. Boyd could try to wriggle out of this implication by pointing out that since future contingent propositions and CCFs are neither true nor false, God, in believing them, cannot be said to hold a literally *false* belief. But this escape route is of no avail. For if God believes *p*, he believes that it is true that *p*. But on Boyd's view the proposition *It is true that p* is presently false; therefore, God does hold a false belief. Moreover, CCFs, if they are not true, are—on the customary semantics for such propositions—uniformly false, so that in believing, say, that the Israelites would repent under certain circumstances, God holds a false belief. Therefore, even if future contingent propositions are neither true nor false, it turns out that on Boyd's view God is not omniscient.

According to the Principle of Bivalence, for any proposition *p*, *p* is either true or false. By affirming divine omniscience while denying God's knowledge of the future, Boyd has painted himself into the corner of denying that the Principle of Bivalence holds for future contingent propositions and CCFs. Now as a biblical theologian, is Boyd really prepared to defend so extraordinary and widely rejected a claim as the assertion that the Principle of Bivalence fails for future contingent propositions? In my book *The Only Wise God*, I assessed this claim and found it unwarranted, faced with formidable objections, and having absurd consequences.[1] It will be interesting to see how Boyd responds to my three arguments on behalf of premise (2) that "there are true CCFs" in my essay in this volume.

It needs to be clearly understood that Boyd cannot affirm that there are *any* such true propositions, for then the definition of omniscience requires that God know them, in which case God has knowledge of the determinate truth about an "unsettled" aspect of reality, which Boyd denies. If Boyd rejoins that the future contingents known to God are "settled" after all, then contingency (Boyd's "possibilities") is not incompatible with being "settled." That would contradict Boyd's view that God's knowing future contingents is as logically impossible as God's making a stone too heavy for him to lift.

This raises the question of what Boyd means when he says that future reality is "composed of both settled and open aspects" (p. 14). Frankly, I do not know what Boyd means by these metaphors—and I have a strong suspicion that he does not either. The best sense that I can make of his claim is that on all other views, God has *decreed* everything that will come to pass. In a sense, that is true; but then the question is whether God cannot decree, as Molinists

---

[1] See my book *The Only Wise God* (Grand Rapids, Mich.: Baker, 1987; Eugene, Ore.: Wipf & Stock, 2000), pp. 55-60.

affirm, that some events come to pass *contingently*. It is noteworthy that Boyd equates God's *settling* something with God's *determining* or *controlling* it. But on the Molinist view God does *not* decree how free agents behave in the circumstances in which he places them. There is thus the real possibility that the events foreknown by God will fail to happen; but if they were to fail to happen, God would have known that instead. Thus, this sense of being "settled" does not exclude possibilities from reality but, on the contrary, affirms them.

Boyd, then, faces two philosophical challenges: (1) to defend the claim that the Principle of Bivalence fails for future contingent propositions and CCFs, and (2) to show that his view alone is able to affirm real possibilities in the world.

Unfortunately, Boyd does not take up these challenges but chooses instead to focus on biblical passages. Even here, however, his philosophical naiveté hampers his exegesis. Consider, first, the biblical warrant for God's knowledge of future contingents. Boyd's strategy is to show that the texts do not justify *exhaustive* knowledge of the future on God's part. The problem with Boyd's procedure is not merely that it takes on the appearance of arguing that someone could pick his way unharmed through an avalanche by theoretically calculating the trajectory of each rock; the problem is that the defender of divine foreknowledge need only show that God knows just *one* future contingent proposition or CCF, for in that case (1) there is no logical incompatibility between divine foreknowledge and future contingents, (2) the Principle of Bivalence does not fail for such propositions, and (3) it becomes ad hoc to claim that other such propositions are not also true and known to God.

So take just one example of each sort of proposition, say, "Before the cock crows twice, you will deny me three times" (Mk 14:30) and "None of the rulers of this age understood this; for if they had, they would not have crucified the Lord of glory" (1 Cor 2:8). Both statements are bivalent and true. So are they contingent? They cannot describe events caused by God, since they concern sinful acts, of which God cannot be the author. Neither are they plausibly determined by secondary causes. Boyd's attempt to explain away Jesus' prediction of Peter's denials as an inference from his flawed character is fanciful. Granted that Jesus could infer that Peter would fail him, how could he infer that Peter's failure would come in the form of denials, rather than, say, flight or silence, and how could he infer *three* denials before the cock crowed *twice?* In the absence of middle knowledge, Boyd's claim that God "orchestrated" the circumstances implies that God took away the freedom of the servant girl and all the others in the courtyard of the high priest's house, as well as of those at the arrest of Jesus. Thus, perversely, the open view winds up destroying contingency and freedom—what we end up with is, in fact, Paul Helm's compatibilistic account of divine foreknowledge! Similarly, it is implausible to think that the demonic forces referred to in 1 Corinthians 2:8 were determined by secondary causes so that this is not a CCF. Thus, Boyd's handling of the evidence on behalf of divine foreknowledge of future contingents is desperate.

Moreover, he fails to consider the full scope of the evidence. As I explain in my essay, it is impossible to have a biblically sound doctrine of providence on the open view. Consider the account of Saul's death in 1 Samuel 31:1-6 and 1 Chronicles 10:8-12. Both writers describe Saul's suicide. But then the Chronicler adds this stunning comment: "Therefore the Lord slew him and turned the kingdom over to David" (1 Chron 10:14). Now how is the open theologian to make sense of this assertion? Saul's suicide was considered a sinful and disgraceful deed and therefore could not have been causally determined by God. Yet his suicide, says the Chronicler, was God's doing. Or think of Joseph's statement to his brothers in Egypt: "You meant evil against me, but God meant it for good in order to bring about this present result" (Gen 50:20). Again, the brothers' crime could not have been caused by God; and yet God sovereignly directed events toward his previsioned end. Open theology is impotent to explain this coalescence of human freedom and divine sovereignty. Ironically, open theology is forced to revert to Calvinistic determinism to account for God's providence and thus actually winds up destroying human freedom. By contrast, Molinism provides a perspicuous account of divine sovereignty and human freedom in terms of God's middle knowledge.

The second half of Boyd's biblical argument is his citation of passages implying God's ignorance of future contingents. Certainly there are such passages; the whole question is how we should understand them. Here two points need to be made.

First, a consistent application of Boyd's hermeneutic leads to a defective concept of God. It is striking how similar Boyd's literalistic hermeneutic is to that of Mormon theologians, who employ it to justify their belief in a God who is not only ignorant of future contingents but is a physical being with human form. Like Boyd, the Mormon theologian insists on taking the biblical descriptions of God at face value. "Look here," he says, "the Scripture *says* that God was walking in the cool of the garden. Walking necessitates having legs. God *says* he has eyes and ears and arms and hands. If God can't convince us by explicitly saying that he can and does have bodily parts, *how could he convince us if he wanted to?*" It is difficult to see how one can adopt Boyd's naive literalism with respect to divine knowledge and yet reject it with respect to divine corporeality.[2] Mormon theologians realize this and have therefore opened the doors of Brigham Young University to openness theologians to present guest lectures there.

The fundamental flaw of this hermeneutic is its failure to appreciate that the Bible is not a textbook in systematic theology or philosophy of religion but that it is largely a collection of *stories* about God's dealings with men. These stories are told from the human perspective and evince all the liveliness of the storyteller's art. God is sometimes portrayed as ignorant not only of future contingents but even of present states of affairs and past events (e.g., Gen 3:9-11; 18:21). It is hard to exaggerate how pervasive in Scripture anthropomorphic portrayals of God are. Not only are there the obvious anthropomorphisms, like God's having arms and legs, but the unconscious anthropomorphisms, such as God's "seeing" the distress of his people or "hearing" their prayer or "striking" his enemies. Contrary to Boyd, we have every reason to be suspicious of a literal interpretation of passages that portray God as finite or limited.

But then what, Boyd demands, is the truth communicated by such anthropomorphic portrayals of God? That leads me to my second point: Molinism can make sense of the passages adduced by Boyd in defense of his view. In general, the truth communicated to us by these passages is that God's sovereignty does not consist of blind decrees operating irrespective of free human responses; rather, God's decrees take into account and are conditioned by the free acts of creatures. This truth is expressed anthropomorphically from the human point of view in terms of God's disappointment or frustration or relenting on planned action. Thus, I agree with Boyd that such passages do undermine a Calvinistic conception of an all-determining God. But Boyd's problem is that the only alternatives he knows are either Calvinistic determinism or openness. His essay shows no awareness of a Molinist alternative.[3] Luis de Molina developed his view precisely in response to the theological determinism of Calvin and Luther, and the brilliance of his achievement is that he did so without sacrificing divine sovereignty. Unfortunately, contemporary open theology sprang up as a reaction to Calvinism in ignorance of the Molinist alternative. Are openness theologians so entrenched in their perspective that, now

---

[2]What is awkward for Boyd is that there are far more passages implying divine corporeality than divine ignorance of future contingents and there are fewer passages affirming divine incorporeality than divine foreknowledge.

[3]Boyd's analogy of the three chess players does not even take cognizance of the Molinist alternative but contrasts only foreordination, simple foreknowledge, and openness. Boyd's limited deity makes the problem of evil worse, not easier, for it becomes inexplicable why God just sits by, wringing his hands, while letting evils go on unchecked without any morally sufficient reason for not stopping them.

having learned of Molinism, they will persist in their overreaction to Calvinism? Or are they willing to embrace the more moderate *rapprochement* afforded by Molina?

AN AUGUSTINIAN-
CALVINIST RESPONSE

Paul Helm

*T*he main issue raised by Gregory Boyd's essay is not the meaning of this
or that text of the Bible, nor is it some point of theological or philosophical
clarification; it is the issue of method. Because the difference between open
theism and classical theism is a fundamental difference of interpretation of
what Scripture has to say about God, Boyd cannot settle the matter simply by
appealing to Scripture.

A-Data and D-Data
Scripture contains many such statements as the following:
☐ "And before him no creature is hidden, but all are naked and laid bare to
the eyes of the one to whom we must render an account." (Heb 4:13)
☐ "[God] accomplishes all things according to his counsel and will." (Eph 1:11)
☐ "We know that all things work together for good for those who love God,

who are called according to his purpose." (Rom 8:28)

☐ "Lord, you know everything: you know that I love you." (Jn 21:17)

Let us call these passages the "all things" data, *A-data* for short.

There are, in addition, those texts that Boyd considers in the main part of his essay—texts in which the Lord interacts with his people in very humanlike ways. Let us call these the "dialogue" data, *D-data* for short. Boyd's strategy is to diminish the force of the A-data while bringing the D-data into center stage. In other words, his method is to allow the D-data to control the A-data and to interpret all A-data in the light of the D-data at least insofar as these data bear on the doctrine of God. The method of classical theism is to work in the other direction: to place the A-data at center stage and to interpret the D-data in the light of the A-data.[1]

Neither side is going to convince the other side by swapping texts, however expertly or fully such swapping is attempted. Current debates about the canon of Scripture or about the present-day use of the Old Testament are debates about the status of the Bible (or of fundamental parts of it); they are debates not about the Bible's authority as such but about the range and nature of that authority. So, too, the debate between classical theism and the open position is not about individual texts but about which texts are to be given hermeneutical priority in formulating a doctrine of God.

So while I admire the detail of Boyd's essay and the ingenuity he shows in his interpretation of the various texts he examines, I want to suggest that, regrettably, such effort is, in the context of this particular debate, so much wasted effort. For the question is, which motif—the control-and-knowledge motif or the creative-flexibility motif—is (as Humpty Dumpty might have said) to be master? Accordingly, Boyd claims that on this question the open position does not distinguish between literal and anthropomorphic language but that "generally speaking, it interprets the second motif the same as it does the first. It believes that both motifs can and should be interpreted as describing what God and creation are really like" (p. 23). But anyone can see that this is not the case and that it cannot be the case, simply because the two sorts of data present prima facie contradictions. In this situation something must give, and in Boyd's treatment of the A-data, something does give. To start with, his treatment is highly selective. There are certain obvious passages of Scripture

───────────────────

[1]I have elsewhere tried to show how classical theists such as Calvin attempt (successfully, I believe) to do justice to the passages of Scripture which imply that God changes. See, e.g., my essay "God in Dialogue," in *Interpreting the Bible*, ed. A. N. S. Lane (Leicester, U.K.: Apollos, 1997), and my contribution to *God and Time: Four Views*, ed. Greg Ganssle (Downers Grove, Ill.: InterVarsity Press, 2001).

that can be classified as A-data to which he does not refer. But in the second place, in order to avoid the contradiction between the A-data and the D-data when each are understood without qualification, he has to interpret the A-data somewhat elastically. Thus Boyd says that the scriptural motif that exalts God as the sovereign Lord of history "clearly entails that much of the future is settled ahead of time and is therefore known by God as such" (p. 15). And here it is evident that Boyd is not taking the A-data with the same literalness as he does the D-data. For the A-data do not assert that *much* of the future is settled ahead of time; they assert that *all* of it is.

Theism and Philosophy

How are we to approach the difference in method between classical theism and open theism? A favorite ploy—going back at least to Adolf Harnack, and currently employed with considerable gusto by the open theists—is to blame philosophy, particularly Greek philosophy, for the crime of imposing alien forms of thought on the pure Word of God. Boyd himself appears to endorse this idea when he says "exegesis should always drive our philosophy, instead of the other way around" (p. 14). He says that classical theism is driven by a philosophical presupposition that has its source in ancient Greek philosophy of what is worthy of God (pp. 35, 40). But of course Boyd himself cannot avoid philosophical preconceptions and preferences in constructing his open position.

How so? It is a plausible principle that if *p* is a philosophical position, then the denial of *p* is also a philosophical position. So if it is a philosophical position that human persons are essentially immaterial, then the denial of that position is likewise philosophical. If it is a philosophical position that God cannot change, then the denial of that position—the claim that God can change—is likewise philosophical. And if I understand the position correctly, Boyd and the open theists assume from the outset that God changes in a way similar to that in which you and I change. They may say that they do nothing of the sort, that their view of God is drawn by careful induction from relevant biblical data. But the biblical data, however carefully interpreted, will only yield this theological conclusion, the open conclusion, if the protagonists of that position assume *ab initio* that such a view of God is cogent. So if we cannot dismiss one view as being corrupted by false philosophy and yet maintain that the other view is purely biblical, how are we to proceed?

Theism and Christian Supernaturalism: The Analogy of Faith

I suggest that what is at the heart of the contrast between open theism and classical theism is not only or principally a different understanding of the nature of God, or even a difference of interpretation of this or that passage of Scripture, but a profoundly different appreciation of the plight of humankind and the saving grace of God. (This same point applies also to those who espouse Arminianism or middle knowledge in the interests of maintaining libertarian free will, as I will argue in my own contribution.)

On the open view, however in detail divine saving grace is understood and defined, it is that action of God which is causally necessary for human salvation but never causally sufficient. The human will can always frustrate the grace of God. Let us suppose, with all evangelical Protestants, that faith alone in Christ alone is the instrumental cause of a person's justification. Then on the open view, God's grace can only ever be causally necessary for the production of such faith; it can never be causally sufficient. What, in addition, is causally necessary, is an autonomous free choice on the part of the would-be believer—a choice that, if exercised against the divine overtures of grace, could frustrate God's loving purposes toward that individual. But if the choice is exercised in compliance with these overtures, then divine grace and the choice are together causally sufficient for faith in Christ.

For the open position, the plight of humans cannot be so great (for they possess indeterministic freedom to choose for or against Christ), and the grace of God need not be so great either, for often people freely choose for Christ. There is no need of a covenant of redeeming grace to which God is immutably faithful or of divine promises on which the sinner can utterly rely. In particular, there is no need for a saving grace from God that is efficacious in renewing an alienated will. This is why, ultimately, the issue of openness in connection with the doctrine of God, isolated from other facets of the Christian faith, implies a shallow view of the need of humans and the power of God. On a more radical view, human need is such that men and women cannot want to want God, and his grace is needed not only to help them to want to want him, but to ensure that they do so. So the claim that such incompatibilistic freedom is consistent with divine omniscience, as Boyd claims at the start of his essay, even if correct, does not get to what should be the heart of things for the Christian; for only the efficacious grace of God can ensure the salvation of a person in bond-slavery to sin. And for God's grace to be efficacious, God needs to be able to work all things after the counsel of his own will. And in order to do that, he has to be the God of classical theism.

2

THE SIMPLE-FOREKNOWLEDGE VIEW

David Hunt

A standard affirmation among Christians is that God is all-knowing, or *omniscient*. What this means, in short, is that God knows all truths and believes no falsehoods. The doctrine of divine omniscience, like most doctrines, is certainly subject to interpretation, and the consensus in its favor masks considerable disagreement over details. But there are at least two points of interpretation on which the vast majority of believers would surely agree. First, in knowing everything, God doesn't just *happen* to get things right, so that his omniscience is at bottom a matter of luck; instead, it's his very *nature* to be all-knowing, so that it's not even possible for him to be mistaken in any respect. Second, when it is said that God is all-knowing, the "all" refers to the *future* as well as the past and present: God's knowledge contains no gaps that must await future developments before they can be filled in. Because most Christians understand God's omniscience this way, most subscribe to the doctrine of divine *foreknowledge:*

> (F) God has complete and infallible knowledge of the future.

The present chapter is dedicated to defending this traditional doctrine.

Why does (F) even need to be defended? There are in fact a number of difficulties that have been raised against this doctrine. Three of these seem to me to be particularly important, and the bulk of this chapter will be devoted to addressing them. Each comes in the form of an argument designed to show that (F) is incompatible with some other truth to which Christians are deeply committed. The first purports to prove that (F) rules out human beings' possession of genuine free will; the second alleges that (F) is incompatible with the idea that God himself is a personal being capable of intentional action; and the third argues that (F) fails to enhance God's providential position in any way, thus depriving God of what should be the principal theological benefit of foreknowledge. I will refer to these three objections to (F) as the Problem of Human Freedom, the Problem of Divine Agency and the Problem of Divine Providence, respectively.

Of course many who find one or more of these objections persuasive are atheists who see, in the difficulties they raise for (F), yet another reason for rejecting the theistic God. But others are Christians for whom the apparent intractability of one or more of these problems provides a motive for tinkering with (F)—while trying to keep the tinkering within theologically acceptable limits! There are two general directions that such tinkering can take. One is toward curtailing divine foreknowledge to exclude the problematic cognitions (in particular, knowledge of so-called future contingencies).[1] Call this *diminished foreknowledge*. The other direction is taken by those who insist that the three problems can be resolved without diminishing divine foreknowledge but who argue that this can be done only if the manner in which God knows future events is elaborated in some special way—say, by grounding his foreknowledge in "middle knowledge" or by removing God from time so that he can view the past, present and future from an atemporal vantage point.[2] Call

---

[1]This is a relatively recent development for which it is hard to find any patristic or medieval representatives. Twentieth-century philosophers who advocate this position, in one form or another, include Peter Geach, *Providence and Evil* (Cambridge: Cambridge University Press, 1977), chap. 3; Richard Swinburne, *The Coherence of Theism* (Oxford: Clarendon, 1977), chap. 10, esp. pp. 172-78; Richard Purtill, "Fatalism and the Omnitemporality of Truth," *Faith and Philosophy* 5 (1988): 185-92; and William Hasker, *God, Time and Knowledge* (Ithaca, N.Y.: Cornell University Press, 1989), pp. 119-26, 187-90.

[2]The doctrine of divine "middle knowledge" was developed by Luis de Molina, a sixteenth-century Spanish Jesuit. See his *On Divine Foreknowledge*, pt. 4 of *Concordia*, trans. Alfred J. Freddoso (Ithaca, N.Y.: Cornell University Press, 1988). Among those responsible for the recent revival of interest in middle knowledge are Alvin Plantinga, *The Nature of Necessity* (Oxford: Clarendon, 1974), chap. 9; Alfred J. Freddoso, introduction to Molina's *On Divine Foreknowledge*, pp. 1-81; Edward Wierenga, *The Nature of God: An Inquiry into Divine Attributes* (Ithaca, N.Y.: Cornell University Press, 1989), chap. 5; Thomas P. Flint, *Divine Providence: The Molinist Account*, Cornell Studies in the Philosophy of Religion (Ithaca, N.Y.: Cor-

this *augmented foreknowledge*. Advocates of diminished foreknowledge deny (F), while the partisans of augmented foreknowledge accept (F) and then add to it.

In contrast to both diminished and augmented foreknowledge, I shall champion the cause of *simple foreknowledge*. Before explaining what I mean by this, let me say what I do *not* mean. The expression *simple foreknowledge* is sometimes used to designate a particular *means* by which God knows the future, namely, via a direct apprehension of the future itself. A useful way of thinking about such knowledge is to imagine that God is equipped with a "time telescope" that allows him to observe temporally distant events. Now I must admit that I find this a very natural and attractive way of thinking about God's knowledge of the future: not the least of its virtues is that it explains how God might come by his beliefs about the future in such a way that these beliefs could count as *knowledge* rather than correct guesses. But the fact is that I'm not at all sure *how* God knows the future, and I don't want my defense of (F) to be hostage to or dependent on a particular view on this subject. So my "official" position on the mechanism of divine foreknowledge will be agnostic. What I *am* committed to defending in this chapter is the view that God simply *knows the future* (leaving open the question of how he does it). By "simple" foreknowledge, then, I shall mean the view that the *simple* affirmation of (F)—uncomplicated by exceptions, additions, qualifications et cetera—is by itself wholly compatible with human freedom, divine agency and enhanced providential control. If the reader finds it useful in following the arguments to think of God inspecting the future through a "time telescope," this should do little harm so long as it is understood that this is not part of the thesis that I am defending here.[3]

It is important to understand that this defense of simple foreknowledge, if successful, will not show that diminished or augmented foreknowledge is *wrong;* indeed, I have myself a good deal of sympathy for some versions of

---

nell University Press, 1998); and William Lane Craig (see his contribution to the present volume). The idea that God exists outside time is the "classic" position taken by Augustine, Thomas Aquinas and others. For recent defenses, see Eleonore Stump and Norman Kretzmann, "Eternity," *Journal of Philosophy* 78 (1981): 429-60; Paul Helm, *Eternal God: A Study of God Without Time* (Oxford: Oxford University Press, 1988); and Brian Leftow, *Time and Eternity* (Ithaca, N.Y.: Cornell University Press, 1991).

[3]For the "time telescope" model of simple foreknowledge, see William Hasker, *God, Time and Knowledge,* chap. 3. I have also used the term this way in my "Divine Providence and Simple Foreknowledge," *Faith and Philosophy* 10 (July 1993): 394-414. For an "agnostic" position closer to the one I am adopting here, see William Lane Craig, *The Only Wise God* (Grand Rapids, Mich.: Baker, 1987), chap. 11.

augmented foreknowledge. What a successful defense *would* show is that any alternative to simple foreknowledge must be justified on grounds *other* than its ability to escape the Problem of Human Freedom, the Problem of Divine Agency and the Problem of Divine Providence. These problems do not by themselves provide compelling reasons for embracing a diminished or augmented alternative to simple foreknowledge, since they can all be solved with the resources of simple foreknowledge alone.

The Case for Divine Foreknowledge

Before stating and analyzing these three problems for (F), we need to have a better idea of what is at stake. The mere fact that most believers *do* accept (F) does not mean that they *should* accept it. What then can be said on behalf of this doctrine?

There are four points that seem to me to provide powerful initial support for (F). In the *first* place, there is considerable biblical evidence for divine foreknowledge. God's ability to know what will happen before it happens is integral to who he is; Isaiah even makes it the chief mark by which the true God may be distinguished from false gods (Is 41:22-23). The reported instances in which God exercises this power are so numerous (and familiar) that only a couple of examples will be mentioned here.

The first example illustrates something of the *variety* of events accessible to divine foreknowledge. In Genesis 40 Joseph recognizes in his fellow prisoners' dreams a divine communication regarding Pharaoh's future decision to restore the chief butler and condemn the chief baker; then in the next chapter Joseph interprets Pharaoh's own dream to foretell seven years of plenty and seven years of famine. In this pair of examples we see God's foresight encompassing both the outcome of Pharaoh's most intimate thought processes *and* the long-term effects of large-scale climatic forces. The second set of examples, worth including on any short list of "proof-texts" because the knower in this case is God's own incarnate Son, is taken from the first half of Matthew 26. Here we find Jesus predicting, in quick succession, that he will be betrayed on the feast of the Passover (v. 2) by a disciple (v. 21) "who has dipped his hand into the bowl with me" (v. 23); that it is Judas in particular who will betray him (v. 25); that his other disciples will desert him (v. 31); and that Peter will deny him three times before morning (v. 34)—none of which looks like it could be foreknown with certainty in the absence of some supernatural insight into the future.

In addition to dozens of specific examples like these, the Bible contains many summary claims about the incredible range of God's foreknowledge. The psalmist notes how God knows beforehand the least significant things he is going to do ("Even before a word is on my tongue, O LORD, you know it completely," Ps 139:4), while another passage from Isaiah speaks of the cosmic sweep of divine foreknowledge ("I am God, and there is no one like me, declaring the end from the beginning and from ancient times things not yet done," Is 46:9-10). In short, the doctrine of divine foreknowledge appears firmly rooted in the plain meaning of scores of biblical texts.

So much for the first reason for accepting (F). The *second* reason is that the central Christian understanding of God as a supreme and perfect being arguably requires (F). There is at least some dissonance (if not an outright contradiction) in our thinking about God if we suppose him to be unsurpassably great while also attributing to him ignorance of some future event. Unless we affirm (F), we can't say (as we surely want to say) that God is as great as a being can possibly be.

The *third* point in favor of (F) is that divine sovereignty and providence require God to be supremely knowledgeable as well as supremely powerful. There is, to be sure, considerable theological controversy over how much control God *does* exercise: the Bible reveals a God who is "in control" in some pretty robust sense but not "controlling" in the manner of a puppeteer or ventriloquist. But we needn't enter this controversy, since even those who minimize God's control over events typically insist that God has the *ability* to control everything—it's just that he freely refrains from exercising that ability (for familiar reasons). If he has so much as the ability, however, he needs the knowledge, since power without knowledge is blind.

Fourth and finally, the overwhelming consensus of the Church's leading thinkers is that (F) is correct. The first Christian philosopher on record, Justin Martyr, writing in the second century, suggests that God is delaying the Last Judgment because "in His foreknowledge He sees that some will be saved by repentance, some who are, perhaps, not yet in existence."[4] St. Augustine, sometimes referred to as the "third founder" of Western Christianity (after Christ and Paul), is quite unequivocal: "For to confess that God exists, and at the same time to deny that He has foreknowledge of future things, is the most manifest folly. . . . For one who is not prescient of all future things is not God."[5] The same position is taken by all the leading medieval theologians, like Boethius, St. Anselm, St. Thomas Aquinas and so on.[6] Martin

---

[4]Justin Martyr *First Apology*, chap. 28.
[5]Augustine *The City of God* 5.9.
[6]See, e.g., Boethius *The Consolation of Philosophy* 5.6; Anselm *De Concordia* 1.1; Thomas Aquinas *Summa Theologica* 1.Q14.A13.

Luther and John Calvin both subscribe unquestioningly to (F), though their tendency is to mention divine foreknowledge only in connection with God's sovereign power, as when Luther writes, "It is then essentially necessary and wholesome for Christians to know that God . . . foresees, purposes and does all things according to His immutable, eternal and infallible will."[7] But (F) is also widely attested by those, like John Wesley, who do not go as far as the Reformers in their denigration of human initiative: "God *foreknew* those in every nation who would believe, from the beginning of the world to the consummation of all things."[8] This list could, of course, go on and on.[9] While lacking the authority of Scripture, the near unanimity of such figures surely counts for something, at least among those of us who identify to one degree or another with "the tradition."

It should be admitted, even by critics, that the case for (F) is indeed impressive. But at the same time it is important to note that none of the four reasons just offered on behalf of (F) is absolutely irresistible. Let's take them in order.

The first reason was the biblical evidence supporting (F). But the fact is that the Bible nowhere makes this claim in precise and unambiguous terms. While (F) is certainly a natural inference from the scriptural evidence, it *is* an inference. This inference begins with the biblical data—particular instances of foreknowledge, like *God knew in advance that Pharaoh would pardon the chief butler*, and collections of instances, like *God knew in advance all the things the psalmist was about to say*—and generalizes from them to the universal claim *God knows in advance absolutely everything that will ever happen*. But such inferences are at least potentially vulnerable to the fallacy of "hasty generalization."

It's also possible that the data on which the inference is based are flawed. At least some cases in which foreknowledge is attributed to God may reflect nothing more than his unexcelled ability to extrapolate from current conditions or his present awareness of what he himself intends to do, rather than reflecting an irreducible power to apprehend the future. So, for example, God might foresee the seven years of plenty and seven years of famine in Egypt not because he espies this event as through a "time telescope," but because his knowledge of meteorological conditions makes him a weather forecaster with-

---

[7] Martin Luther, *The Bondage of the Will*, in Erasmus and Martin Luther, *Discourse on Free Will*, trans. and ed. Ernst F. Winter (New York: Continuum, 1997), p. 106.
[8] John Wesley, Sermon 58.
[9] Even Arminius is on the list: "The understanding of God is certain and infallible; so that he sees certainly and infallibly, even, things future and contingent, whether he sees them in their causes, or in themselves" (Disputation 17).

out equal or because he has decided to manipulate the weather to this end.

Other predictions might be best understood *conditionally,* conveying information about what will happen *if* things keep going in the direction in which they are now headed. A critic of (F) might even suggest that Jesus' prediction of Judas's betrayal really has the following force: "I know you very well, Judas—better even than you know yourself—and you are going to betray me unless you change your present course." (It's not always easy to distinguish a simple prediction from a conditional one, as Jonah found out when God failed to destroy Nineveh as expected.) It doesn't seem very plausible that *all* the proof-texts for divine foreknowledge can be explained away in such fashion, but the critic of (F) at least has an opening to make the attempt.

The second reason offered on behalf of (F) was the contribution such knowledge makes to divine perfection. But while the Bible does attribute to God a very impressive range of properties, it nowhere sums up these properties into the single concept of a perfect or maximally excellent being, strictly construed. Where we *do* find this concept featured prominently and explicitly is in Neo-Platonism, a pagan philosophical system. Perhaps then the idea of an unexcellably perfect being is an unscriptural phantom of reason, and we put too much stock in our own intellectual powers when we endorse it and then endeavor to derive from it the doctrine of divine foreknowledge.

The third reason rested on the general usefulness of knowledge. The idea was that additional knowledge gives the knower a comparative advantage when it comes to achieving his ends, and that exhaustive knowledge would therefore give God a *superlative* advantage (without which he could not qualify as God). What this overlooks is that greater knowledge contributes to greater control only when the knowledge is *relevant* to the achievement of control. There may, however, be many facts about the future that are irrelevant to God's present purposes, and knowing *these* facts would endow him with no practical advantage. It appears, then, that our interest in maintaining divine providence and sovereignty might be satisfied with something weaker than (F).

The fourth and final reason was simply the weight of the traditional consensus in (F)'s favor. Unlike God, however, the authorities cited earlier are not infallible: maybe they just got this one wrong. Perhaps the whole tradition became implicated in this error when the church fathers fell under the spell of Greek philosophy and began to see the Scriptures through an alien conceptual lens, with the result that (F) became a self-perpetuating mistake that none of these great thinkers had the insight to challenge. That's at least possible, even if we think it's pretty unlikely.[10]

So where does this leave us with respect to (F)? We have seen that a strong, broad-based case can be made on behalf of (F). We have also seen that each reason making up this case has a point at which it is potentially vulnerable. Of course a merely potential vulnerability would have to be *exploited* successfully before giving us any grounds for abandoning (F). I leave it to the opponents of (F) to exploit the vulnerabilities we have identified—I won't do their job for them! Notice, though, that even a successful attack on all four of the reasons offered on behalf of (F) wouldn't show that (F) is false; it would only show that (F) is not supported by these particular reasons, leaving it an open question whether it derives support from other reasons (or is true without being backed by reasons at all). The crucial issue, given the prima facie case that has been made on behalf of (F), is whether there are any good reasons for thinking that (F) is *false*.

This is where the Problem of Human Freedom, the Problem of Divine Agency and the Problem of Divine Providence come in. Let us then turn to a consideration of these three problems. If any of them does succeed in rebutting (F), we might at that point wish (as part of our review of where we went wrong) to return to the potential vulnerabilities in the case for (F), ruefully admitting our errors: "Aha, so we *did* misinterpret those proof-texts," "We *were* mistaken in our concept of God and the inferences we made from it," and so on. But until that happens, we are within our rights in regarding (F) as presumptively true.

The Problem of Human Freedom

1. Formulating the problem. The Problem of Human Freedom was recognized as a serious difficulty almost as soon as Christian beliefs began attracting logical scrutiny. Because of its long history and its centrality to the concerns of this book, it will occupy more of our attention than the other two problems.

Let us follow the problem as Augustine formulates it in his dialogue *On Free Choice of the Will*. It is Augustine's interlocutor, Evodius, who first broaches the subject:

I very much wonder how God can have foreknowledge of everything in the

---

[10]While these critiques of (F) may be found individually in a number of places, this whole package of criticisms is characteristic of "free-will theism." A good source for all of these objections is Clark Pinnock et al., *The Openness of God* (Downers Grove, Ill.: InterVarsity Press, 1994).

future, and yet we do not sin by necessity. It would be an irreligious and completely insane attack on God's foreknowledge to say that something could happen otherwise than as God foreknew. So suppose that God foreknew that the first human being was going to sin. Anyone who admits, as I do, that God foreknows everything in the future will have to grant me that. Now . . . since God foreknew that he was going to sin, his sin necessarily had to happen. How, then, is the will free when such inescapable necessity is found in it?[11]

In the first sentence of this passage Evodius affirms that divine omniscience extends to the future; in the second sentence he emphatically rejects the idea that God's foreknowledge could ever be mistaken. So Evodius is clearly committed to (F). He then proposes to apply this assumption to a particular example: the primal sin by which Adam and Eve turned their wills from the command of God to the prompting of Satan.

The problem this raises is developed in the last two sentences of the passage, which can be put in argument form as follows:

(1) If God foreknows that Adam will sin, then it's necessary that Adam will sin.

(2) If it's necessary that Adam will sin, then Adam will not sin of his own free will.

∴ If God foreknows that Adam will sin, then Adam will not sin of his own free will.

This conclusion is not explicitly stated in the text, but it's present by implication. (An argument with an implied but unstated conclusion is called an *enthymeme*.) Nor does Evodius bother to spell out the implications of the argument for agents other than Adam. Since the argument does not turn on any features peculiar to this particular example (something distinctive about Adam, the conditions under which he was acting, etc.), a similar argument can be constructed for *any* human action. So the argument's full ramifications are these: if (F) is true, no one ever does anything of his own free will.

Why does Evodius, as a Christian, find this conclusion so disturbing? Clearly Evodius would *not* be troubled by the argument if he thought that God has foreknowledge but humans lack free will or if he thought that humans have free will but God lacks foreknowledge. Instead, Evodius (like most Christians) believes both of the following:

(3) God foreknows that Adam will sin.

---

[11]Augustine *On Free Choice of the Will* 3.2. All quotations from this work are taken from the translation by Thomas Williams (Indianapolis: Hackett, 1993).

(4) Adam will sin of his own free will.

But these are inconsistent with the conclusion of the above argument. Augustine himself recapitulates the problem for Evodius like this: "And so you fear that this argument forces us into one of two positions: either we draw the heretical conclusion that God does not foreknow everything in the future; or, if we cannot accept this conclusion, we must admit that sin happens by necessity and not by will."[12] If the argument based on (1) and (2) is accepted, we must reject either (3) or (4). But if we want (with Evodius) to keep both (3) and (4), we must find something wrong with the argument. Since the argument is formally valid (it is a "hypothetical syllogism," exemplifying the valid inference form $A{\rightarrow}B$, $B{\rightarrow}C$, therefore $A{\rightarrow}C$), the argument can be rejected only by rejecting one of its premises, (1) or (2).

Our situation, then, is this: we must find a principled way to deny (1), (2), (3) or (4); more specifically, as Christians, we must find a *theologically acceptable* way to deny one of these propositions. What has given this problem its hoary status as one of the great philosophical puzzles is that it's just not obvious which of these propositions can be rejected. Premise 3 is not a promising candidate, since it certainly looks like all the reasons that were marshaled in favor of (F) provide equal support for (3). After all, if (F) is true, God surely doesn't have complete and infallible knowledge of the future at some times and not at others; God has such knowledge at *all* times. Since he has it at all times, he has it the day before he creates Adam, when Adam's sinning is yet future; but then it follows that (3) is (then) true. It's also hard to see how (4) could be denied. Adam's sin (like any sin) is surely *blameworthy*—if it weren't, it would be difficult indeed to make sense out of the bulk of what the Bible has to say about sin. But we are blameworthy for our actions only to the extent that we do what we do of our own free will. (When my free will is abridged—e.g., because I'm overwhelmed by an external force, I'm acting under duress, I'm suffering a muscle spasm, I'm paralyzed with fear, I don't know what I'm doing, etc.—my responsibility is correspondingly diminished.) So how could (4) fail to be true?

But if (3) and (4) seem undeniable, so do (1) and (2). We need to look at these, especially (1), with some care. Doing so will help us appreciate how really baffling is the dilemma that Evodius is asking Augustine to help him resolve.[13]

---

[12]Ibid., 3.3.

[13]Influential formulations of the Problem of Human Freedom are also to be found in Boethius, Anselm, Aquinas, Scotus, William Ockham and Jonathan Edwards. There is a considerable

2. Accidental necessity. If God foreknows that Adam will sin, then Adam will sin—that's beyond dispute. But in what sense is it *necessary* (given God's foreknowledge of it) that Adam will sin? It isn't *logical* necessity that is in question here: Adam's refraining from sin, unlike his marrying the number 47 or discovering the best way to barbecue a rainbow, does not violate any strictly logical principles. Rather, (1) concerns what the medieval thinkers called *accidental* necessity. Since the word *accidental* in this context is roughly synonymous with *contingent* (i.e., something that is the case but might not have been the case), this phrase may strike some as an oxymoron: how could something that is accidental be necessary or something that is necessary be accidental?

Here's how. Conditions that are not themselves necessary (because they could have turned out differently) may, once those conditions are in place, limit what else is possible. Suppose, for example, that it is not necessary that I pitch this stone over the side of this cliff; I can prevent myself from doing so, and if I nevertheless go ahead and throw the stone, this is still something I *could have* prevented myself from doing. My launching the stone into space is an "accident"—not, of course, in the ordinary English sense of "unintended" or "fortuitous" (let's assume I threw the stone on purpose) but in the sense that things did not have to go this way. Once they have gone this way, however, certain things that *were* in my power (before I threw the stone) are *no longer* in my power.

In the first place, having already thrown the stone, it is no longer possible for me to undo or revoke the fact that I threw the stone; it's too late for that. In general, everything that is past is (now) necessary in this sense. (This idea is captured in such common expressions as "What's done is done," "There's no use crying over spilt milk," and so on.) In the second place, there is nothing I can now do to prevent the *consequences* of this past event, such as the fact that the stone will soon be lying at the bottom of the canyon. If I realize as it disappears into the chasm that I just threw away a gold nugget, I can only regret this result, which is now, quite literally, out of my hands. At this point in time, between the throwing of the stone and its landing on the rocks below, both the throwing of the stone (a past event) and its arrival at the bottom of

amount of contemporary literature on this issue, sparked in large part by Nelson Pike's restatement of the problem in his article "Divine Foreknowledge and Voluntary Action," *Philosophical Review* 74 (January 1965): 27-46. Since the publication of Pike's paper, well over 100 articles on the topic have appeared in professional philosophy journals. A collection of some of the most important of these may be found in John Martin Fischer, ed., *God, Foreknowledge and Freedom* (Stanford, Calif.: Stanford University Press, 1989). William Hasker is currently working on a survey of the controversy for publication in the *International Journal for Philosophy of Religion*.

the cliff (a future event) are irrevocable.

This is roughly the situation that (1) alleges to obtain with respect to God's antecedent knowledge and Adam's subsequent action. Imagine that Adam has just been formed by God from the dust of the ground. When he comes into existence, God already knows that he will disobediently eat of the tree of the knowledge of good and evil. This is not something God knows as a matter of logical necessity; if something else had been true, God would instead have known *that*. But given that he knows *this* and that he has known it from eternity, there is nothing Adam can now do to prevent (or "postvent"!) this fact. He's come on the scene too late for that. But if Adam is stuck with the fact that God already knows he will sin, he's also stuck with the consequences of this fact. A notable consequence of God's foreknowing that Adam will sin is that *Adam will sin;* so Adam is stuck with this fact as well. God's prior knowledge, which Adam is stuck with because it was in place before he even began to exist, does not leave open the possibility that Adam will act other than God knows he will act. As Adam opens his eyes and gazes upon Eden for the first time, both God's (past) foreknowledge that he will sin and Adam's (future) sinning confront Adam as fixed and irrevocable.

One caveat must be issued before we accept this justification of (1). The only reason offered for thinking that Adam's future sinning is unavoidable is that it is entailed by something else that Adam can't avoid (namely, God's past foreknowledge of his sinful choice), and the only reason offered for thinking that *this* is unavoidable for Adam is that it belongs to the *past*. But surprising as it may seem, it is not unqualifiedly true that God's knowing yesterday what will happen tomorrow *is* a fact about the past. To say that someone *knows* something that is (in part) to say that the person *believes* something that is *true*. Both truth *and* belief are necessary for knowledge. You can *believe* something that is false, but you can't *know* something that is false—only *truths* can be known. But the mere fact that something *is* true doesn't mean you know it—you must actually *believe* this truth if knowledge of it is to be credited to you. This has important implications for God's prior knowledge that Adam will sin. To say that God *knew* that Adam will sin is to say at least this: *(i)* God *believed* that Adam will sin and *(ii)* it is *true* that Adam will sin. Whereas *(i)* is about the past, *(ii)* is about the future; so the fact that God *knew* that Adam will sin is partly about the past and partly about the future.

Let us say that a "soft fact" about the past is one whose *grammar* points to the past (e.g., through use of the past tense) but whose *content* belongs at least in part to the future, whereas a "hard fact" about the past is a fact that is *entirely* about the past. *God knew that Adam will sin* is therefore a soft fact about the past. This is significant because a soft fact, unlike a hard fact, is not accidentally necessary just by virtue of being about the past; since a soft fact concerns (at least in part) the future, then unless there is some independent reason to think that the future it points to is inevitable, the fact as a whole might yet turn out false. This undercuts our only reason for thinking that God's prior knowledge of Adam's sin is accidentally necessary at the time Adam comes into existence, and so undercuts our only reason for thinking that the consequences of God's knowledge, including the fact that Adam will sin, are fixed and inevitable.

But (1) is easily rescued from this temporary setback. If *God knew that Adam will sin* is not a hard fact about the past, *God believed that Adam will sin* certainly looks like it *is* a hard fact about the past, and the latter (as we have seen) is true whenever the former is true. So the soft fact *God knew that Adam will sin* includes the hard fact *God believed that Adam will sin*. Moreover, because God is infallible and his beliefs can't fail to be true, the fact that God *believed* that Adam will sin is just as effective at "locking in" Adam's future sinning as the fact that God *knew* that Adam will sin. So (1) is acceptable after all, in virtue of this hard-factual component of divine foreknowledge. This detour into hard-versus-soft facts was not a waste of time, however, since the hard-fact-soft-fact distinction helps us understand *why* (1) is true and also paves the way for an objection we will be considering in section four.[14]

Accidental necessity is by no means a straightforward notion, but once we understand what is being said in (1), it is very hard to see how it could be denied. We can now treat (2) more briefly, since we have already done the work required to understand what the first part of this premise is asserting. *If it is necessary that Adam will sin*—if, that is, it is now accidentally necessary (irrevocable, unavoidable, not-able-to-be-other-than) that Adam will sin—*then Adam will not sin of his own free will*. The idea, surely, is this: "free choice" is a sham if there is really only one course of action open to an agent. But this is exactly the situation facing Adam: from the moment he first drew breath, it was accidentally necessary that he would eat of the tree of knowledge. The Fall is "locked in" by God's prior knowledge, and Adam is stuck with the results. So Adam does not sin of his own free will, given that God's beliefs before Adam even came into existence precluded any genuine possibility that Adam might not sin.

---

[14]Pike (see n. 13) couches the argument in terms of God's belief rather than God's knowledge. This is one respect in which his formulation makes the logic of the argument clearer, not to mention harder to refute, than it is in some of the earlier formulations of the problem.

Well, there we have it: (1) and (2), no less than (3) and (4), appear to be rock solid. But they are mutually contradictory; hence at least one of them must somehow be false! Which one could it possibly be?

3. The Boethian and Calvinist solutions. It may surprise the reader to learn this late in the game that every one of these propositions, which we have been at such pains to justify, has in fact been the subject of serious criticism. A moment ago we were despairing over how to select one of these seemingly undeniable propositions for rejection; now we find ourselves being overwhelmed by an excess of candidates! Let's begin our review of how we could have misread the situation so badly with some comments on (3) and (4).

Not only are (3) and (4) more problematic than they appear, but *most* of the figures cited earlier as part of the traditional consensus favoring (F) dissent from one or both of these propositions. Ironically, even Evodius's mentor, Augustine, withheld his full endorsement from (3)—the very thing he tells Evodius it would be heretical to deny!—and later came to withhold it from (4) as well. How is this possible? Was Evodius simply mistaken in thinking that he as a Christian needed to affirm both (3) and (4)?

With respect to (3), those who reject (F) in favor of *diminished* foreknowledge would of course regard Evodius as mistaken. But denying (3) *because one denies (F)* is obviously unhelpful to the business of defending (F) against the Problem of Human Freedom! Is there another ground for denying (3) that might contribute toward the defense of (F) rather than presupposing its falsity? Well, suppose that God knows the future without *fore*knowing it. This would be the case if God (and his knowledge) exists outside of time. On this conception of God he could still know everything that is yet future *relative to us;* but since he is not himself in time, these things would not be future *relative to him,* and so he would not know them *as* future. This was in fact Augustine's view of God, as he makes clear elsewhere.[15] But since it is the Late Roman philosopher and theologian Boethius who gave this position its classic formulation, I shall refer to it as the *Boethian* view.

And how exactly does the Boethian move help matters when it comes to the Problem of Human Freedom? As Boethius himself explains it, an atemporal deity, "embracing all the infinite spaces of the future and the past, considers them in his simple act of knowledge as though they were now going on." Since God's knowledge of Adam's sin does not precede the sin, it's not part of a fixed past dictating how Adam's future decisions and actions must go. "Why

---

[15]For example, *Confessions* 11; *De Trinitate* 15; *De diversis quaestionibus ad Simplicianum* 2.2.2.

then do you require those things to be made necessary which are scanned by the light of God's sight, when not even men make necessary those things they see? After all, your looking at them does not confer any necessity on those things you presently see."[16] God sees everything at once from a vantage point outside time and history, and this is no more deleterious to the freedom of the actions God observes from this vantage point than is your sitting on a hill observing the picnickers, kite-flyers, baseball players and so on at the nearby park deleterious to *their* freedom. The Boethian solution, in short, responds to the Problem of Human Freedom by denying (3), yet it does so in such a way that (F) is preserved.

As for (4), most of those cited in support of (F) would also resist this proposition to one degree or another, if not deny it outright. *On Free Choice of the Will*, ostensibly written in defense of the will, is as much about its bondage as it is about its freedom, with its final chapters devoted to the postlapsarian "ignorance and difficulty" by which our wills are hampered. Augustine's doubts about human autonomy hardened further in the course of his involvement in the Pelagian controversy, until he could write at the end of his career: "On the solution to this question I tried hard to maintain the free decision of the human will, but the grace of God was victorious."[17] Since Calvin is popularly associated with antipathy toward (4), let us call this the *Calvinist* solution.

The Calvinist position is rooted in our utter dependence on God and our utter incapacity to do anything good without the aid of divine grace. If God is truly sovereign, what room is there for "little gods" exercising their own autonomous agency over against God? Few proponents of this position are as intemperate in their rejection of (4) as is Luther, who ends *The Bondage of the Will* by declaring that "free will lies vanquished and prostrate."[18] But even where free will is frankly asserted, as in Aquinas, it is often so subsumed under divine causality and hedged about with "enabling" and "effective" grace that it's hard to know how (4) can continue to be affirmed in any straightforward sense.[19]

Should we jump at the chance to evade the Problem of Human Freedom that is offered us by the apparent deniability of (3) and (4)? I don't believe we should. My reticence on this score is not, however, rooted in the assumption that (3) and (4) are both *true.* Just for the record, I rather like the atemporal view of God, for various reasons I won't go into here; so I am inclined to join

---

[16]Boethius *Consolation* 5.6.
[17]Augustine *Retractations* 2.1.
[18]Luther, *Bondage of the Will*, p. 134.
[19]See, e.g., Flint's judgment of Thomism's difficulties accommodating a robust sense of free will in his *Divine Providence,* pp. 88-94.

Augustine and Boethius (not to mention Anselm, Aquinas, et al.) in denying (3) while affirming (F). (I am not inclined to deny or seriously qualify premise (4) just because I don't understand free will clearly enough to see that other things to which I am committed are really incompatible with it.) But denying (3)—or (4), for that matter—does not yield a satisfactory solution to the Problem of Human Freedom, even if the proposition denied is in fact false. Let me explain.

Sometimes we have good reason to believe that there must be something wrong with an argument before we are in a position to see *what* is wrong with it. Consider, for example, the most famous of Zeno's paradoxes of motion, in which it is argued that Achilles, renowned for his speed, could not win a race against a tortoise if the tortoise were given a head start, no matter how small. This is because Achilles, to pass the tortoise, would first have to catch it, and this would involve his traversing an infinite number of distances: first, the distance to the tortoise's initial position x; then the distance to the new position $x + j$ the tortoise reached while Achilles was getting to x; then the distance to the new position $x + j + k$ the tortoise reached while Achilles was getting to $x + j$ and so on. One way that Zeno's problem can be formulated is this:

(a)   If Achilles can overtake the tortoise, then it's possible for someone to finish traversing each of an infinite number of intervals.

(b)   If it's possible for someone to finish traversing each of an infinite number of intervals, then it's possible to perform an infinite number of tasks in a finite amount of time.

(c)   It's not possible to perform an infinite number of tasks in a finite amount of time.

∴   Achilles cannot overtake the tortoise.

And what's wrong with that? Well, we might be pretty sure (at least prior to encountering Zeno's argument!) that

(d)   Achilles *can* overtake the tortoise.

Since the denial of *(d)* follows from *(a)-(c)*, one of the propositions *(a)-(d)* must be false.

Suppose now that someone were to propose that the problem can be solved by rejecting *(d)*. Wouldn't this be utterly preposterous? Of course it would; but be careful *why* you regard it as preposterous. Perhaps it's because you are so sure that *(d)* is true: it's preposterous to address Zeno's argument by denying *(d)* because it's preposterous to deny *(d)*. But suppose archeologists digging near Mycenae unearth a tablet, dated circa 700 B.C., bearing the title (in archaic Greek) "The True Story of Achilles' Heel." It turns out that Homer's references to the "fleet-footed Achilles" were just a joke: the real Achilles had an enormous bone spur on one heel, making it too painful for him to walk unaided, let alone run. So *(d)* is false after all. Does this solve Zeno's paradox? Of course not. What is paradoxical is that you could begin with someone believed to be quite fast—faster than a tortoise, at any rate—and then demonstrate, in the way Zeno does, that this person could not outrun a tortoise after all. Denying *(d)* simply removes Achilles from complicity in this paradox; it does nothing to resolve it. Whether or not *(d)* is (also) false, we can be confident that something is seriously wrong with *(a)-(c)*, even if we're not sure just what it is.

It seems to me that we face exactly the same situation when it comes to the argument for the incompatibility of divine foreknowledge and human freedom that Augustine puts in the mouth of Evodius. If God had attached tiny wires to Adam so that he could manipulate him as one would a marionette or if he had caused a fog to settle over Adam's mind so that he didn't know what he was doing, then we could readily see how this might change Adam's circumstances so that he did not eat the apple of his own free will. But there is something fishy about the idea that Adam's action, while in every other respect satisfying the most exacting requirements for free will, might nevertheless count as unfree *simply* because God foreknew what he would do.

I am therefore in hearty agreement with the way one of my coauthors, William Lane Craig, put the point in an earlier book:

> How does the addition or deletion of the factor of God's simply knowing some act in advance affect the freedom of that act? [The claim that it does] posits a constraint on human freedom which is entirely unintelligible. Therefore, it must be false. Somewhere there is a fallacy in the argument, and we need only examine it carefully to find the error.[20]

Denying (3) or (4) does not get to the nub of the problem raised by Evodius's argument any more than denying *(d)* in the case of Zeno's argument does—even if (3), (4) and *(d)* are all false. Because Zeno's argument is so dubious, it cannot provide a reason for denying *(d)*; even if there is some independent reason for denying *(d)* (e.g., the unearthed tablet), we know that there is trouble somewhere in *(a)-(c)* as well. Likewise, because Evodius's argument is so dubious, it cannot provide a reason for denying (3) or (4); even if there is

---

[20]Craig, *Only Wise God,* pp. 68-69. Craig also makes the comparison with Zeno's paradoxes of motion.

some independent reason for denying (3) or (4)—of the sort canvassed by Augustine and friends—we have good reason to suspect trouble somewhere in (1) and (2) as well.[21]

I believe it is precisely because Augustine understood this that he never drew on his own doubts about (3) and (4) when formulating a response to the Problem of Human Freedom. We will return to Augustine's analysis of the problem in a moment. But first, let's reexamine the prospects for rejecting (1), since the irrelevance of (3) and (4) means that the fallacy must lie either here or in (2).

4. The Ockhamist solution. The defense of (1) offered in section two depended crucially on Adam's future sinning's being entailed by a *hard* fact about the past, a fact that Adam was stuck with from the moment he first drew breath. We saw that while God's *foreknowing* that Adam will sin does not qualify as a hard fact, this fact includes God's *forebelieving* that Adam will sin; and this latter fact *does* look like a hard fact that entails Adam's future sinning. The fourteenth-century philosopher and logician William Ockham nevertheless maintained that appearances here are deceiving.[22] The fact that *God believes that Adam will sin,* he averred, is also a soft fact, remaining "soft" until Adam actually sins; and if *this* fact is unavailable to Evodius's argument, we can safely conclude that God's foreknowing that Adam will sin does not involve *any* hard fact which both entails and also predates Adam's sinning. So the argument breaks down at (1).

This Ockhamist position has developed into what is probably the major strategy used by contributors to the contemporary philosophical debate in their attempt to evade the Problem of Human Freedom.[23] But given our earlier reasons for thinking that *God believes that Adam will sin* is indeed a hard fact, on what grounds do Ockham and his modern followers assert the contrary? There are three principal ways that the Ockhamist position might be defended.

Strategy 1. One way to argue that *God believes that Adam will sin* is a soft

---

[21]I provide a more extensive argument for this way of regarding the Problem of Human Freedom in my article "What *Is* the Problem of Theological Fatalism?" *International Philosophical Quarterly* 38 (March 1998): 17-30.

[22]Ockham's views on this subject may be found in his *Predestination, God's Foreknowledge and Future Contingents,* trans. Marilyn McCord Adams and Norman Kretzmann (New York: Appleton-Century-Crofts, 1969).

[23]It is also the strategy underlying the first two published responses to Pike's 1965 restatement of the argument: John Turk Saunders, "Of God and Freedom," *Philosophical Review* 75 (April 1966): 219-25; and Marilyn McCord Adams, "Is the Existence of God a 'Hard' Fact?" *Philosophical Review* 76 (October 1967): 492-503. Others who have endorsed this strategy include Alvin Plantinga, William Lane Craig, Joshua Hoffman, Gary Rosenkrantz, Alfred J. Freddoso, Jonathan Kvanvig, Bruce Reichenbach, Edward Wierenga and Thomas Talbott.

fact is to do so in the same way we argued that *God knows that Adam will sin* is a soft fact, namely, by first unpacking what it is for God to hold a belief about the future and then showing that this fact is constituted not just by what is *now* the case but also (in part) by what will be the case *later.* This direct approach can succeed, I believe, only if it can be shown how one and the same state of the divine mind—the one that, as matters actually stand, constitutes God's believing that Adam will sin—would instead count as a *different* belief (namely, the belief that Adam will *not* sin) if Adam does not sin.

While this may seem pretty dubious, there is at least some theoretical space for this maneuver. Linda Zagzebski has formulated a position she calls "Thomistic Ockhamism" under which God's cognitive act is part of his very essence; John Fischer has suggested applying Hilary Putnam's notion of "wide content" to divine foreknowledge; and I have laid out a "dispositional omniscience scenario" in which God knows everything without actively thinking about it all the time.[24] These thumbnail descriptions will convey very little to the reader unfamiliar with the relevant literature; I offer them only as evidence that such approaches exist. But if any succeeds, the Ockhamist is home free; for if God's belief is constituted as *the belief that Adam will sin* only retroactively, once Adam actually sins, then nothing about God's prior belief would appear to be inconsistent with either Adam's freedom to sin or his freedom not to sin.

It is noteworthy that all three of the suggestions for implementing this strategy mentioned in the preceding paragraph represent attempts by *critics* of Ockhamism to understand how God's beliefs about the future could possibly be "soft."[25] None of the leading defenders of Ockhamism has invested in this strategy.[26] Perhaps they regard it, with reason, as a poisoned pawn, attractive for its offer to make the Ockhamist thesis intelligible but fatal in its theological

---

[24]Linda Zagzebski, *The Dilemma of Freedom and Foreknowledge* (Oxford: Oxford University Press, 1991), chap. 3, sec. 4; John Martin Fischer, "Freedom and Foreknowledge," *Philosophical Review* 92 (January 1983): 94; David Hunt, "Does Theological Fatalism Rest on an Equivocation?" *American Philosophical Quarterly* 32 (April 1995): 153-65. I develop this conception of omniscience more fully, and weigh its advantages and disadvantages, in my "Dispositional Omniscience," *Philosophical Studies* 80 (December 1995): 243-78.

[25]Zagzebski does defend the coherence of Thomistic Ockhamism, but this is not her preferred solution to the Problem of Human Freedom, and her assessment of Ockhamism is largely negative.

[26]The exceptions are Eddy M. Zemach and David Widerker, "Facts, Freedom and Foreknowledge," *Religious Studies* 23 (March 1987): 19-28. They employ the "functionalist" approach mentioned by Fischer, with a result quite congenial to Zagzebski's Thomistic Ockhamism. This is an exception that proves the rule, however, since Widerker later went on to write one of the sharpest critiques of Ockhamism: David Widerker, "Troubles with Ockhamism," *Journal of Philosophy* 87 (1990): 462-80.

implications: after all, if Jesus' prior belief about what Judas will do is constituted as *the belief that Judas will betray me* only retroactively, once Judas actually betrays him, then it's pretty baffling how Jesus could make the prediction
reported in Matthew 26:25 *prior* to Judas's betraying him. But the Ockhamists'
lack of interest in this first strategy may also reflect nothing more than their
confidence in the remaining two strategies. These other strategies derive from
two criteria proposed by Ockham himself, under which a fact is soft in virtue
of how it is related to certain other facts: "that proposition that is about the
present in such a way that (i) it is nevertheless *equivalent* to one about the
future and (ii) its truth *depends* on the truth of the one about the future does
not have [corresponding to it] a necessary proposition about the past."[27] Let's
see how *(i)* and *(ii)* can be parlayed into critiques of (1).

Strategy 2. Some Ockhamists have argued that, however difficult it is to
understand *how* God's forebeliefs could be soft, we can be confident *that* they
are soft, since there is a simple argument by which this can be *demonstrated*. If
this is so, then the fact that we can't understand what divine belief could possibly *be* if it is to count as soft is irrelevant—there's a lot we don't and indeed
can't understand about God, and this is one of those things.

But *can* it be shown that God's forebeliefs are soft? Here's the argument.
God's infallibility ensures that

God believed that Adam will sin → Adam will sin

while his omniscience guarantees that

Adam will sin → God believed that Adam will sin

It follows that

God believed that Adam will sin ↔ Adam will sin

The fact that God believed that Adam will sin is therefore *logically equivalent*
to the fact that Adam will sin: there is no "possible world" in which these facts
are not indissolubly linked. Because *Adam will sin* is certainly not a hard fact
about the past, and *God believed that Adam will sin* is logically equivalent to it,
the latter cannot be a hard fact about the past either, Q.E.D.[28]

I do not find this argument at all convincing. If *God believed that Adam will
sin* and *Adam will sin* were the *same fact*, it would be easy to see why they
would both have to be soft (if either were soft) or both hard (if either were
hard). But they are obviously *different facts*: the first is about *what God*

---

[27]Ockham, *Predestination*, p. 38.
[28]Arguments substantially of this type may be found in Alvin Plantinga, "On Ockham's Way
Out," *Faith and Philosophy* 3 (July 1986): 247-51; and Ted A. Warfield, "Divine Foreknowledge and Human Freedom Are Compatible," *Nous* 31 (March 1997): 80-86. Craig also
endorses this line in *The Only Wise God*, pp. 67-68.

believed and the second is about *what Adam will do*. The right conclusion to draw, it seems to me, is that a hard fact can be logically equivalent to a soft fact when these are not the *same fact*, as in the present case. I therefore reject this second defense of Ockhamism.[29]

Strategy 3. Ockham also thought God's holding a belief about the future could not be a hard fact because his holding that belief is *dependent* on the way the future turns out. Adam doesn't sin *because* God believed he would sin; rather, God believes that Adam will sin *because* Adam will sin. This makes God's prior belief unavailable for blocking Adam's alternatives. Since God's belief depends on what Adam does, if Adam *were* to refrain from sinning, God *would not* have believed that he would sin, and there would not then have been any prior divine belief to rule out Adam's refraining. Because God's fore-belief varies with Adam's future action, it can't be classified as a hard fact until Adam actually opts for one action over the other.[30]

But this argument is again unconvincing. Let us agree that were Adam to do otherwise, God would have believed otherwise; the problem is that the foregoing argument provides no reason to think that Adam *can* do otherwise. Suppose I fail to save a child from a burning building because I am knocked unconscious by a falling beam. Then it's true that, *had* I saved the child, I *would not* have been knocked unconscious; but this does nothing to alter the fact that, as matters actually stand, I *could not* save the child. Nor is the result any different when the past is dependent on the future, as in the foreknowledge case.

Imagine that *tachyons* (particles that travel backward in time) have been adapted for household use and that my friend the tycoon has installed one of the new tachyonic doorbells at his mansion. Arriving for a dinner party, I press the button outside the front door; this causes a buzzer inside the house to sound five minutes *earlier,* giving the butler a headstart in getting to the door. Now let's go back to my arrival at the door. Is it possible for me to refrain from ringing the

---

[29]For a reply to Plantinga, see Dale Eric Brant, "On Plantinga's Way Out," *Faith and Philosophy* 14 (July 1997): 334-52. For replies to Warfield, see William Hasker, "No Easy Way Out: A Response to Warfield," *Nous* 32 (1998): 361-63; David Hunt, "On Augustine's Way Out," *Faith and Philosophy* 16 (January 1999): 14-16; and Anthony Brueckner, "On an Attempt to Demonstrate the Compatibility of Divine Foreknowledge and Human Freedom," *Faith and Philosophy* 17 (January 2000): 132-34. See also David Widerker, "Two Forms of Fatalism," in *God, Foreknowledge and Freedom,* ed. John Martin Fischer (Stanford, Calif.: Stanford University Press, 1989), pp. 97-110.

[30]This is Plantinga's principal objection to the argument in his *God, Freedom and Evil* (New York: Harper & Row, 1974). Craig also sees this as the central fallacy in the argument, as he explains in *Only Wise God*, pp. 69-74.

bell, given that it has already sounded? Suppose you say yes, justifying your answer as follows. Since the buzzer's having sounded depends on my pressing the button, if I were to refrain from pressing the button, the buzzer would not have sounded. My alternatives, then, are to press the button (in which case the buzzer sounded) or to refrain from pressing the button (in which case the buzzer did not sound): both possibilities are open to me. What this justification overlooks, however, is that the buzzer has *already sounded;* so the state of affairs that consists of my refraining from pressing the button (and the buzzer's not having sounded), a state that was unproblematic enough before the buzzer sounded, is now impossible. Indeed, insofar as I *am* able to refrain from pressing the button, this is only to the extent that the buzzer's having sounded does *not* depend on my pressing the button. If I had backed away from the door, deciding at the last moment not to attend the dinner, the buzzer that sounded five minutes earlier would have to be explained in some other way (e.g., the mechanism malfunctioned, there was a disturbance in the "tachyonic field," another dinner guest arrives and rings the bell instead). But whatever its cause, the sounding of the buzzer is a hard fact that I cannot now revoke.

The same is true for *God's belief* five minutes ago that I will ring my friend's doorbell. Does it make any difference that God's belief depends on what I do and that it would have been different if I were to act differently? No, for he has already held this belief, and my action must be consistent with this fact about the past. But whereas the sounding of the buzzer leaves me with alternatives to pressing the button, since it might sound without my causing it to ring, God's believing that I will press the button does not leave me any alternatives to pressing the button, since he can't hold that belief and I fail to press the button. This defense of Ockhamism, like the first two, is a dead end.

Despite its popularity among critics of the argument, I cannot see how the Ockhamist solution is even remotely plausible. Fortunately there is one more solution to consider.

5. *The Augustinian solution.* If we are right to accept (1) and also right to think of the argument in which it figures as the theological equivalent of Zeno's paradoxes (so that we cannot look to premise 3 or 4 for a solution), then the problem must lie in (2). At the end of section two, I stated briefly a reason for accepting (2). Since we must now reassess this reason, it will be useful to formulate and name it. Let the "Principle of Alternate Possibilities" (or PAP) be the name and this the formulation:

(PAP) A person X does an action A of his own free will only if X could have done otherwise.

If it is accidentally necessary before X is even born that X will do A, then X never has it in his power to do other than A; but then it follows from (PAP) that X does not do A of his own free will. So (2) must be true. The only way to deny this premise is to deny (PAP).

This is the route Augustine himself takes. While rejecting (3) because he endorses the atemporal version of (F) and qualifying (4) in the interests of divine grace, Augustine sees that denying either or both of these propositions does not get to the heart of the problem Evodius is posing for him. So rather than opting for an easy accommodation to the argument's conclusion, Augustine undertakes to refute the argument, and he does so by disputing (PAP). What he concludes, in brief, is that there is a sense in which (PAP) is true and a sense in which (PAP) is false, and the sense in which it is true does not support (2). Without that support, there is absolutely no reason to think that (2) *is* true; so Evodius's argument fails.

One way it might come about that an agent cannot do otherwise is if prior states of the universe (e.g., ones that obtained even before the agent was born) *causally determine* what the person does. Some philosophers who believe (or fear) that scientific naturalism commits them to regarding all of our actions as causally determined, but who are also unwilling to dismiss free will and moral responsibility as an illusion, have attempted to recast these notions in such a way that they are compatible with the absence of real alternatives. It is fair to say that this "compatibilist" understanding of free will is the predominant one among secular philosophers today.

It is important to understand that this is *not* the position from which Augustine challenges (PAP). Among the ideas discussed by Augustine and Evodius in *On Free Choice of the Will* is the possibility that human actions are the result of "natural necessity," where a paradigm of natural necessity is the falling of a stone.[31] For a scientific naturalist, human beings are just as much a part of nature as stones, and our behavior is no less a product of "natural necessity," only much more complex; so this is just the kind of necessity that must be shown compatible with free will if the scientific naturalist is to preserve our ordinary concept of ourselves as free and responsible agents. But Augustine emphatically rejects such "compatibilism": it is because the stone falls by "natural necessity" that it does not fall by free choice and is not blameworthy for falling. If Adam's fall, like the stone's fall, were determined by "natural necessity," Adam too would be neither free nor blameworthy for sinning. So at least

---

[31]Natural necessity and the example of the falling stone are discussed in Augustine *On Free Choice of the Will* 3.1.

in the case where natural necessity or causal determinism is responsible for the fact that an agent cannot do otherwise, Augustine would not dispute (PAP).

The argument based on divine foreknowledge raises a completely different set of considerations. Augustine points out that the necessity that attaches to our actions in virtue of God's prior knowledge and infallibility is not at all like the necessity that attaches to the stone's fall in virtue of its prior suspension in midair and its subjection to the relevant natural laws.

> Just as your memory does not force the past to have happened, God's foreknowledge does not force the future to happen. And just as you remember some things that you have done but did not do everything that you remember, God foreknows everything that he causes but does not cause everything that he foreknows. . . . Let us rather confess that nothing in the future is hidden from God's foreknowledge, and that no sin is left unpunished by his justice, for sin is committed by the will, not coerced by God's foreknowledge.[32]

Augustine's point here is this: if God causes, forces or coerces Adam to sin, Adam would indeed be blameless; but God's merely foreknowing what Adam will do does not cause, force or coerce him. It is true that God's foreknowing Adam's action, like his causing Adam's action, leaves Adam with no alternatives—Adam can no more escape divine omniscience than he can resist divine omnipotence. But the mere absence of alternate possibilities is irrelevant. Causing, forcing or coercing someone interferes with that person's agency; simply knowing what the person will do is not an interference of any sort, and its implications for free agency are benign. So (PAP), which treats all alternative eliminators equally, is unacceptable as a general principle.[33]

It seems to me that a number of things recommend Augustine's position, of which I will mention two. First, Augustine's solution speaks directly to our suspicions about argument (1)-(2). Divine foreknowledge deprives Adam of alternatives, but we just can't believe that it deprives him of free will. Augustine's advice, in effect, is to trust our intuitions about this case. We think there is a problem here because the normal case in which an agent lacks alternatives (that he would otherwise possess) is one in which he is the victim of outside interference; the absence of alternatives is therefore a generally reliable indicator that an agent's free will has been abrogated. But foreknowledge cases *show*

---

[32]Augustine *De libero arbitrio* 3.4.
[33]I defend this reading of Augustine's position in my "Augustine on Theological Fatalism: The Argument of *De Libero Arbitrio* III.1-4," *Medieval Philosophy and Theology* 6 (Spring 1996): 1-30. I argue that this is the best available response to the Problem of Human Freedom in my "On Augustine's Way Out," pp. 3-26.

us that this is not universally true: because divine foreknowledge does not cause or compel what it knows, it is an exception to the general rule. (Divine *power* might cause or compel the future, but that's another story!)[34]

Second, Augustine's solution is consistent with recent critiques of (PAP) in the philosophical literature. This is important because it shows that the Problem of Human Freedom is not uniquely theological and that Augustine's solution is of general application—it's not a piece of special pleading whose only virtue is that it gets the traditional theist off the hook. Here's a nontheological story, first told by the philosopher Harry Frankfurt, in which (PAP) also yields the wrong result: Black wishes to see Smith dead, he knows that Jones shares this wish, and he thinks it likely that Jones will act on this wish. Unwilling to take any chances, Black deploys a science-fiction device capable of monitoring or controlling a person's thoughts and programs it to monitor Jones's intentions with respect to murdering Smith. If the device indicates that Jones is *not* going to murder Smith on his own, the device then interferes with Jones's mental processes to ensure that he murders Smith after all; but if the device indicates that Jones *is* going to murder Smith on his own, it simply monitors the course of events without interference. As it turns out, Jones goes ahead and murders Smith on his own, and nothing happens to trigger the device's intervention.

What are we to make of this case? It sure looks like Jones cannot do otherwise than kill Smith—either he will do it on his own or he will do it because the device forces him. But we are also strongly inclined to hold that Jones kills Smith of his own free will. Frankfurt justifies this judgment on the following grounds: Black's device "played no role at all in leading [Jones] to act as he did"; indeed, "everything happened just as it would have happened without Black's presence in the situation and without his readiness to intrude into it"; so the device is "irrelevant to the problem of accounting for a person's action" and "does not help in any way to understand either what made [Jones] act as he did or what, in other circumstances, he might have done."[35] But what is

---

[34]Of course God as creator is causative of the things that he knows, but he doesn't cause them by knowing them, and his knowledge outstrips what he does cause: "he can foreknow even those things which he himself does not do, such as whatever sins there may be" (Augustine *The Predestination of the Saints* 10.19). Aquinas, in *Summa Theologica* 1A.Q14.A8, defends the thesis that God's knowledge is the cause of things, even citing Augustine (*De Trinitate* 15.13.22) in support. But at least one pair of commentators (Eleonore Stump and Norman Kretzmann, "God's Knowledge and Its Causal Efficacy," in *The Rationality of Belief and the Plurality of Faith*, ed. Thomas D. Senor [Ithaca, N.Y.: Cornell University Press, 1995], pp. 94-124) argues that even Aquinas is concerned primarily with the *existence* of creatures rather than the contingent facts that come to characterize them.

[35]Harry Frankfurt, "Alternate Possibilities and Moral Responsibility," *Journal of Philosophy* 66 (December 1969): 836-37.

here true of Black's device is equally true of God's foreknowledge that Jones will kill Smith. (As Augustine puts it in *The City of God*, "a man does not therefore sin *because* God foreknew that he would sin.")[36] Though both Black's device and God's foreknowledge eliminate all alternatives to Jones's action, neither does so in such a way as to jeopardize Jones's free agency.[37]

The philosophical debate over Frankfurt-style cases and their implications for (PAP) is complex and ongoing; it obviously cannot be resolved here. I will simply record my conviction that cases in which God foreknows what someone will do are immune to every difficulty that critics have raised against normal Frankfurt-style cases like the one involving Black, Smith and Jones. So even if the current debate sparked by Frankfurt is inconclusive, divine foreknowledge provides compelling grounds for rejecting (PAP) and, so, for rejecting argument (1)-(2).[38]

Ockham, as it turns out, was right about the relevance to the Problem of Human Freedom of the fact that God's believing that Adam will sin depends on Adam's future sinning and not the other way around. But he was wrong to think that the dependence of God's past belief on Adam's future action contributes to a solution to this problem by showing how Adam might possibly do otherwise despite God's prior belief that he would sin. Instead it shows how one form of accidental necessity—the one generated by divine foreknowledge—has no adverse consequences for free will, despite its elimination of alternative possibilities.

6. Conclusion. So (F) survives this first attack. I think we can be pretty confident of this even before we identify an actual flaw in the argument, just as we can be confident that the reality of motion survives Zeno's "paradox" without resting our confidence on a sophisticated analysis of where Zeno goes wrong. It's just implausible on its face that mere advance knowledge, even of the infallible and divine variety, should be able to transform an action that would in

---

[36] Augustine *The City of God* 5.10.

[37] Others who have tied a solution to the Problem of Human Freedom to Frankfurt's attack on (PAP) include Linda Zagzebski, *Dilemma of Freedom and Foreknowledge,* chap. 6, sec. 2; and John Martin Fischer, *The Metaphysics of Free Will* (Cambridge, Mass.: Blackwell, 1994), pp. 180-83. Fischer, however, holds that (PAP) gives the wrong result not just when alternatives are eliminated by divine foreknowledge, but also when they are eliminated by causal determinism. Zagzebski and I would disagree, as would Eleonore Stump: see Stump's "Intellect, Will and the Principle of Alternate Possibilities," in *Christian Theism and the Problems of Philosophy,* ed. Michael Beaty (Notre Dame, Ind.: Notre Dame University Press, 1990), pp. 254-85.

[38] I argue that divine-foreknowledge cases provide the perfect counterexamples to (PAP) in my "Frankfurt Counterexamples: Some Comments on the Widerker-Fischer Debate," *Faith and Philosophy* 13 (July 1996): 395-401.

other circumstances be free into one that is not free. But the argument poses an interesting philosophical problem that is well worth grappling with. The result of my own grappling with the argument is the rejection of (2), and I recommend this result to the reader (for the reasons given). But it does seem to me that someone might be well within their rights to reject the argument without knowing quite where the fallacy lies. In any case, the Problem of Human Freedom provides no grounds for abandoning commitment to simple foreknowledge.

The Problem of Divine Agency

This brings us to the second argument against (F). This argument, as well as the third one we will look at below, raises problems that are at least implicit in much traditional discussion of God's providential governance of the world; but I don't know of any classic theological text where it is given so pithy a formulation as the one Augustine puts in the mouth of Evodius. I will instead introduce the Problem of Divine Agency by way of a story.

Suppose that your quirky uncle Clarence—the one who invented the time machine when everyone said it was impossible—shows up at your seventeenth-birthday party with an unusual gift. "I know you've been anxious about some upcoming decisions," he tells you. "So on my last trip into the future, I took along a video camera and recorded some of the key moments in the rest of your life." He hands you a brightly wrapped box. "This will tell you, for example, whether you get into Harvard and whether you accept. Happy viewing!" You thank him, lock the present in a drawer and return to the party.

Later that night you unwrap the videocassette and put it in the VCR. It begins with a trivial scene Uncle Clarence apparently included just to prove the tape's authenticity. There you are at the refreshment table, an hour or so after he gave you the cassette, about to upset the punchbowl . . . and there it goes—all over the floor, your pants and Mrs. Flint's dress. Just before the scene ends, you notice Uncle Clarence's reflection caught in a mirror at the end of the room, camera in hand, recording the incident. You decide to erase that part of the tape. But what about Harvard? That question is soon answered. The next scene shows you opening the letter from the admissions committee. You've been accepted! What a relief. But wait, you are now opening another letter, this one from Cornell. You've been accepted there as well, and Cornell is including a full scholarship. You had always dreamed of attending Harvard, but Harvard offered no money. What will you decide to do? The question is answered as the camera shows you towing a U-Haul trailer into Ithaca, New York, with one eye on the road and one eye on a campus map showing the location of the freshman residence hall to which you have been assigned at Cornell. And that's just the beginning of the tape. The next scene shows a wedding . . .

Let's interrupt the story at this point, because we've followed it far enough to introduce the problem on which we want to focus. You must now *live* the scenes that you have watched on tape. What will that be like? In ordinary life you deliberate among alternative courses of action, reach decisions that resolve your uncertainty and then act on your newly acquired intentions. That's what it is to be an active participant in your life rather than a passive spectator or an actor reading a script. But it looks like your viewing of the tape has condemned you to the latter category, at least with respect to the episodes filmed by Uncle Clarence. How can you engage in deliberation when you already know how it will turn out? How can you resolve uncertainty with a decision when there is no uncertainty to resolve? How can you acquire an intention to act in a particular way if your prior knowledge makes intention-acquisition pointless? By showing you what the future holds, the video short-circuits the route by which you usually approach your own actions, namely, through deliberation, decision-making and intentional agency. This leaves deeply problematic how you can even *be* an agent with respect to those future actions.

Now consider the theological parallel to this story, in which your viewing Uncle Clarence's video is replaced by God's reviewing his exhaustive knowledge of future events. Doesn't the same problem arise for him as arose for you? He knows *everything* that he is going to do, not just selected episodes from the future (like the ones Uncle Clarence thought fit to record on videotape). So there is *nothing* with respect to which he can deliberate, decide or intend. "Knowledge is power"—or so we thought. Instead, maximal knowledge appears to make God maximally impotent.[39]

What should we think of this problem? It's certainly hard to escape the *feeling* that I would approach my future actions rather differently if I already knew what I am going to do; what is less clear is whether I *should* approach them differently and whether what may be true of me can be extended to *God*. I believe that the answer to *both* questions is no, making the Problem of Divine

<hr>

[39]See Tomis Kapitan's provocatively titled article "Action, Uncertainty and Divine Impotence," *Analysis* 50 (March 1990): 127-33. See also his "Can God Make Up His Mind?" *International Journal for Philosophy of Religion* 15 (1984): 37-47, and "Agency and Omniscience," *Religious Studies* 27 (March 1991): 105-20. Others who have pressed this problem include Richard Taylor, "Deliberation and Foreknowledge," *American Philosophical Quarterly* 1 (January 1964): 73-80; and Richard R. La Croix, "Omniprescience and Divine Determinism," *Religious Studies* 12 (September 1976): 365-81.

Agency doubly defective. But to see this, we need to put the worries underlying this problem in argument form.

Let's assume for present purposes that (F) is true. Then since God foreknows *everything,* his own future actions are among the things he foreknows. So

(1)   If God is an intentional agent, then it is possible for him to acquire the intention to perform an action while already believing that he will perform that action.

(2)   It's impossible for anyone to acquire the intention to perform an action while already believing that he will perform that action.

∴   God is not an intentional agent.

If this is an unacceptable conclusion, we must reject the assumption that God foreknows his own exercises of intentional agency, and this means in turn rejecting (F). Right?

Wrong. Both premises of this argument are fatally flawed. Premise (1) is not just flawed, but transparently so. Acting intentionally requires that one *have* the appropriate intention, but there is absolutely no reason why it should be part of the very nature of intentional action that one *acquire* the intention. Even if as an empirical fact human beings never possess intentions that they did not come to acquire at some time or other, this empirical fact about human intention-acquisition has no obvious implications for divine intentionality. Whatever intentions God has, he presumably has them from eternity, just as he has his knowledge from eternity. So there is no time at which God knows what he is going to do but hasn't yet formed the intention to do so. There is no reason, then, to think that (1) is true and so no reason to think that God runs afoul of what (2) claims to be impossible.[40]

But if God does not acquire intentions in the way that we do, doesn't that at least make it difficult to understand how he can be an intentional agent in anything like the way that we understand ourselves to be? Not at all. In normal cases in which a human agent X performs an intentional action *A,* the following conditions are satisfied:

(a)   X holds a belief *B* that it's up to her whether or not she does *A.*

---

[40]On whether intentions must be acquired, see my debate with Tomis Kapitan in *Religious Studies:* Hunt, "Omniprescient Agency," *Religious Studies* 28 (September 1992): 351-69; Kapitan, "The Incompatibility of Omniscience and Intentional Action: A Reply to David P. Hunt," *Religious Studies* 30 (January 1994): 55-66; Hunt, "The Compatibility of Omniscience and Intentional Action: A Reply to Tomis Kapitan," *Religious Studies* 32 (January 1996): 49-60.

(b)   X endorses a judgment *J* about the advisability of doing *A* instead of some-
        thing else.

(c)   X does *A* with the intention *I* to do *A*.

(d)   Belief *B* and judgment *J* help explain why X has intention *I*.

(e)   X's having intention *I* is preceded by a time at which she does not have
        intention *I*.

Now it seems to me that if God satisfies all these conditions *except (e)*, it is perverse to suggest that he fails to qualify as an intentional agent or that the sense
in which he is an intentional agent is nothing like the sense in which we are
intentional agents. I would add that even in the human case, where *(a)-(e)* are
all true, it is only *(a)-(d)* that make an action intentional; *(e)* is simply a
byproduct of the fact that human beings are temporally limited and do not start
out life knowing everything, so that they come to acquire intentions to act in
certain ways only as the relevant information becomes available to them in
time. That's an accident of the human situation, not an essential constituent of
intentional agency per se.

In case this blow to (1) isn't enough to put the argument down for the
count, let's make it a one-two punch. Premise (2) is also objectionable—so
even if God does acquire (any of) his intentions, this is still compatible with his
already having known what he will do.

Why should the belief that one will perform a particular action make it
impossible to acquire the intention to perform that action? The idea is apparently something like this. The point of intention-acquisition is to *settle* the
question of what one is going to do; but knowing what one is going to do *also*
settles this question. So if one already knows what one is going to do, there is
nothing left to be settled by intention-acquisition. Intention-acquisition is therefore pointless if not impossible when one already knows what one is going to
do. All that remains for the unfortunate soul endowed with detailed knowledge
of his future actions is to go through the motions laid out in the script; since all
questions about one's future course of action have already been settled, the
intentionality essential to genuine agency is stultified.[41]

To see what is wrong with this assessment, let us return to Uncle Clarence's
videotape. After the scene in which you are granted tenure at Purdue, there is

---

[41]Compare this with the following remarks from Clark Pinnock's contribution to *Openness of
God*, p. 123: "Future decisions cannot in every way be foreknown, because they have not
yet been made. God knows everything that can be known—but God's foreknowledge does
not include the undecided."

just one more episode on the tape, this one apparently coming some years later. You are living in what looks like a Stone Age village somewhere in the jungle. The naked tribespeople seem accustomed to your presence; you are astonished to hear yourself communicating with them in what strikes your younger self—the one viewing the videotape—as an unintelligible system of clicks and grunts. It isn't until you observe yourself returning to your hut, opening a Bible and beginning to write laboriously in an unknown language that you realize what has happened: you have joined Wycliffe as a Bible trans-lator! Your shock and consternation know no bounds. What ever could have possessed you to give up the comfortable academic position you had striven so long to attain? That must have been one doozy of a midlife crisis! But this is evidently what the future holds in store for you.

What's your situation now, having viewed the tape to the end? You know that sometime around age forty-five you are going to face a defining moment in your life as two very different visions of the good life contend for your alle-giance. You also know the ultimate outcome of that struggle. There is a sense, then, in which the question whether the mission field will prevail over the ivied walls of academe is already *settled* for you. It is settled in the sense that you are now prepared to assent to the truth of a certain proposition: *I will choose Wycliffe over Purdue.* But you are most emphatically *not* prepared to assent to the choice itself. Your seventeen-year-old self is absolutely horrified at how your forty-five-year-old self is going to mess things up. A missionary is the very last thing you want to be! It is clear that your will is far from settled, even if your belief *is* settled by the irrefutable evidence of Uncle Clarence's videotape.

We can now sum up the problem with (2). While foreknowledge and inten-tion-acquisition both resolve unsettled beliefs, what one comes to believe as a result of foreknowledge is a *propositional* belief about *what will happen,* whereas what one comes to believe as a result of intention-acquisition is a *practical* belief about *what to do.* The former does not entail the latter; so even if the propositional belief is acquired first, it may still be necessary to go through the actual process of intention-acquisition (including protracted delib-eration, if that is what is required) in order to achieve the practical belief. It's clear, for example, that all the work of acquiring the practical belief *to join Wycliffe* lies ahead of your seventeen-year-old self and that there is consider-able point to your doing so, even though you already possess the proposi-tional belief. There is no need in the case of (2) to appeal to unique features of the divine situation, since this premise is false for human agents as well. What makes God *or anyone* an agent is the power to decide *what to do.* God's omniscience does not deprive him of this power, since it determines only his propositional beliefs, leaving his practical beliefs—the ones relevant to agency—wide open.[42]

So (2), like (1), must be rejected. I conclude that (F) easily survives the challenge posed by the Problem of Divine Agency.

The Problem of Divine Providence

We now come to the last of our three problems: the Problem of Divine Providence. By "providence" I mean activity God undertakes with a view toward achieving his intended ends, whether in individual lives or on a cosmic scale. And what exactly is the problem with providence? Well, suppose the Problem of Divine Agency has been neutralized, so that we are no longer troubled by the mistaken notion that (F) might interfere with God's intentional action. But it isn't enough that divine foreknowledge doesn't *worsen* God's agential position—shouldn't it *improve* his position? Shouldn't the vast amounts of additional information with which his foreknowledge provides him make some difference to what he can do, making him more competent in some way than he would be if he lacked knowledge of the future? One would certainly think so; yet some critics of (F) have argued that foreknowledge is utterly useless to God.

One such critic is William Hasker. "The doctrine of divine foreknowledge, in its most widely held form," Hasker argues, "is of *no importance whatever* for the religiously significant concerns about prayer, providence, and prophecy."[43] And why is this? Hasker considers a case in which a young woman prays to God for guidance regarding two potential husbands. Can God's knowledge of the future contribute anything to the advice he gives her? Apparently not:

> for the future situation which God foreknows is, of course, a situation in which she *already* is married to one of the two men (or, perhaps, to neither)—and since the decision's *actually having been made* is presupposed by God's *knowledge* of the future, he cannot possibly *use* that knowledge in deciding how to *influence* that decision. . . . In the logical order of dependence of events, one might say, by the "time" God knows something will happen, it is "too late" either to *bring about* its happening or to *prevent* it from happening.[44]

---

[42]For more on this problem, including its connection to the Problem of Human Freedom, see my "Two Problems with Knowing the Future," *American Philosophical Quarterly* 34 (April 1997): 273-85.

[43]Hasker, *God, Time and Knowledge*, p. 55.

[44]Ibid., pp. 57-58.

Hasker isn't denying here that God can bring about or prevent future events, nor is he denying that at least some of the things God knows might prove useful as he decides whether (and if so, how best) to influence events; what he *is* denying is that anything God knows about the *future* can contribute to God's decision. Could knowledge of what will happen help God act so as to *prevent* what he sees will happen? That doesn't seem right, since his intervention would then be undermining the very knowledge on which it is based.[45] Or could knowledge of what will happen help God act so as to *bring about* what he sees will happen? Here God's intervention reinforces rather than undermines what he foreknows, but in doing so it raises a problem of *circularity:* his intervention is based on his knowledge, which is based on the future, which is based on his intervention. It is because the future is the *result* of whatever has or has not been done to influence it that *knowledge* of the future comes to God "too late" (in the logical rather than temporal order) for God to draw on it in his own efforts to influence the future.

The basic objection seems to be that *(i)* God can't put his foreknowledge to use without generating an explanatory circle and *(ii)* such circles are impossible. Neither part of the objection is immune to challenge. The philosopher David Lewis, in an important article on the similar loops spawned by time-travel stories, argues that while such loops are *inexplicable* they are nevertheless *possible.*[46] These are deep waters, and I'm not at all confident that I can see to the bottom of them; so while I think it's far from obvious that Hasker is right about *(ii)*, I propose to leave it alone. On the other hand, *(i)* is readily refutable. In fact, I'm inclined to think that God can get quite a *lot* of (noncircular) use out of his knowledge of future contingencies. But the defense of this position, which I have undertaken elsewhere, can get pretty complicated.[47] So let me adopt here the much simpler and more modest project of developing a *single* case in which foreknowledge would be useful to God. Having shown this, I will leave it to the reader to judge whether reality might support many or few such cases.

Suppose that an eccentric billionaire named Bill receives a fundraising letter from Wycliffe and responds with the following proposal. He is prepared to

---

[45]As John Sanders puts it, "Once God has foreknowledge he cannot change what will happen for that would make his foreknowledge incorrect." See his "Why Simple Foreknowledge Offers No More Providential Control Than the Openness of God," *Faith and Philosophy* 14 (January 1997): 29.

[46]David Lewis, "The Paradoxes of Time Travel," *American Philosophical Quarterly* 13 (April 1976): 145-52.

[47]Hunt, "Divine Providence," pp. 396-416.

transfer $1,000,000,000 to Wycliffe's account if a representative of Wycliffe can guess which number between 1 and 100 he is going to choose. The staff of Wycliffe's home office begin a marathon prayer session, in the course of which they become certain that Bill will choose the number 47. This certainty comes from God, who foresees that Bill will indeed choose the number 47. The next day Wycliffe's fundraising director, Charity, arrives at Bill's office, where a team of lawyers has drawn up a legally binding transfer of the promised sum contingent on her guessing the right number. She hands over a sealed envelope containing a slip of paper on which the number 47 has been written. Bill then thinks for a few seconds before writing a number on a legal pad. He holds it up so everyone can see: it is the number 47. Charity's envelope is then opened to reveal the match. The forces of Satan howl in dismay as Bill duly transfers the billion dollars to Wycliffe.

It is hard to see how Hasker's objections have any purchase on this case. Information that is available to God through simple foreknowledge but that is not available through diminished foreknowledge is being used to give God a "providential edge." God's use of this information does not guarantee that he will get what he wants—Wycliffe's staff might always resist God's leading—but if it were *unavailable* to him there would be no leading for them to resist. At the very least, he raises the odds (1/100 without intervention, somewhat better if he offers advice based on intimate knowledge of Bill's psychology) that he will get the outcome he desires. *And* he puts this knowledge to use without involving himself in any explanatory loops. Charity's submitting the number 47 to Bill's lawyers presupposes God's guidance at the staff prayer meeting, which presupposes God's foreknowledge that Bill will choose the number 47, which presupposes Bill's choosing the number 47, which presupposes . . . what? Who knows why Bill chose that particular number? Whatever the answer, it's not because Charity handed his lawyers an envelope with the number 47 written inside. There is no circularity here with which we need to be concerned.

Among the various objections that opponents might wish to raise about this example, I would guess that the following two would be the most common and important.

Objection 1. If God's foreknowledge informs a divine intervention that occurs *after* the foreknown event takes place, he could have secured the same result by waiting for the event to occur and then cognizing it with his present knowledge; there is nothing foreknowledge helps him do that he couldn't have done without it. But if his foreknowledge informs an intervention that occurs *before* the foreknown event takes place, as it does in our example, the intervention might have causal effects on the foreknown event or in some other way close the explanatory chain so that we are facing an invidious loop after all. Suppose, for example, that Bill has a spy in the Wycliffe organization who jimmies open the locked drawer where the sealed envelope was placed overnight for safekeeping and then steams it open. Now consider various ways things might go at this point:

(A)   Learning from the spy that Wycliffe has selected the number 47, and wishing all along to donate the money to Wycliffe, Bill therefore chooses the number 47. Here's the explanatory circle we wanted to avoid.

(B)   Wishing to keep his money, Bill chooses a different number. But of course he can't, since God's prescience would then be mistaken. This scenario is incoherent.

(C)   The spy—a Frenchman accustomed to European script—misreads the 47 as 41. The next day Bill is about to choose the number 41 when he receives an urgent message from the spy: Wycliffe has chosen 41! Bill quickly casts about for a different number, and 47 is the first one that pops into his head. This restores coherence, but only by reinstating the explanatory circle.

Reply to objection 1. My task was to describe an unproblematic scenario for God's providential use of foreknowledge; the fact that there might be *other* scenarios that *are* problematic is irrelevant to the question of whether my original scenario (sans spy) is acceptable. But even if Bill has a spy at Wycliffe, God's foreknowledge would still give him the same providential edge. If *(A)-(C)* are metaphysically impossible, we can be sure that reality won't include such situations. The spy's mission will therefore fail. (Perhaps it even fails because God intervenes to that end. If *you* wanted to help Wycliffe get the $1,000,000,000 and you knew about the spy, wouldn't you try to thwart him if you could?) Because it is metaphysically impossible for the spy to succeed, God's foreknowledge will have the same providential benefits it had in the original case.

Objection 2. If (F) is true, God foreknows not only Bill's choice of number but also the Wycliffe staff's responsiveness to his guidance, Charity's delivering the number to Bill's office, Bill's decision not to renege on his agreement and so on. So even if Bill's choosing the number 47 does not depend on God's intervention, God knows *other* things that depend on his intervention. We overlook this problem, Hasker explains, because we

think, albeit unconsciously, of God's foreknowledge along the lines of the limited foreknowledge we ourselves sometimes have, when we see certain events coming that are *not* contingent upon anything we may choose to do or to refrain from doing. In such cases the actions that we take in view of our foresight lead to no paradox. But if we could foresee *everything,* then for us, as for God, it would be too late to do anything about it.[48]

In the divine case, it would appear, the circle is ineliminable.

Reply to objection 2. The situation as Hasker describes it is prima facie odd. He allows that God might gain some providential advantage if his knowledge of the past and present were augmented with *limited* foreknowledge—say, if Bill's choosing the number 47 were the only future contingency in his epistemic repertoire; but he insists that God would *lose* this advantage if he had *unlimited* foreknowledge, as (F) claims.

But why should the acquisition of even *more* knowledge make God's providential position *worse?* Mere *possession* of information about the future is harmless (as was shown in our discussion of the Problem of Divine Agency); only its *use* can generate explanatory loops. But why suppose that God must *use* this problematic extra knowledge? David Basinger has an answer: "[If] God purposely avoids the consideration of relevant data to which he has access, it is . . . possible that he will make decisions that fail to actualize his desired ends to the extent they could have been actualized if he had considered all of the relevant data available." Among such data is "foreknowledge of what he will do in fact and what will follow in fact."[49] Since a God with unlimited foreknowledge knows not only that Bill will choose the number 47 but also that Wycliffe will get the billion dollars in the end and since the latter is relevant information that God would use and not merely possess, we've got an invidious loop on our hands.

I'm just not convinced that this *is* "relevant data," however. The fact that you *want* to get into Harvard and that submitting an application is a *necessary means* to this end is a *reason* for submitting an application; the fact that you *will* get into Harvard (because you learn this from Uncle Clarence's video) is *not* a reason for applying. (Nor is this fact a reason *not* to apply—"I don't have to; I'm going to get in anyway!") In the Wycliffe example, either God's basing his intervention at the staff meeting on knowledge of what will result from his intervention *does* generate an invidious explanatory circle or it *doesn't.* If it's the latter, then Basinger hasn't raised any problems for (F); but if it's the former, this is itself good reason to think that God would (could) not use this

[48]Hasker, *God, Time and Knowledge,* p. 62.
[49]David Basinger, *The Case for Freewill Theism* (Downers Grove, Ill.: InterVarsity Press, 1996), pp. 127-28.

item of foreknowledge in the way Basinger claims. By providing God with *complete* information about the future, unlimited foreknowledge gives God the flexibility to use what is useful and ignore the rest. This is an advantage not enjoyed by a God with knowledge of the past and present alone.[50]

This problem is not quite as consequential as the first two: God's inability to employ his foreknowledge providentially would not show that (F) is *false,* it would only show that this doctrine's importance lies elsewhere (e.g., in its contribution to God's metaphysical excellence). But there are nevertheless a couple of reasons for taking the problem seriously. First, it is much tougher than the other two. While I'm pretty confident in what I have said about the Problem of Human Freedom and the Problem of Divine Agency, the Problem of Divine Providence presents a scenario that is every bit as tangled as the most complex time-travel story, and I'm not at all sure that I have it right. At the very least there is much more that needs to be said about this one.

Second, it is worth defending simple foreknowledge on this score because its alleged failure to provide God with any providential advantage has led critics to squeeze it from both sides. Want more providential control than is afforded by diminished foreknowledge? Then you'll need to augment foreknowledge with "middle knowledge." Think that middle knowledge is incoherent? Then there's nothing to be gained by insisting that God has more than diminished foreknowledge. It is important to see that this is a false dilemma. While simple foreknowledge clearly offers *less* providential control than middle knowledge, it does offer *more* than past-and-present knowledge. This means that there *is* a middle ground to stand on should the problems with middle knowledge prove insuperable.

Conclusion

In defending free agency (both human and divine) from various threats posed by (F), I have said very little about *what it is* that I am defending. This was intentional. I have tried to get by with an unelaborated, pretheoretical understanding of free agency—*simple* free agency, one might say—in much the way I tried to operate with a similar understanding of (F) as *simple* foreknowledge. One virtue of this approach is that I don't need to pretend more knowledge than I actually possess. Perhaps some of my coauthors know what free agency

---

[50]Basinger and I have an exchange on this subject: David Hunt, "Divine Providence and Simple Foreknowledge," *Faith and Philosophy* 10 (July 1993): 396-416; David Basinger, "Simple Foreknowledge and Providential Control: A Response to Hunt," *Faith and Philosophy* 10 (July 1993): 421-27; David Hunt, "Prescience and Providence: A Reply to My Critics," *Faith and Philosophy* 10 (July 1993): 430-40.

is and how God knows the future—I'm quite sure that I don't! But I also hope to gain some insight into these questions by wrestling with the three problems raised against (F). This brings me to a second virtue of this minimalist approach, which is that I am relatively free to be instructed by these three problems. How must I think about divine foreknowledge and free agency if these are to be compatible with each other? Rather than starting off with a rich account of foreknowledge and agency and applying these to the defense of (F), I see my Christian commitment to (F) as providing me with an opportunity to develop a (richer) account of foreknowledge and agency. The best way to do this is to presuppose as little as possible and see where the argument leads.

The most general conclusion to which the argument has led, in my estimation, is that it is the *explanatory* rather than *temporal* order that is important to agency. We overlook this because the two orders normally coincide: when A explains or causes B, A is typically *earlier* than B. Commitment to (F) forces us to consider what happens when these two orders come apart. We have seen that God's beliefs about the future may *settle* the question of what will happen, thereby eliminating alternatives to what he believes; but we have also seen that this need not disrupt the actual exercise of agency (whether human or divine). Thus Clark Pinnock is partly right and partly wrong when he writes, "Total knowledge of the future would imply a fixity of events. Nothing in the future would need to be decided. It also would imply that human freedom is an illusion, that we make no difference and are not responsible."[51] He is right in the first sentence but wrong (I believe) in the implications he derives from it in the second and third sentences.

The conclusion that free agency is compatible with a "closed" future is not open-ended; it extends only as far as the cause or explanation of the future is to be found in the agent (and not in something prior to the agent). Thus our examination of these three problems has given us no grounds for holding that free agency is compatible with causal determinism (which posits sufficient prior conditions for all an agent's actions). Nor does it support compatibilism with respect to *divine* determinism. A book on divine *sovereignty* and human freedom might force us to entertain that prospect! But because divine foreknowledge neither causes nor explains what it knows, it does not require us to adopt an attenuated understanding of free agency under which an agent may be "free" even when his actions are causally determined by a force outside himself, whether God or the universe.

I began this chapter with the ordinary believer's commitment to (F). The

---

[51]Pinnock et al., *Openness of God,* p. 121.

bottom line is that there is no good reason, at least among the three problems we examined, for the believer to jettison this commitment. That's a happy result from a theological standpoint. The fact that this result has, as I believe, interesting implications for free agency provides a nice philosophical bonus.

AN OPEN-THEISM RESPONSE

Gregory A. Boyd

*T*here is much in David Hunt's carefully argued essay with which I agree. There are a few crucial areas where I find myself in disagreement, however. I shall first review two areas of agreement and then discuss three areas where I disagree.

The Bible and God's Foreknowledge
I agree with Hunt (as well as with William Lane Craig and Paul Helm) that the Bible contains examples of God's foreknowing what shall come pass. Hunt "infers" from these examples that God possesses exhaustively definite foreknowledge about all that shall come to pass.[1] Yet he candidly acknowledges that "the Bible nowhere makes this claim" and therefore concedes that the claim is "at least potentially vulnerable to the fallacy of 'hasty generalization' "

---

[1]The open view holds that God knows the future exhaustively, but not that this knowledge is *exhaustively definite,* for the future, in our view, is partly composed of indefinite possibilities.

(p. 70). I appreciate Hunt's candor.

I myself believe that this is precisely the fallacy committed by those who hold to the classical view of foreknowledge. The teaching and examples in Scripture certainly warrant the conclusion that *some* of the future is settled in God's mind. Indeed, I believe the Bible warrants the conclusion that God can settle as much of the future ahead of time as he sovereignly sees fit. But, as I attempted to show in my original essay, the Bible with just as much force also warrants the conclusion that God has sovereignly decided to *not* settle *all* of the future. Some of the future is open, as is evidenced by the fact that God speaks and thinks about it in subjunctive terms; that he changes his intentions in response to changing circumstances; that he expresses regret, disappointment, surprise and frustration regarding what comes to pass; and so on.

Invalidity of Some Standard Arguments

With noteworthy patience and philosophical care, Hunt refuted a number of arguments that are sometimes used in an attempt to demonstrate the compatibility of exhaustively definite foreknowledge and human freedom. I found myself in agreement with most of Hunt's refutations. In particular, his refutation of the argument based on the distinction between "hard" and "soft" facts was insightful. (Helm effectively dealt with this as well.) It could be argued that God's *knowledge* that, for instance, Adam would sin constitutes a "soft" fact. But it cannot be cogently argued that God's *belief* that Adam would sin constitutes a "soft" fact. This is as "hard" a fact about the past (viz., a past mental state of God) as anything could be. And since the beliefs of an omniscient being are by definition infallibly correct, we have to conclude that by "accidental necessity," Adam's future sinning was "locked in" before he was created, in which case he could not be free.

I turn now to three areas of disagreement.

A "Diminished" View of Foreknowledge?

Hunt labels the open view's concept of foreknowledge "diminished foreknowledge" (p. 66). He further suggests that there is "some dissonance (if not outright contradiction) in our thinking about God if we suppose him to be unsurpassably great while also attributing to him ignorance of some future event" (p. 69).

Clearly, if God were ignorant of anything, we could not call him "unsurpassably great." We would have to conclude that his knowledge was indeed "diminished," and hence we would have to deny that he is omniscient. But the open view of the future vehemently denies that God is ignorant of *anything.* If a future event was in fact settled and God was ignorant of this, *that* would be "diminished foreknowledge." But if a future event is possible, not yet settled, we hardly attribute ignorance to God by saying he knows it as possible. For we are simply saying, with all Christians, that God knows all of reality *exactly like it is.*

The mistake Hunt makes—and the one repeated by Craig, Helm and many other critics of the open view—is confusing a difference of opinion about *the content of reality* with a difference of opinion about *the scope of God's knowledge.* On this mistaken logic, open theists could just as easily argue that classical theists "diminish" the scope of God's knowledge because in their view God is "ignorant" of the reality of genuine possibilities!

Foreknowledge and Providential Control

This first objection is closely related to a second objection. Hunt believes that although the simple-foreknowledge view gives God less control than either the middle-knowledge perspective or the Reformed perspective, it gives God more control than the "diminished foreknowledge" (viz., the open-theists') perspective. I respectfully disagree. Two points may be made.

First, open theists agree with the historic orthodox understanding that God possesses unlimited or "infinite" intelligence. If thought through consistently, this entails that God's intelligence doesn't get "thinned out," as it were, by having to attend to any number of possibilities. He may attend to and anticipate a trillion possible story lines as though each was the only possible story line he had to attend to. This means that God loses no providential advantage by virtue of the fact that he faces a future partly composed (by his own design!) of possibilities. Whatever story line comes to pass, God perfectly anticipated it— *as though* this was the only possible story line that could be actualized. When the story line of history is completed, it will look to us finite beings as though God eternally foreknew just this one story line.

An open theist can thus celebrate, as much as can any classical theist, the wonder of God's incomprehensible foreknowledge. We can celebrate the unsurpassable sovereign advantage this foreknowledge affords God. It's just that we also celebrate that God is so intelligent, he didn't need to have only one story line to pay attention to in order to perfectly anticipate it. In the open view, God doesn't *under*-know the future, he *over*-knows it. The criticism that God loses providential control by having more than one possible story line to attend to is really based on an anthropomorphic presupposition that God's intelligence is not infinite. *Humans* lose control to the extent that we must anticipate possibilities rather than simply know certainties, for we have only so much intelligence to go around. But for a God of infinite intelligence, there is virtually no advantage in anticipating *settled* story lines versus *possible* story lines.

Second, precisely because some of the future is open in our view, God has more, not less, providential control than in the simple-foreknowledge position. In the simple-foreknowledge view, God cannot alter what is going to come to pass, for it is eternally settled. In the open view, God can "alter the future," for "the future" is not exhaustively settled. Because the future is partly composed of possibilities, God can warn us (as in biblical prophecy) about future circumstances and can lead us to alter what otherwise would come to pass. We "trust that God holds the future" not because he is certain of what *will* transpire. What confidence does that bring? Perhaps the future of which God is certain has one of our children being kidnapped! We rather "trust that God holds the future" because he perfectly knows and anticipates all that *may* transpire. The "may" gives space for God to intervene and lead us in a different direction.

The Frankfurt Analogy

My final objection to Hunt's essay concerns his endorsement of the Frankfurt analogy. As said above, Hunt effectively refutes a number of ways people have attempted to render exhaustively definite foreknowledge with free agency. Yet he believes that exhaustively definite foreknowledge and free agency are compatible, and he pins his hope for a plausible philosophical defense of this compatibility on one argument. Those who defend libertarian freedom often assume that "A person X does an action A of his own free will only if X could have done otherwise." Hunt agrees that if this principle is valid, then God's foreknowledge that X will do A means that X did not do A freely. For God's foreknowledge "locks in" the fact that X will do A, thus ruling out the possibility of X's doing -A. But Hunt rejects this principle. Person X may do A freely, even though it is not possible for X do to -A. Hunt's case for the compatibility of exhaustively definite foreknowledge and free agency rests on the cogency of his case against this principle.

The only support Hunt offers in his essay for this rejection is an analogy, first submitted by Harry Frankfurt. Suppose one person (Black) wants another person (Smith) dead. He knows that a third person (Jones) wants to kill Smith. Black therefore deploys a science-fiction device that is capable of monitoring and, if need be, controlling Jones's mental processes. Hence, even if Jones had second thoughts about killing Smith, the device would ensure that he would do so. As it turns out, Jones freely follows through on his intention to kill Smith. Hunt argues that this analogy demonstrates that it is possible to do something freely, even though one couldn't have done otherwise, for Jones would have killed Smith in any case. As Hunt puts it, "Though both Black's device and God's foreknowledge eliminate all alternatives to Jones's action, neither does so in such a way as to jeopardize Jones's agency" (p. 90).

In my estimation, Frankfurt's analogy is fatally flawed. The central problem is that it defines a free decision in terms of behavior rather than in terms of mental processes. It is true that in *terms of external behavior,* Jones had no alternative to murdering Smith. But it is not true that Jones had no alternative *in terms of his internal mental (and spiritual) processes.* Though he didn't know it, Jones's choice was either to murder Smith of his own volition or to not. Had he listened to his conscience and decided not to murder Smith, the science-fiction device would have made him kill Smith anyway, but in this case it wouldn't be a murder Jones freely committed. A perfectly fair and informed jury would never hold Jones morally responsible for doing what the device made him do.

I therefore conclude that Hunt has failed in his attempt to demonstrate the compatibility of exhaustively definite foreknowledge and free agency. And since I largely agree with Hunt's own refutation of other possible defenses, I remain under the conviction that exhaustively definite foreknowledge is not logically compatible with free agency. Person X is free (and thus morally responsible) regarding an action A if and only if it is genuinely possible for him to do -A. Hence, in perfectly knowing X, God would know that both A and -A are possible. The future is open to X's doing A or -A.

A MIDDLE-KNOWLEDGE RESPONSE

William Lane Craig

*D*avid Hunt's provocative position is that fatalism is true—but not to worry, for fatalism is compatible with libertarian freedom!

In examining Hunt's position, the first question we need to ask is, why should we think that fatalism is true? Has Hunt explicated a sense of temporal necessity that does not reduce to either the unalterability or the causal closedness of the past?

He has not. Hunt merely appeals to examples to evoke in us the feeling of the past's necessity. When Hunt concludes, "In general, everything that is past is (now) necessary in this sense" (p. 75), we are left wondering, "In what sense is that?" Let ACT stand for "act in a certain way and, if one were to act in that way, some past fact would not have been a fact." If Hunt means that it is not possible for me to ACT, then Hunt's generalization from a single example is hasty.

We can envision instances in which I could ACT. If, for example, I have a time machine that enables me to travel back in time, then I can ACT. Now in the absence of a time machine, it is doubtless not within my power to ACT with respect to a broad range of past facts. But that does not imply that there are *no* past facts relative to which I can ACT. Unless we are logical fatalists, we must agree that at least the past fact of a future contingent proposition's being true is something now past that is still such that I can ACT with respect to it. But then I can also ACT with respect to God's past beliefs. For, necessarily, if I were to refrain from some action A, then a true future contingent proposition p stating that I shall do A would have been false. And, necessarily, if p had been false, then God would not have believed p. It therefore follows that were I to refrain from A, God would not have believed p.

Now Hunt is quite willing to admit the truth of counterfactuals of the form

1. If I were to refrain from A, then God would not have believed p.

and presumably of the form

2. If I were to refrain from A, then p would not have possessed the truth value *True*.

But he insists that I do not, in fact, have the power to refrain from A. For both God's belief that p and p's possession of the truth value *True* are "hard" facts about the past, and it is not within my power to ACT with respect to hard facts about the past.

What is a "hard fact"? Hunt says that it is "a fact that is *entirely* about the past" (p. 76). What does that mean? Hunt does not explain. He seems to be striving to articulate what Alfred Freddoso has called *temporally indifferent* propositions. In Freddoso's analysis, a temporally indifferent propositions is one that could be true at a first, an intermediate, or a last moment of time.[1] Hence, a temporally indifferent proposition that is true at a time t will be entirely about t.

If, with Hunt, we identify hard facts with the facts described by temporally indifferent propositions true at a past moment of time, then p's possessing the value *True* is not a hard fact. Accordingly, it may be the case that it is within my power to ACT with respect to that fact. But then I also have the power to ACT with respect to God's belief that p. For the statement "God believes p" is not temporally indifferent either, since it could not be true at a last moment of; time. Therefore, "God believed p" is not a hard fact about the past.

---

[1]See Alfred J. Freddoso, "Accidental Necessity and Logical Determinism," *Journal of Philosophy* 80 (1983): 257-78. These conditions apply to logically contingent propositions.

Furthermore, why we should accept the equation between a fact's being "entirely about the past" and its being temporally necessary? If time travel is possible, then facts that are entirely about the past are not beyond the power of the time traveler to affect. Analogously, temporally indifferent propositions based on divine foreknowledge like *Isaiah prophesies the destruction of Jerusalem* may be such that it is within the power of later agents to ACT with respect to them.[2] Accordingly, this fact is not temporally necessary before the relevant agents freely destroy Jerusalem. This is admittedly weird; but then time travel and divine foreknowledge are exotic notions, and we should not be surprised if they lead to startling implications.

The crucial difference between these cases and Hunt's alleged parallel, *If I had saved the child, then I would not have been knocked unconscious,* is that his example gratuitously deviates from the standard counterfactual semantics. The type of counterfactual at issue here is called a *backtracking counterfactual* because the truth of the antecedent requires that the past be different than it was. Now such backtracking counterfactuals are deviant from the standard semantics for counterfactuals. On the standard semantics, the past is held constant, and one asks what would then happen in the possible worlds that are most similar to ours in which the counterfactual's antecedent is true. This is called "the standard resolution of vagueness" among possible worlds in which the antecedent is true. On the standard semantics, true counterfactuals having the antecedent Hunt imagines have consequents like "then he would have survived the fire." In order to claim that a backtracking counterfactual is true, one needs some justification for adopting a special resolution of vagueness. Otherwise we get counterintuitive results from our semantics.[3] It is a matter of considerable controversy when a special resolution of vagueness is justified. I have

---

[2]See discussion in my book *Divine Foreknowledge and Human Freedom,* Brill's Studies in Intellectual History 19 (Leiden: Brill, 1991), pp. 180-83. (N.B., I should have used the present tense in my examples there, since only present-tense statements are immediate.) According to the analysis I offer, a proposition is temporally necessary if and only if it expresses a hard fact and temporally contingent if and only if it expresses a soft fact. A fact is soft if and only if it is a past or present event or actuality that is counterfactually dependent on some future event or actuality in such a way that the earlier event or actuality is a consequence of which the later event or actuality is the condition. A fact is hard if and only if it is a present or past event or actuality that is not so dependent. On the relevant sense of conditions and consequences, see Roger Wertheimer, "Conditions," *Journal of Philosophy* 65 (1968): 355-64.

[3]For example, someone on the thirty-fifth floor of a building might assert, "If I were to jump out the window, I would not fall to my death." Why not? "Because if I were to jump out the window, I would have placed a safety net outside!" One can imagine the chaos that would result if we were to embrace arbitrarily the truth of such backtracking counterfactuals instead of those yielded by the standard resolution of vagueness!

elsewhere argued that it is warranted only in cases in which the event described in the antecedent is a condition of which the event in the consequent is the consequence. In Hunt's example, my not being knocked unconscious is not a consequence of my saving the child; indeed quite the reverse is the case.[4] In the absence of any justification of a special resolution of vagueness, we have no reason to think that Hunt's counterfactual is true. By contrast, in the case of divine foreknowledge, a special resolution *must* be used, for given God's essential omniscience, there is *no possible world* in which the antecedent is true and he does not believe what the antecedent states.

As for Hunt's second example of the tachyonic doorbell, he just assumes that no special resolution of vagueness is in order. But in the case of time-traveling signals, backtracking counterfactuals can be justified.[5] As for God's belief that I shall press the button, what is impossible is the *conjunction* of God's belief and my failing to press the button. But my failing to press the button is not impossible. If I were to have refrained, God would have believed differently.

Hunt also takes for granted that temporal necessity is closed under entailment, that is to say, that the necessity of the premises is passed on to the conclusion of his argument. But we have the very best of reasons for thinking that temporal necessity as Hunt imagines it is not closed under entailment—namely, fatalism posits a constraint on our actions that is completely unintelligible. It is curious that Hunt actually cites me approvingly on this point but then turns around and says that "divine foreknowledge deprives Adam of alternatives" (p. 88), though not of free will. If divine foreknowledge leaves Adam causally free, what mysterious force deprives him of alternatives? In fact there can be no such mysterious force, for that would be to posit some causal constraint on Adam. But if there is no such mysterious force, what deprives Adam of the power to act other than as he will? It seems, then, that even if Hunt could enunciate some sense in which God's believing *p* is temporally necessary, temporal necessity must not be closed under entailment, so that the

---

[4]What makes his illustration deceptive is that my not being knocked unconscious is a necessary condition of my saving the child in the sense of material implication: "If I saved the child, I was not knocked unconscious." But merely logical conditions do not disclose genuine relations of condition-consequence (everything is both a condition and a consequence of itself in a merely logical sense), and the truth of this indicative conditional statement does not justify the backtracking counterfactual envisioned by Hunt.

[5]Of course, in the case at hand a special resolution of vagueness may not be warranted, for were I to refrain, someone else might press the button or the buzzing might be due to malfunction. But in some such time travel cases, a special resolution may be preferable or necessary.

events described by *p* do not occur necessarily.

So much for fatalism. What about Hunt's solution to it? That solution is predicated on a Frankfurtian conception of libertarian freedom that rejects the Principle of Alternative Possibilities. Since I am not causally constrained to do some action *A*, I do *A* freely, even if it is not within my power to freely refrain from doing *A*. Thus, my doing *A* necessarily is not incompatible with my doing *A* freely.

The problem with Hunt's solution is that it appears to be inconsistent with Frankfurtian freedom itself. For as Thomas Flint observes, Harry Frankfurt's examples leave intact the libertarian intuition that if I do *A* freely, then I could have failed to do *A* freely.[6] But Hunt's fatalism does not allow this. For given God's foreknowledge, I cannot fail to do *A* freely. I must do *A*, and I must do *A* freely—that is, without causal constraint—since all the historical antecedents of *A* are also foreknown by God and, hence, are necessary. Thus, Hunt's solution is inconsistent with the very concept of freedom it presupposes. Frankfurt's examples involve my either doing *A* freely or doing *A* under causal constraint. But these options are not open under Hunt's fatalism. All he can affirm is that every free action of mine is done without causal determination. But the fatalist has already conceded that; that point is not in dispute. The issue is, what sense of freedom remains if I cannot freely refrain from *A?* Frankfurt's answer to that question is one that is not open to the theological fatalist.

---

[6]Thomas P. Flint, *Divine Providence,* Cornell Studies in the Philosophy of Religion (Ithaca, N.Y.: Cornell University Press, 1998), pp. 166-67.

AN AUGUSTINIAN-CALVINIST RESPONSE

Paul Helm

*D*avid Hunt initially concentrates on defending the consistency of the following propositions:

(3)   God foreknows that Adam will sin.

(4)   Adam will sin of his own free will.

But he adopts an interesting dialectical attitude toward them. He says, "Sometimes we have good reason to believe that there must be something wrong with an argument before we are in a position to see *what* is wrong with it" (p. 80), and he then offers Zeno's paradox of Achilles and the tortoise as a case in point. Even though we may not be able to see where the fallacy lies, we are convinced that there must be a fallacy since we are convinced that Achilles is faster than the tortoise.

Hunt claims that we face exactly the same situation when it comes to the argument for the incompatibility of divine foreknowledge and human freedom. He says that "there is something fishy about the idea that Adam's action, while in every other respect satisfying the most exacting requirements for free will, might nevertheless count as unfree *simply* because God foreknew what he would do" (p. 81). His argument is outlined here:

(i)   God foreknows that Adam will sin (assumption).

(ii)   The supposition that God's knowing some act in advance adversely affects the (incompatibilistic) freedom of that act is fishy and unintelligible.

(iii)   Therefore *(i)* is consistent with Adam's sinning of his own free will.

As far as I can see, Hunt offers no argument for *(ii)* beyond calling the claim that God's foreknowledge of Adam's sin renders it unfree (i.e., not an indeterministic act) "fishy."

This does not seem to be a very persuasive argument. In fact, it looks remarkably like a case of begging the question. The question is, Is divine foreknowledge incompatible with human freedom? To say that a positive answer to this question is fishy (or, following William Lane Craig, is "unintelligible") and then to dismiss it without argument is a plain begging of the question.

The parallel with Zeno's paradox of Achilles and the tortoise is not apt. There is nothing in the least paradoxical about the claim that divine foreknowledge is inconsistent with human indeterministic action, as is testified by the generations of discussion of the issue and by the diverse viewpoints represented in this book. It is a serious problem meriting serious discussion.

Further, there is an inherent weakness in the case of the appeal to the Achilles paradox. For once this particular ball starts to roll, it is difficult to stop it. Take any metaphysical question: Is time unreal? Is the human self a simple entity? Do material things have essences? Does God exist? Do I have counterparts in other possible worlds? All these questions can, it seems, be given the Achilles treatment. Thus it may be claimed that the idea that time is unreal is unintelligible, fishy. Therefore whatever the arguments for that view, there must be flaws in them even though we cannot at present find them. Therefore it is reasonable to believe that time is real. And so on.

If Hunt's appeal to the precedent of Zeno's paradox of Achilles and the tortoise works in the case of (3) and (4), should it not also do to rule (1) out of court, since what (1) says—that if God foreknows that Adam will sin, then Adam cannot sin of his own free will but instead his action of sinning is necessitated—looks equally fishy and unintelligible. How could God's foreknowledge of an action necessitate that action? In fact Hunt comes close to adopting this attitude when he says, "Divine foreknowledge deprives Adam of alternatives, but we just can't believe that it deprives him of free will" (p. 88; see also the conclusion to his discussion of "The Problem of Human Freedom"). So it is a puzzle why we need to devote philosophical attention to (1) if it is sufficient to appeal to the Achilles paradox in the case of (3) and (4). Why doesn't Achilles also do the job on (1)?

Despite this, Hunt does give attention to (1), and I agree with him wholeheartedly in his able rejection of the Ockhamist strategy as an attempt to disable the consequences that the necessity of the past has for human freedom. Rejecting Ockhamism, Hunt by this stage accepts (1), (3) and (4). So the problem must lie with (2)—that if it's necessary that Adam will sin, then Adam will not sin of his own free will. At this point, in his attack on (2), Hunt, following Harry Frankfurt, rejects the "Principle of Alternate Possibilities" (PAP). Adam sins of necessity if God foreknows what he will do, and his sinning by necessity is inconsistent with (PAP). But (PAP) is not necessary for a satisfactory account of freedom. And so Adam may sin of necessity while retaining his freedom.

If (PAP) is rejected, then Hunt may justifiably claim that "divine foreknowledge deprives Adam of alternatives, but we just can't believe that it deprives him of free will" (p. 88). Let us suppose that Hunt is correct in this. It seems that one who upholds the Augustinian-Calvinist perspective could co-opt Hunt as an ally at this point, by arguing in the following way:

(1)   Human freedom is compatible with the denial of (PAP). (Hunt's conclusion)

(2)   The denial of (PAP) is consistent with causal determinism, since (PAP) is inconsistent with causal determinism.

(3)   Therefore, freedom is consistent with causal determinism.[1]

Whether or not Hunt would welcome this argument is hard to say since throughout his (rather misleading) account of Augustine's attitude to compatibilism, he opposes compatibilism. What Hunt says about Augustine is misleading because throughout his account of what goes on in Augustine's early treatise *On Free Choice of the Will,* Hunt claims that Augustine rejects (PAP) but not on causally determinist grounds (p. 8). It is true that Augustine rejects

---

[1]For argument on this, see John Martin Fischer and Mark Ravizza, S.J., *Responsibility and Control* (Cambridge: Cambridge University Press, 1998), pp. 34-41. Of course on the Frankfurt view, freedom does not require causal determinism.

the idea that human actions are the result of natural necessity, but of course natural necessity does not exhaust the varieties of determinism or of compatibilism, not even among modern secular naturalists—not, at least, if the paradigm of natural necessity is the falling of a stone. The view that human actions are the causal outcome of beliefs and desires, say, gives us a very unstone-like version of determinism and (for a compatibilist) of compatibilism. And certainly in his later writings Augustine denies (PAP) on the grounds that it is inconsistent both with that version of compatibilism he favors and with the sufficiency and efficacy of divine grace, as Hunt himself notes (p. 93 n. 40).

So if Hunt denies (PAP), he is committed to some version or other of determinism. His argument shows that divine foreknowledge is consistent both with determinism and with Frankfurtian freedom. So is Hunt among those who share the Augustinian-Calvinist perspective?

Fatalism Again

Finally, since the word *fatalism* occurs more than once in Hunt's characterization of Augustinianism, it is worth saying something about this in addition to the remarks I will make in response to Craig. It is obvious that not every doctrine that denies indeterministic free will is a case of fatalism, since determinism denies it and determinism is distinct from fatalism. Fatalism is the doctrine that whatever will be will be, holding (in one prominent version) that the denial of free will follows from the laws of logic alone. It holds that some future event X will occur no matter what. But determinism denies this. (As we have seen, the Frankfurtianism that Hunt favors also entails the denial of indeterministic free will. So if this denial is sufficient to make a doctrine fatalistic, then Hunt will find himself in the serried ranks of the theological fatalists.) This suggests that the phrase *theological fatalism* is not sufficiently discriminating. What Hunt and Craig call theological fatalism would be better characterized as one of at least three distinct views—theological determinism, theological Frankfurtianism or theological decretalism. Though these last two views entail determinism, they need not entail theological determinism.

Divine Providence

The other two problems for simple foreknowledge with which Hunt deals concern the problem of divine agency and the problem of divine providence. As I could not make much of the problem of divine agency, I shall round off these comments by a brief remark on divine providence.

Hunt attempts a refutation of William Hasker's claim that the doctrine of divine foreknowledge is of no importance whatever for prayer, providence and prophecy. Hunt offers an ingenious story to show that what God knows about the future might offer practical help on the basis of what he foresees. But this example does not meet Hasker's point, which is that foreknowledge as a corollary of divine omniscience—"foreknowledge that embraces all actual free choices, including those that are yet to be made"—is of no practical importance.[2] Selective foreknowledge, of the sort that God might make known to others so that they can bring about changes not yet within the ken of God, is not within Hasker's ken either.

---

[2]William Hasker, *God, Time and Knowledge* (Ithaca, N.Y.: Cornell University Press, 1989), p. 55.

3

THE MIDDLE-KNOWLEDGE VIEW

William Lane Craig

*T*he climax of Charles Dickens's wonderful classic *A Christmas Carol* comes when Scrooge, shaken by the scenes shown him by the Spirit of Christmas Yet to Come, pleads, "Answer me one question. Are these the shadows of the things that Will be, or are they shadows of things that May be, only?"[1] The ghost does not speak a word in answer to Scrooge.

And with good reason! For had the spirit responded, "These shadows are merely scenes of things that could be," Scrooge might well have breathed a sigh of relief and gone on with his life as before. "After all," he might quite rightly reflect, "almost anything *could* happen! No need to lose sleep about that!" On the other hand, if the spirit had told him candidly, "No, these shadows are not scenes of things that will be" (as we know to be true from the story's end), then Scrooge might have felt no cause for alarm at all, since none of what he had witnessed would in fact come to pass. In that case, he might not have been led to repent and change his life.

Scrooge's problem was that he was asking the wrong question; he had

---

[1]Charles Dickens, *A Christmas Carol and Other Stories,* The Modern Library (New York: Random House, 1995), p. 97.

failed to exhaust the alternatives. For between what *could* be and what *will* be lies what *would be*. What the spirit was revealing to Scrooge was what *would* happen if Scrooge did not repent and change. The spirit was not exhibiting mere possibilities (it was *possible* that Scrooge would sell his business and open a flower stand in Covent Garden, but who cares about that?), nor was he showing Scrooge what was in fact going to happen (Dickens assures us that Tiny Tim did *not* die). Rather the spirit was warning Scrooge that if he did not repent, all these terrible things would come to pass.

In philosophical terminology, the spirit was revealing to Scrooge a bit of *counterfactual* knowledge. Counterfactuals are conditional statements in the subjunctive mood: for example, "If I were rich, I would buy a Mercedes"; "If Barry Goldwater had been elected president, he would have won the Vietnam War"; and "If you were to ask her, she would say yes." Counterfactuals are so called because the antecedent or consequent clauses are typically contrary to fact: I am not rich, Goldwater was not elected president, and the U.S. did not win the Vietnam War. Nevertheless, sometimes the antecedent and/or consequent is true. For example, your friend wants to ask the girl of his dreams for a date and, emboldened by your reassurance that "If you were to ask her, she would say yes," does ask her and she does say yes.

Counterfactual statements make up an enormous and significant part of our ordinary language and are an indispensable part of our decision making: For example, "If I pulled out into traffic now, I wouldn't make it"; "If I were to ask J. B. for a raise with his mood, he'd tear my head off"; "If we sent the Third Army around the enemy's right flank, we would prevail." Clearly life-and-death decisions are made daily on the basis of the presumed truth of counterfactual statements.

The Doctrine of Middle Knowledge
Christian theologians have typically affirmed that in virtue of his omniscience, God possesses counterfactual knowledge. He knows, for example, what would have happened if he had spared the Canaanites from destruction, what Napoleon would have done had he won the Battle of Waterloo, and how Jones would respond if I were to share the gospel with him. Not until Friedrich Schleiermacher and the advent of modern theology did theologians think to deny God knowledge of true counterfactuals. Everyone who had considered the issue agreed that God has such knowledge.

What theologians did dispute, however, was, so to speak, *when* God has such counterfactual knowledge. The question here did not have to do with the moment of time at which God acquired his counterfactual knowledge. For whether God is timeless or everlasting throughout time, in neither case are there truths that are unknown to God until some moment at which he discovers them. As an omniscient being, God must know every truth there is and so can never exist in a state of ignorance. Rather the "when" mentioned above refers to the point in the *logical* order concerning God's creative decree at which God has counterfactual knowledge.

This idea of a logical order with regard to God's decrees is a familiar one to Reformed theologians. For although all God's decrees occur at once rather than sequentially, there is a logical order among the decrees. For example, infralapsarians say that God decreed Christ's death on the cross in order to remedy humanity's fall into sin, so that logically God's decree of the cross comes after his decree of the fall. By contrast, supralapsarians say that God's primary aim for humankind was redemption via the cross, and therefore he decreed the fall in order to have something to redeem humans from. On this scheme, the decree of the cross is logically prior to the decree of the fall. Thus even though it was agreed on all hands that God's decrees occur all at once, theologians debated how they were to be logically arranged.

A similar dispute existed among post-Reformation theologians with respect to the place of God's counterfactual knowledge. Everybody agreed that logically prior to God's decree to create a world, God has knowledge of all necessary truths, including all the possible worlds he might create. This was called God's *natural knowledge*. It gives him knowledge of what *could* be. Moreover, everyone agreed that logically subsequent to his decree to create a particular world, God knows all the contingent truths about the actual world, including its past, present and future. This was called God's *free knowledge*. It involves knowledge of what *will* be. The disputed question was where one should place God's counterfactual knowledge of what *would* be. Is it logically prior to or posterior to the divine decree?

Catholic theologians of the Dominican order held that God's counterfactual knowledge is logically *subsequent* to his decree to create a certain world. They maintained that in decreeing that a particular world exist, God also decreed which counterfactual statements are true. Logically prior to the divine decree, there are no counterfactual truths to be known. All God knows at that logical moment are the necessary truths, including all the various possibilities.

At that logically prior moment God knows, for example, that there is a possible world in which Peter denies Christ three times, and another possible world in which Peter affirms Christ, and yet another world in which it is Matthew who denies Christ three times, and so on. God picks one of these worlds to be actual, and thus subsequent to his decree it is true that Peter will deny

Christ three times. Moreover, God knows this truth because he knows which world he has decreed. Not only so, but in decreeing a particular world to be real, God also decrees which counterfactuals are true. Thus he decrees, for example, that if Peter had instead been in such-and-such circumstances, he would have denied Christ two times. God's counterfactual knowledge, like his foreknowledge, is logically posterior to the divine creative decree.

By contrast, Catholic theologians of the Jesuit order inspired by Luis de Molina maintained that God's counterfactual knowledge is logically *prior* to his creative decree. This difference between the Jesuit Molinists and the Dominicans was no mere matter of theological hair-splitting! The Molinists charged that the Dominicans had in effect obliterated human freedom by making counterfactual truths a consequence of God's decree, for on the Dominican account it is God who determines what each person will do in whatever circumstances he finds himself. By contrast, the Molinists, by placing God's counterfactual knowledge prior to the divine decree, made room for creaturely freedom by exempting counterfactual truths from God's decree. In the same way that necessary truths like 2 + 2 = 4 are prior to and therefore independent of God's decree, so also counterfactual truths about how creatures would freely choose under various circumstances are prior to and independent of God's decree.

Not only does the Molinist view make room for human freedom, but it affords God a means of choosing which world of free creatures to create. For by knowing how persons would freely choose in whatever circumstances they might be in, God can—by decreeing to place just those persons in just those circumstances—bring about his ultimate purposes *through* free creaturely decisions. Thus, by employing his counterfactual knowledge, God can plan a world down to the last detail and yet do so without annihilating creaturely freedom, since what people would freely do under various circumstances is already factored into the equation by God. Since God's counterfactual knowledge lies logically in between his natural knowledge and his free knowledge, Molinists called it God's *middle knowledge.*

On the Dominican view, there is one logical moment prior to the divine creative decree at which God knows the range of possible worlds that he might create; then he chooses one of these to be actual. On the Molinist view, there are two logical moments prior to the divine decree: first, the moment at which he has natural knowledge of the range of possible worlds, and second, the moment at which he has knowledge of the proper subset of possible worlds that, given the counterfactuals true at that moment, are feasible for him to create. The counterfactuals which are true at that moment thus serve to delimit the range of possible worlds to worlds feasible for God.

For example, there is a possible world in which Peter affirms Christ in precisely the same circumstances in which he in fact denied him. But given the counterfactual truth that if Peter were in precisely those circumstances he would freely deny Christ, then the possible world in which Peter freely affirms Christ in those circumstances is not feasible for God. God could *make* Peter affirm Christ in those circumstances, but then his confession would not be free.

Thus on the Molinist scheme, we have the following logical order:

Moment 1: . . .   O   O   O   O   O   O   O   . . .
Natural knowledge: God knows the range of possible worlds.

Moment 2: . . .   O   O   O   . . .
Middle knowledge: God knows the range of feasible worlds.

Divine creative decree

Moment 3:   O
Free knowledge: God knows the actual world.

Arguments for Middle Knowledge

Why should one think that the Molinist scheme is correct? Three lines of argument—biblical, theological and philosophical—may be adduced in support of the Molinst position. Let us consider each in turn.

Biblical arguments. Biblically speaking, it is not difficult to show that God possesses counterfactual knowledge. One of the Jesuit theologians' favorite proof-texts was 1 Samuel 23:6-10, which tells of David's using of a divining device (an ephod) to inquire of the Lord whether Saul would attack Keilah, where David was ensconced, and whether the men of Keilah would deliver David over to Saul. In both cases, the device registered an affirmative answer, whereupon David fled the city, so that the predictions did not in fact come true. What the device had mediated to David was not, therefore, simple foreknowledge but counterfactual knowledge. God was letting David know that if he *were* to remain at Keilah, then Saul *would* come after him, and that if Saul *were* to come after David, then the men of Keilah *would* deliver him over to Saul. The answers given by the divining device were thus correct answers, even though the events did not come to pass, since the answers were indicative of what would happen under certain circumstances.

Although most scriptural prophecy is unconditional, sometimes prophecies are explicitly conditional, like the one David received at Keilah. Consider, for example, Jeremiah's prophecy to King Zedekiah in Jeremiah 38:17-18:

> Thus says the LORD, the God of hosts, the God of Israel, If you will only surrender to the officials of the king of Babylon, then your life shall be spared, and this city shall not be burned with fire, and you and your house shall live. But if you do not surrender, . . . then this city shall be handed over to the Chaldeans, and they shall burn it with fire, and you yourself shall not escape from their hand.

In his omniscience God knew what would happen whichever course of action Zedekiah chose. Indeed, when we construe certain prophecies as counterfactual warnings, rather than as categorical declarations of simple foreknowledge, we can explain how it is that in Israel the test of a true prophet is the fulfillment of his predictions (Deut 18:22) and yet some predictions given by true prophets do not actually come to pass because the people forewarned responded in an appropriate way (Is 38:1-5; Amos 7:1-6; Jon 3:1-10). In such cases, the prophecy from God was counterfactual knowledge of what would happen under the prevailing circumstances; but were intercessory prayer or repentance to occur, then God would not carry out what had been threatened.

We also find counterfactual knowledge exhibited by Christ. For example, he tells Peter, "Go to the sea and cast a hook; take the first fish that comes up; and when you open its mouth, you will find a coin; take that and give it to them for you and me" (Mt 17:27). This passage is most naturally understood as an expression of Jesus' knowledge that if Peter were to carry out Jesus' instructions, he would find things as the Lord predicted. Again, Jesus commands the disciples, after a futile night of fishing, "Cast the net to the right side of the boat, and you will find some [fish]" (Jn 21:6). The miraculous catch that ensued shows that Jesus knew exactly what would happen if the disciples obeyed his command. Sometimes Jesus makes counterfactual statements himself: "If I had not come and spoken to them, they would not have sin. . . . If I had not done among them the works that no one else did, they would not have sin" (Jn 15:22, 24). "If my kingdom were of this world, my followers would be fighting to keep me from being handed over to the Jews" (Jn 18:36). "Woe to that one by whom the Son of Man is betrayed! It would have been better for that one to not have been born" (Mt 26:24). These are only a few of many examples.

I think it is plain, then, that the God of the Bible exhibits counterfactual knowledge. Given God's infallibility, it will not do to explain these examples as mere hunches on God's part. If God believes that Saul would besiege Keilah if David were to stay there, then that counterfactual statement is known by God to be true, since it is logically impossible for God to subscribe to false beliefs.

Unfortunately, this does not answer the question of whether God has middle knowledge. For the scriptural passages show only that God possesses counterfactual knowledge, and, as I have said, until modern times all theologians agreed that God possesses counterfactual knowledge. The dispute among them concerned when in the logical order of things this knowledge comes: is it before or after the divine decree? Since Scripture does not reflect upon this question, no amount of proof-texting can prove that God's counterfactual knowledge is possessed logically prior to his creative decree. This is a matter for theological-philosophical reflection, not biblical exegesis. Thus, while it is clearly unbiblical to deny that God has simple foreknowledge and even counterfactual knowledge, those who deny middle knowledge cannot be accused of being unbiblical.

Theological arguments. The strongest arguments for the Molinist perspective are theological. Once one grasps the concept of middle knowledge, one will find it astonishing in its subtlety and power. Indeed, I would venture to say that it is the single most fruitful theological concept I have ever encountered. In my own work, I have applied it to the issues of Christian particularism, perseverance of the saints and biblical inspiration.[2] Thomas Flint has used it to analyze infallibility; and Del Ratzsch has used it to explore evolutionary theory.[3] An article begs to be written on a Molinist perspective of quantum indeterminacy and divine sovereignty. With respect to the concerns of this book, middle knowledge provides an illuminating account of divine foreknowledge and providence.

Divine Foreknowledge

The doctrine of divine foreknowledge raises two questions: First, is divine foreknowledge compatible with future contingents? And second, how can God know future contingents? Though I think that acceptable answers to these questions are available to the defender of simple foreknowledge, it is worth

---

[2]On Christian particularism, see William Lane Craig, " 'No Other Name': A Middle Knowledge Perspective on the Exclusivity of Salvation Through Christ," *Faith and Philosophy* 6 (1989): 172-88. On perseverance of the saints, see William Lane Craig, " 'Lest Anyone Should Fall': a Middle Knowledge Perspective on Perseverance and Apostolic Warnings," *International Journal for Philosophy of Religion* 29 (1991): 65-74. On biblical inspiration, see William Lane Craig, " 'Men Moved by the Holy Spirit Spoke from God' (2 Peter 1:2): A Middle Knowledge Perspective on Biblical Inspiration," *Philosophia Christi* 1 (1999): 45-82.

[3]Thomas P. Flint, "Middle Knowledge and the Doctrine of Infallibility," in *Philosophy of Religion*, vol. 5 of *Philosophical Perspectives,* ed. Jas. E. Tomberlin (Atascadero, Calif.: Ridgeway, 1991), pp. 373-93; Del Ratzsch, "Design, Chance and Theistic Evolution," in *Mere Creation,* ed. William Dembski (Downers Grove, Ill.: InterVarsity Press, 1998), pp. 289-312.

laying out a Molinist perspective as well.

The compatibility of divine foreknowledge and future contingents.
With respect to the first question, it must be the case that divine foreknowledge and future contingents (in particular, human free acts) are compatible for the simple reason that Scripture teaches both.[4] When so-called openness theologians dispute this compatibility, their denial is clearly driven not by biblical exegesis but by a philosophical argument derived from ancient Greek fatalism and dressed in theological guise; biblical exegesis is being bent to support a conclusion already determined by philosophical considerations. This is ironic since these same theologians loudly decry the polluting influence of Greek philosophical thought upon the biblical tradition. In fact, it is they themselves who have been seduced by philosophical reasoning of Greek provenance, which was stoutly resisted by the early church fathers. If openness theologians are not convinced by the proffered solutions to fatalism, then it is the better part of intellectual humility simply to confess that one lacks the philosophical insight to solve the problem (cf. Ps 139:6) and hold the biblical doctrines in tension rather than deny the Scripture's clear teaching that God does know the future.[5]

So what is the argument that allegedly demonstrates the incompatibility of divine foreknowledge and human freedom? Letting x stand for any event, the basic form of the argument is as follows:

(1)   Necessarily, if God foreknows x, then x will happen.
(2)   God foreknows x.
(3)   Therefore, x will necessarily happen.

Since x happens necessarily, it is not a contingent event. In virtue of God's foreknowledge, everything is fated to occur.

The problem with the above form of the argument is that it is just logically fallacious. What is validly implied by (1) and (2) is not (3) but (3'):

(3')   Therefore, x will happen.

The fatalist gets things all mixed up here. It is correct that in a valid, deductive argument the premises necessarily imply the conclusion. The conclusion follows necessarily from the premises; that is to say, it is impossible for the premises to be true and the conclusion to be false. But the conclusion itself need

---

[4]See D. A. Carson, *Divine Sovereignty and Human Responsibility: Biblical Perspectives in Tension,* New Foundations Theological Library (Atlanta: John Knox, 1981).
[5]For a discussion of the biblical data pertinent to divine foreknowledge, see William Lane Craig, *The Only Wise God* (Grand Rapids, Mich.: Baker, 1987), part 1.

not be necessary. The fatalist illicitly transfers the necessity of the *inference* to the conclusion *itself.* What necessarily follows from (1) and (2) is just (3'). But the fatalist in his confusion thinks that the conclusion is itself necessarily true and so winds up with (3). In so doing he simply commits a common logical fallacy.

The correct conclusion, (3'), is in no way incompatible with human freedom. From God's knowledge that I shall do *x*, it does not follow that I must do *x* but only that I shall do *x*. That is in no way incompatible with my doing *x* freely.

Undoubtedly, a major source of the fatalist's confusion is his conflating *certainty* with *necessity.* In the writings of contemporary theological fatalists, one frequently finds statements which slide from affirming that something is *certainly* true to affirming that something is *necessarily* true. This is sheer confusion. Certainty is a property of persons and has nothing to do with truth, as is evident from the fact that we can be absolutely certain about something that turns out to be false. By contrast, necessity is a property of statements or propositions, indicating that a proposition cannot possibly be false. We can be wholly uncertain about statements that are, unbeknownst to us, necessarily true (for example, some complex mathematical equation or theorem). Thus, when we say that some statement is "certainly true," this is but a manner of speaking indicating that we are certain the statement is true. People are certain; propositions are necessary.

By confusing certainty and necessity, the fatalist makes his logically fallacious argument deceptively appealing. For it is correct that from (1) and (2) we can be absolutely certain that *x* will come to pass. But it is muddle-headed to think that because *x* will certainly happen then *x* will necessarily happen. We can be certain, given God's foreknowledge, that *x* will not fail to happen, even though it is entirely possible that *x* fail to happen. Event *x* could fail to occur, but God knows that it will not. Therefore, we can be sure that it will happen— and happen contingently.

Contemporary theological fatalists recognize the fallaciousness of the above form of the argument and therefore try to remedy the defect by making (2) also necessarily true:

(1)   Necessarily, if God foreknows *x*, then *x* will happen.

(2')   Necessarily, God foreknows *x*.

(3)   Therefore, *x* will necessarily happen.

So formulated, the argument is no longer logically fallacious, and so the question becomes whether the premises are true.

Premise (1) is clearly true. It is perhaps worth noting that this is the case not because of God's essential omniscience or inerrancy but simply in virtue of the definition of "knowledge." Since knowledge entails true belief, anybody's knowing that x will happen necessarily implies that x will happen. Thus, we could replace (1) and (2') with the following:

(1*)   Necessarily, if Smith truly believes that x will happen, then x will happen.

(2*)   Necessarily, Smith truly believes that x will happen.

And (3) will follow as before. Therefore, if any person ever holds true beliefs about the future (and surely we do, as we smugly remind others when we say, "I told you so!"), then, given the truth of (2), fatalism would also follow from merely human beliefs, a curious conclusion!

Indeed, as ancient Greek fatalists realized, the presence of any agent at all is really superfluous to the argument. All one needs is a true, future-tense statement to get the argument going. Thus, we could replace (1) and (2') with this:

(1**)   Necessarily, if it is true that x will happen, then x will happen.

(2**)   Necessarily, it is true that x will happen.

And we shall get (3) as our conclusion. Thus, philosopher Susan Haack quite rightly calls the argument for theological fatalism "a needlessly (and confusingly) elaborated version" of Greek fatalism, and she says that the addition of an omniscient God to the argument constitutes a "gratuitous detour" around the real issue, which is the truth or falsity of future-tense statements.[6]

In order to avoid the above generalization of their argument to all persons and to mere statements about the future, theological fatalists will deny that the second premise is true with respect to humans or mere statements, as it is for God. They will say that Smith's holding a true belief or some future-tense statement's being true is not necessary in the way that God's holding a belief is necessary.

That raises the question as to whether (2') is true. At face value, (2') is obviously false. Christian theology has always maintained that God's creation of the world is a free act, that God could have created a different world—in which x does not occur—or even no world at all. To say that God necessarily foreknows any event x implies that this is the only world God could have created and thus denies divine freedom.

But theological fatalists have a different sort of necessity in mind when they

---

[6]Susan Haack, "On a Theological Argument for Fatalism," *Philosophical Quarterly* 24 (1974): 158.

say that God's foreknowledge is necessary. They are talking about *temporal necessity,* or the necessity of the past. Often this is expressed by saying that the past is unpreventable or unchangeable. If some event is in the past, then it is now too late to do anything to affect it. It is in that sense necessary. Since God's foreknowledge of future events is now part of the past, it is now fixed and unalterable. Therefore, it is said, (2') is true.

But if (2') is true in that sense, then why are not (2*) and (2**) true as well? The theological fatalist will respond that Smith's belief's being true or a future-tense statement's being true is not a fact or an event of the past, as is God's holding a belief.

But such an understanding of what constitutes a fact or event seems quite counterintuitive. If Smith believed in 1997 that "Clinton will be impeached," was it not a fact that his belief was true? If Smith held that same belief today, would it not be a fact that his belief is no longer true (since Clinton has left office)? If Smith's belief changes from being true to being false, then surely it was a fact that it was then true and is a fact that it is now false. The same obviously goes for the mere statement "Clinton will be impeached." This statement once had the property of being true and now has the property of being false. In any reasonable sense of "fact," these are past and present facts.

Indeed, a statement's having a truth value is plausibly an event as well. This is most obvious with respect to statements like "Flight 4750 to Paris will depart in five minutes." That statement is false up until it is five minutes prior to departure, it becomes true at five minutes till departure, and then it becomes false again immediately thereafter. Other statements' being true may be more long-lasting events, like "Flight 4750 to Paris will depart within the next hour." Such a statement's being true is clearly an event on any reasonable construal of what constitutes an event.

No theological fatalist whom I have read has even begun to address the question of the nature of facts or events which would make it plausible that Smith's truly believing a future-tense statement and a future-tense statement's being true do not count as past facts or events. But then we see that theological fatalism is not inherently theological at all. If the theological fatalist's reasoning is correct, it can be generalized to show that every time we hold a true belief about the future or every time a statement about the future is true, then the future is fated to occur—surely an incredible inference!

Moreover, we have the best of reasons for thinking that (2') is defective in some way: namely, fatalism posits a constraint on human freedom that is unintelligible. For the fatalist admits that the events God foreknows may be causally indeterminate; indeed, they could theoretically be completely uncaused, spontaneous events. Nevertheless, such events are said to be somehow constrained. But by what? Fate? What is that but a mere name? If my action is causally free, how can it be constrained by God's merely knowing about it?

Sometimes fatalists say that God's foreknowledge places a sort of logical constraint on my action. Even though I am causally free to refrain from my action, there is some sort of logical constraint upon me, rendering it impossible for me to refrain. But insofar as we can make sense of logical constraints, these constraints are not analogous to the sort of necessitation imagined by the theological fatalist. For example, given the fact that I have already played basketball at least once in my life, it is now impossible for me to play basketball for the first time. I am thus not free to go out and play basketball for the first time. But this sort of constraint is not at all analogous to theological fatalism. For in the case we are envisioning, it is within my power to play basketball or not. Whether or not I've played before, I can freely execute the actions of playing basketball. It's just that if I have played before, my actions will not *count* as playing for the first time. By contrast, the fatalist imagines that if God knows that I shall not play basketball, then even though I am causally free, my actions are mysteriously constrained so that I am literally unable to walk out onto the court, dribble and shoot. But such noncausal determinism is utterly opaque and unintelligible.

The argument for fatalism must therefore be unsound. Since (1) is clearly true, the trouble must lie with (2'). And (2') is notoriously problematic. For the notion of temporal necessity to which the fatalist appeals is so obscure a concept that (2') becomes a veritable mare's nest of philosophical difficulties. For example, since the necessity of (1) is logical necessity and the necessity of (2') is temporal necessity, why think that such mixing of different kinds of modality is valid? If the fatalist answers that logical necessity entails temporal necessity, so that (1) can be construed merely in terms of temporal necessity, then how do we know that such necessity is passed on from the premises to the conclusion in the way that logical necessity is? Indeed, since x is supposed to be a future event, how *could* it be temporally necessary? And even if x is temporally necessary, how do we know that this sort of necessity is incompatible with an action's being free? So long as a person's choice is causally undetermined, it is a free choice even if that person is unable to choose the opposite of that choice.[7] So even if x were temporally necessary, such that not-x cannot occur,

---

[7]See Harry Frankfurt, "Alternative Possibilities and Moral Responsibility," *Journal of Philosophy* 66 (1969): 829-39; Thomas V. Morris, *The Logic of God Incarnate* (Ithaca, N.Y.: Cornell University Press, 1986), 151-52. Morris imagines a man with electrodes secretly implanted in his brain who is presented with the choice of doing either A or B. The electrodes are inactive so

it is far from obvious that x is not freely performed or chosen.

All of the above problems arise even if we concede (2') to be true. But why think that this premise is true? What is temporal necessity anyway, and why think that God's past beliefs are now temporally necessary? Theological fatalists have never provided an adequate account of this peculiar modality. I have yet to see an explanation of temporal necessity according to which God's past beliefs are temporally necessary that does not reduce to either the *unalterability* or the *causal closedness* of the past.

But interpreting the necessity of the past as its unalterability (or unchangability or unpreventability) is clearly inadequate, since the future, by definition, is just as unalterable as the past. To *change* the future would be to bring it about that an event which will occur will not occur, which is self-contradictory. It is purely a matter of definition that the past and future cannot be changed, and no fatalistic conclusion follows from this truth. We need not be able to *change* the future in order to *determine* the future. If our actions are freely performed, then it lies within our power to determine what the course of future events will be, even if we do not have the power to change the future.

Fatalists will insist that the past is necessary in the sense that we do not have a similar ability to determine the past. Nonfatalists may happily concede the point: backward causation is impossible. But the past's causal closedness does not imply fatalism. For freedom to refrain from doing as God knows one will do does not involve backward causation.

Here we come to the Molinist solution to theological fatalism. The Molinist is quite glad to admit that nothing I can do now will cause or bring about the past. But he will insist that it does lie within my power to freely perform some action a, and if a were to occur, then the past would have been different than it in fact is. Suppose, for example, that God has always believed that in the year 2000 I would accept an invitation to speak at the University of Regensburg. Up until the time arrives I have the ability to accept or refuse the invitation. If I were to refuse the invitation, then God would have held a different belief than the one he in fact held. For if I were to refuse the invitation, then different counterfactual propositions would have been true, and God would have known this via his middle knowledge. Neither the relation between my action and a corresponding counterfactual proposition about it, nor the rela-

---

long as the man chooses A; but if he were going to choose B, then the electrodes would switch on and force him to choose A. In such a case the man is unable to choose B, but his choosing A is still entirely free, since the electrodes do not function at all when he chooses to do A. For an application of the scenario to theological fatalism see David P. Hunt, "On Augustine's Way Out," *Faith and Philosophy* 16 (1999): 3-26.

tion between a true counterfactual proposition and God's believing it, is a causal relation. Thus, the causal closedness of the past is irrelevant. If temporal necessity is merely the causal closedness of the past, then it is insufficient to support fatalism.

To my knowledge, no fatalist has explicated a conception of temporal necessity that does not amount to either the unalterability or the causal closedness of the past. Typically, fatalists just appeal gratuitously to some sort of "Fixed Past Principle" to the effect that it is not within my power to act in such a way, and that if I were to do so, then the past would have been different—which begs the question. On analyses of temporal necessity that are not reducible to either the unalterability or the causal closedness of the past, God's past beliefs always turn out *not* to be temporally necessary.[8] The Molinist accounts for this in terms of God's middle knowledge, which infallibly tracks true counterfactual propositions concerning our free choices.

Thus, the argument for theological fatalism is unsound. The doctrine of middle knowledge helps to make the compatibility of divine foreknowledge and human freedom perspicuous.

The basis of divine foreknowledge of future contingents. What, then, about the second question raised by divine foreknowledge, namely, the basis of God's knowledge of future contingents? Detractors of divine foreknowledge sometimes claim that because future events do not exist, they cannot be known by God. The reasoning seems to go as follows:

(1)   Only events that actually exist can be known by God.
(2)   Future events do not actually exist.
(3)   Therefore, future events cannot be known by God.

Now (2) is not uncontroversial. A good many physicists and philosophers of time and space argue that future events do exist. They claim that the difference between past, present and future is merely a subjective matter of human consciousness. For the people in the year 2015, the events of that year are just as real as the events of our present year are for us; and for those people, it is we who have passed away and are unreal. On such a view God transcends the four-dimensional space-time continuum, and thus all events are eternally present to him. It is easy on such a view to understand how God could therefore know events that to us are in the future.

Nevertheless, I do think that such a four-dimensional view of reality faces

---

[8]See, e.g., Alfred J. Freddoso, "Accidental Necessity and Logical Determinism," *Journal of Philosophy* 80 (1983): 257-78.

insuperable philosophical and theological objections, which I have discussed elsewhere.[9] Therefore, I am inclined to agree with (2) of the above argument. So the question becomes whether there is good reason to think that (1) is true.

In assessing the question of how God knows which events will transpire, it is helpful to distinguish two models of divine cognition: the *perceptualist* model and the *conceptualist* model. The perceptualist model construes divine knowledge on the analogy of sense perception. God looks and sees what is there. Such a model is implicitly assumed when people speak of God's "foreseeing" the future or having "foresight" of future events. The perceptualist model of divine cognition does run into real problems when it comes to God's knowledge of the future, for, since future events do not exist, there is nothing there to perceive.

By contrast, on a conceptualist model of divine knowledge, God does not acquire his knowledge of the world by anything like perception. His knowledge of the future is not based on his "looking" ahead and "seeing" what lies in the future (a terribly anthropomorphic notion in any case). Rather God's knowledge is self-contained; it is more like a mind's knowledge of innate ideas. As an omniscient being, God has essentially the property of knowing all truths; there are truths about future events; thus, God knows all truths concerning future events.

Middle knowledge can help us understand how God knows truths about the future. Divine foreknowledge is based on God's middle knowledge of what every creature would freely do under any circumstances and on his knowledge of the divine decree to create certain sets of circumstances and to place certain creatures in them. Given middle knowledge and the divine decree, foreknowledge follows automatically as a result.

Of course, the skeptic may ask how God knows counterfactuals concerning human free choices if those choices do not exist. Molinists could respond either that God knows the individual essence of every possible creature so well that he knows just what each creature would do under any set of circumstances he might place him in, or that God, being omniscient, simply discerns all the truths there are and, prior to the divine decree, there are not only necessary truths but counterfactual truths, and therefore God possesses not only natural knowledge but middle knowledge as well.

---

[9]See my companion volumes *The Tensed Theory of Time: A Critical Examination*, Synthese Library 293 (Dordrecht, Holland: Kluwer Academic Publishers, 2000) and *The Tenseless Theory of Time: A Critical Examination*, Synthese Library 294 (Dordrecht, Holland: Kluwer Academic Publishers, 2000).

So long as we are not seduced into thinking of divine foreknowledge on the model of perception, it is no longer evident why knowledge of future events should be impossible. A conceptualist model along the lines of middle knowledge furnishes a perspicuous basis for God's knowledge of future contingents.

Thus, both with respect to the problem of theological fatalism and the question of the basis of divine foreknowledge, the Molinist doctrine of middle knowledge provides an illuminating account of God's foreknowledge.

Divine Providence

The Molinist account of divine providence is even more stunning than its account of divine foreknowledge. Here its superiority to the doctrine of simple foreknowledge emerges. Consider the following biblical passages:

> This man [Jesus], handed over to you according to the definite plan and foreknowledge of God, you crucified and killed by the hands of those outside the law. (Acts 2:23)

> For in this city, in fact, both Herod and Pontius Pilate, with the Gentiles and the peoples of Israel gathered together against your holy servant Jesus, whom you anointed, to do whatever your hand and your plan had predestined to take place. (Acts 4:27-28)

Here we have a staggering assertion of divine sovereignty over the affairs of men. The conspiracy to crucify Jesus—which involved not only the Romans and the Jews in Jerusalem at that time, but more particularly Pilate and Herod, who tried Jesus—is said to have happened by God's plan based on his foreknowledge and foreordination. How are we to understand so far-reaching a providence as this?

If we take the term *foreknowledge* as encompassing middle knowledge, then we can make perfect sense of God's providential control over a world of free agents. For via his middle knowledge, God knew exactly which persons, if members of the Sanhedrin, would freely vote for Jesus' condemnation; which persons, if in Jerusalem, would freely demand Christ's death, favoring the release of Barabbas; what Herod, if king, would freely do in reaction to Jesus and to Pilate's plea to judge him on his own; and what Pilate himself, if holding the prefecture of Palestine in A.D. 27, would freely do under pressure from the Jewish leaders and the crowd. Knowing all the possible circumstances, persons and permutations of these circumstances and persons, God decreed to create just those circumstances and just those people who would freely do what God willed to happen. Thus, the whole scenario, as Luke insists, unfolded according to *God's plan.* This is truly mind-boggling. When one reflects that the existence of the various circumstances and persons involved was itself the result of a myriad of prior free choices on the part of these and other agents, and these in turn of yet other prior contingencies, and so on, then we see that only an omniscient mind could providentially direct a world of free creatures toward his sovereignly established ends. In fact, Paul reflects that "none of the rulers of this age understood this; for if they had, they would not have crucified the Lord of glory" (1 Cor 2:8). Once one grasps the doctrine of divine middle knowledge, one is led to adoration and praise of God for his breathtaking sovereignty.

Now what account of divine providence can be given in the absence of middle knowledge? Advocates of divine openness freely admit that without middle knowledge, a strong doctrine of divine providence becomes impossible. But such a viewpoint can make no sense whatsoever of scriptural passages such as those cited above. I am bewildered that partisans of this camp can deny divine foreknowledge while claiming to be biblical, when, as seen above, "foreknowledge" is part of the very *vocabulary* of the New Testament. Nor can it be said that God's plan was hit upon by him late in the game, once he could reasonably guess what the relevant agents would do. For as Paul was wont to emphasize, this was an *eternal plan,* made from the foundations of the world but hidden for ages in God and now realized in the fullness of time, as God sent forth his Son, manifesting the wisdom of God to the principalities and powers who oppose him (Gal 4:4; Eph 3:9-11; cf. 1 Pet 1:20).

The Augustinian-Calvinist perspective interprets the above passages to mean that foreknowledge is based upon foreordination: God knows what will happen because he makes it happen. Aware of the intentions of his will and his almighty power, God knows that all his purpose shall be accomplished. But this interpretation inevitably makes God the author of sin, since it is he who moved Judas, for example, to betray Christ, a sin that merits the hapless Judas everlasting perdition. But how can a holy God move people to commit moral evil and, moreover, how can these people then be held morally responsible for acts over which they had no control? The Augustinian-Calvinist view seems, in effect, to turn God into the devil.

The proponent of simple foreknowledge can make no good sense of God's providentially planning a world of free creatures. For logically prior to the divine decree, God has natural knowledge of all the possible scenarios, but he does not have knowledge of what would happen under any circumstances. Thus, logically posterior to the divine decree, God must consider himself extraordinarily lucky to find that this world happened to exist. ("What a break!" we can imagine God saying to himself, "Herod and Pilate and all those people each reacted just perfectly!") Actually, the situation is much worse than that, for God had no idea whether Herod or Pilate or the Israelite nation or the Roman Empire would even exist posterior to the divine decree. Indeed, God must be astonished to find himself existing in a world—out of all the possible worlds he could have created—in which mankind falls into sin and he himself enters human history as a substitutionary sacrificial offering to rescue them! Of course, I am speaking anthropomorphically here; but the point remains that without middle knowledge, God cannot know prior to the creative decree what the world would be like. If the defender of simple foreknowledge goes on to say that God's foreordination of future events is based upon his simple foreknowledge, then this trivializes the doctrine of foreordination, making it a fifth wheel that carries no load since, as we have seen, the future by definition cannot be changed. Once God knows that an event really is future, there is nothing more left to do; foreordination becomes a redundancy. Surely, there is more substance to the biblical doctrine of foreordination than the triviality that God decrees that what will happen will happen!

Thus of the options available, the Molinist approach provides by far the most elucidating account of divine providence. It enables us to embrace divine sovereignty and human freedom without mysticism or mental reservation, thereby preserving faithfully the biblical text's affirmation of both these doctrines. We therefore have powerful theological motivation for adopting the Molinist perspective.

Philosophical arguments. Finally, I think that we also have good philosophical grounds for thinking that a doctrine of middle knowledge is correct. We may argue as follows:

(1)   If there are true counterfactuals of creaturely freedom, then God knows these truths.

(2)   There are true counterfactuals of creaturely freedom.

(3)   If God knows true counterfactuals of creaturely freedom, God knows them either logically prior to the divine creative decree or only logically posterior to the divine creative decree.

(4)   Counterfactuals of creaturely freedom cannot be known only logically posterior to the divine creative decree.

From (1) and (2) it follows logically that

(5)   Therefore, God knows true counterfactuals of creaturely freedom.

From (3) and (5) it follows that

(6)   Therefore, God knows true counterfactuals of creaturely freedom either logically prior to the divine creative decree or only logically posterior to the divine creative decree.

And from (4) and (6) it follows that

(7)   Therefore, God knows true counterfactuals of creaturely freedom logically prior to the divine creative decree

which is the essence of the doctrine of divine middle knowledge.

Let us say a word in defense of each of the argument's premises. The truth of (1) is required by the definition of omniscience:

(O)   For any agent x, x is omniscient = $_{def.}$ For every proposition p, if p, then x knows that p and does not believe not-p.

What (O) requires is that any agent is omniscient if and only if he knows all truths and believes no falsehoods. This is the standard definition of omniscience. It entails that if there are counterfactual truths, then an omniscient being must know them.

Opponents of divine foreknowledge have suggested revisionary definitions of omniscience so as to be able to affirm that God is omniscient even as they deny his knowledge of future contingents (and counterfactuals of creaturely freedom).[10] William Hasker's revisionist definition is typical:

(O')   God is omniscient = $_{def.}$ God knows all propositions which are such that God's knowing them is logically possible.

Revisionists then go on to claim that it is logically impossible to know propositions about future contingents, as shown by the argument for theological fatalism, and so God may count as omniscient despite his ignorance of an infinite number of true propositions.

As it stands, however, (O') is drastically flawed. It does not exclude that God believes false propositions as well as true ones. Worse, (O') actually requires God to know false propositions, which is incoherent as well as theologically unacceptable. For (O') requires that if it is logically possible for God to know some proposition p, then God knows p. But if p is a contingently false proposition, say, *There are eight planets in the sun's solar system*, then there are possible worlds in which p is true and known by God. Therefore, since it is logically possible for God to know p, he must actually know p, which is absurd.

---

[10]For the following definition see William Hasker, "A Philosophical Perspective," in *The Openness of God: A Biblical Challenge to the Traditional Understanding of God,* ed. Clark Pinnock et al. (Downers Grove, Ill.: InterVarsity Press, 1994), p. 136.

What the revisionist really wants to say is something like this:

(O″)   God is omniscient = $_{def.}$ God knows only and all true propositions which are such that it is logically possible for God to know them.

Unlike (O′), (O″) limits God's knowledge to a certain subset of all true propositions.

The fundamental problem with all such revisionary definitions of omniscience as (O″) is that any adequate definition of a concept must accord with our intuitive understanding of the concept. We are not at liberty to "cook" the definition in some desired way without thereby making the definition unacceptably contrived. Definition (O″) is guilty of being "cooked" in this way. For intuitively, omniscience involves knowing all truth, yet according to (O″) God could conceivably be ignorant of infinite realms of truth and yet still count as omniscient. The only reason why one would prefer (O″) to (O) is because one has an ulterior motivation to salvage the attribute of omniscience for a cognitively limited deity rather than to deny outright that God is omniscient. Definition (O″) is therefore unacceptably contrived.

A second problem with (O″) is that it construes omniscience in modal terms, speaking, not of knowing all truth, but of knowing all truth which is knowable. But omniscience, unlike omnipotence, is not a modal notion. Roughly speaking, omnipotence is the capability of actualizing any logically possible state of affairs. But omniscience is not merely the *capability* of knowing only and all truths; it *is* knowing only and all truths. Nor does omniscience mean knowing only and all knowable truths, but knowing only and all truths, period. It is a categorical, not a modal, notion.

Third, the superiority of (O″) over (O) depends on there being a difference between a truth and a truth that is logically possible to know. If there is no difference, then (O″) collapses back to the general definition (O) and the revisionist has gained nothing. What is a sufficient condition for a proposition to be logically knowable? So far as I can see, the only condition is that the proposition be true. What more is needed? If revisionists think that something more is needed, then we may ask them for an example of a proposition that could be true but logically impossible to know. A proposition like "Nothing exists" or "All agents have ceased to exist" comes to mind; but on traditional theism these propositions are not possibly true, since God is an agent whose nonexistence is impossible. Unless the revisionist can give us some reason to think that a proposition can be true yet unknowable, we have no reason to adopt (O″). It seems that the only intrinsic property that a proposition must possess in order to be logically knowable is truth.

The revisionist will claim at this point that true future contingent propositions are logically impossible for God to know, since if he knows them, then
they are not contingently true, as shown by the fatalistic argument.[11] But here
the revisionist commits a logical howler. He reasons that for any future-tense
proposition p it is impossible that God know p and p be contingently true;
therefore, if p is contingently true, it is not possible that God knows p. But
such reasoning is logically fallacious. What follows is merely that God does not
know p, not that it is impossible that God knows p. Thus, even *granted* the
fatalist's false premise (that it is impossible that God know p and p be contingently true), it does not follow from p's contingent truth that p is such that it is
logically impossible for God to know p. Therefore, even on the defective definition (O″) proposed by the revisionist, God turns out not to be omniscient,
since p is a true proposition that, so far as we can see, is logically possible for
God to know, and yet God does not know p. Thus, the theological fatalist must
deny divine omniscience and therefore reject God's perfection—a very serious
theological consequence, indeed.

So with regard to the first premise of our philosophical argument, omniscience requires that if there are true counterfactuals of creaturely freedom,
God must know them.

Premise (2) asserts that there are true counterfactuals of creaturely freedom.
This premise does not require us to believe that all counterfactuals about creatures' free acts are either true or false. But it does seem plausible that counterfactuals of the following form are either true or false (letting P be any person,
A some action and C any set of circumstances including the whole history of
the world up until the point of decision):

(CCF)   If P were in C, P would freely do A.

It is counterfactuals of this form that we dignify with the title "counterfactuals
of creaturely freedom."

We have every reason to think that there are true counterfactuals of creaturely freedom. In the first place, it is plausible, as I say, that counterfactuals of
the form (CCF) are true or false. For once the circumstances are fully specified,
any ambiguity which might cause us to doubt that the counterfactual has a
truth value is removed. And it is plausible that in many cases P would freely do
A in C, just as the counterfactual states. Second, we ourselves often know the
truth of such counterfactuals. For example, if I were to offer my wife a plate of
chocolate-chip cookies and a plate of liver and onions, I know which one she

———————————————————————————————

[11]Ibid., pp. 147-48.

would choose as surely as I know almost anything! A little reflection reveals how pervasive and indispensable such counterfactual truths are to rational conduct and planning. We base our very lives upon their truth or falsity. Third, as pointed out above, Scripture itself gives examples of such true counterfactuals (think again about Paul's statement in 1 Cor 2:8).

The most common objection urged against the truth of counterfactuals of creaturely freedom is the so-called grounding objection. The basic complaint here is that there is nothing to make such counterfactuals true (since they are supposed to be true logically prior to God's creative decree and even now are usually contrary-to-fact); but without a ground of their truth, they cannot be true.

Thomas Flint, an eminent defender of middle knowledge, has rightly observed that the grounding objection is, in the minds of many philosophers, the principal obstacle to endorsing a Molinist perspective.[12] It is therefore all the more remarkable that this objection is virtually never articulated or defended in any depth by its advocates. No anti-Molinist to my knowledge has yet responded to Alvin Plantinga's simple retort: "It seems to me much clearer that some counterfactuals of freedom are at least possibly true than that the truth of propositions must, in general, be grounded in this way."[13] What Plantinga understands—and what the grounding objectors generally do not—is that behind the grounding objection sticks a theory about the relationship of truth and reality that is both subtle and controversial and that needs to be articulated, defended and applied to counterfactuals of creaturely freedom if the grounding objection is to have any force. Anti-Molinists have not even begun to address these issues.

The theory presupposed by the grounding objection is a particular construal of truth as correspondence known among contemporary philosophers as the theory of *truth-makers*.[14] According to a view of truth as correspondence, a statement is true if and only if reality is as that statement describes. In order to identify the reality corresponding to a true statement, one typically employs the method of disquotation: the statement "Snow is white," for example, is true if and only if snow is white. During the revival of the correspondence theory of truth in the early part of the twentieth century, philosophers such as Ber-

---

[12]Thomas P. Flint, *Divine Providence: The Molinist Account*, Cornell Studies in the Philosophy of Religion (Ithaca, N.Y.: Cornell University Press, 1998), p. 123.

[13]Alvin Plantinga, "Reply to Robert Adams," in *Alvin Plantinga*, ed. Jas. E. Tomberlin and Peter Van Inwagen, Profiles 5 (Dordrecht, Holland: Reidel, 1985), p. 378.

[14]See the seminal article by Kevin Mulligan, Peter Simons and Barry Smith, "Truth-Makers," *Philosophy and Phenomenological Research* 44 (1984): 287-321.

trand Russell and Ludwig Wittgenstein maintained that there must exist not only truth-bearers (whether these be sentences or thoughts or propositions or what have you) which have the property of being true and so corresponding with reality, but also something in reality in virtue of which the sentences or propositions are true. This interpretation of the correspondence theory was taken up again in the 1980s as the theory of truth-makers.

A truth-maker may be defined as *that in virtue of which a sentence or proposition is true.* Immediately we see the potentially misleading connotations of the term *truth-maker.* The word *making* suggests a causal relation involving some concrete object, but truth-makers are not normally so conceived by their advocates. Instead truth-makers are typically construed to be abstract realities like "facts" or "states of affairs"—more often than not, the fact stated as the truth conditions of a proposition, as disclosed by disquotation. Thus, what makes the statement "Snow is white" true is the fact that snow is white or the state of affairs of snow's being white. Such abstract entities do not stand in causal relations. This invalidates at a single swoop the crude construal of the grounding objection expressed in Robert Adams's demand, "Who or what does cause them [counterfactuals of creaturely freedom] to be true?"[15] The question is inept because the relation between a proposition and its truth-maker is not a causal relation.

The grounding objector seems to think that in order to be true, counterfactuals of creaturely freedom must have truth-makers that either are or imply the existence of physical objects. But this assumption seems quite unwarranted, since we can think of other types of possibly true propositions whose truth-makers neither are nor imply physical objects. For example:

1. No physical objects exist.
2. Dinosaurs are extinct today.
3. All ravens are black.
4. Torturing a child is wrong.
5. Napoleon lost the Battle of Waterloo.
6. The U.S. president in 2070 will be a woman.
7. If a rigid rod were placed in uniform motion through the ether, it would suffer a Lorentz-FitzGerald contraction.

Statement 1 could be true and statement 2 is true, yet they preclude truth-makers that imply the relevant physical objects, such as dinosaurs. Statement 3

---

[15]Robert Adams, "Plantinga on the Problem of Evil," in *Alvin Plantinga,* ed. Jas. E. Tomberlin and Peter Van Inwagen, Profiles 5 (Dordrecht, Holland: Reidel, 1985), p. 232. Compare William Hasker's demand, "Who or what is it (if anything) that *brings it about* that these propositions are true?" (William Hasker, "A Refutation of Middle Knowledge," *Noûs* 20 [1986]: 547).

is a universal statement which does not apply just to any ravens that happen to exist and so cannot be made true just by any existing ravens' being black. Statement 4 is a value judgment which implies neither that children do exist nor that any are actually tortured. Statements 5 and 6 are true tensed statements about persons who no longer or do not yet exist and so cannot have such persons among their truth-makers. Finally, statement 7 is a true counterfactual about the ether of nineteenth-century physics, which does not exist. These statements reveal just how naive an understanding grounding objectors have of the notion of truth-makers. For if these statements have truth-makers, their truth-makers are not physical objects out there in the world but are abstract entities like states of affairs or facts.

Now, as I say, it is a matter of debate whether true propositions do have truth-makers. In a recent critique, Greg Restall demonstrates that given the customary axioms of truth-maker theory, it follows that every true proposition is made true by every truth-maker there is, so that, for example, "Grass is green" is made true by snow's being white. In the understatement of the year, Restall muses, "This is clearly not acceptable for any philosophically discriminating account of truthmakers."[16] Truth-maker theorists typically deny the doctrine of *truth-maker maximalism,* the doctrine that every true statement has a truth-maker. I have yet to encounter an argument for the conclusion that counterfactuals of creaturely freedom cannot be among those types of truths lacking a truth-maker. Indeed, when one reflects on the fact that they are *counterfactual,* then such statements seem prime candidates for that type of statement which is true without any truth-maker.

If there are, on the other hand, truth-makers for counterfactuals of creaturely freedom, then the most obvious and plausible candidates are the facts or states of affairs disclosed by the disquotation principle. Thus, what makes it true that "If I were rich, I would buy a Mercedes" is the fact that if I were rich I would buy a Mercedes. Just as there are tensed facts that now exist even though the objects and events they are about do not (as illustrated by statements 5 and 6 above), so there are counterfacts that actually exist even though the objects and events they are about do not. If counterfactuals of creaturely freedom have truth-makers, then it is in virtue of these facts or states of affairs that the corresponding propositions are true. And since these counterfacts are

---

[16]Greg Restall, "Truthmakers, Entailment and Necessity," *Australasian Journal of Philosophy* 74 (1996): 334. Restall offers an account of truth-makers involving abstract entities to solve this problem, but in doing so he leaves his truth-makers undefined. This result only underscores how ham-fisted a handling of truth-makers is presupposed by grounding objectors to middle knowledge.

not the result of God's decree, they exist even logically prior to God's decree to create any physical objects.

In short, I concur with Plantinga in saying that I am far more confident that there are true counterfactuals of creaturely freedom than I am of the theory which requires that they have truth-makers. And if they do, then no reason has been given why these cannot be the facts or states of affairs that are stated as their truth conditions.

Premise 3 of our philosophical argument for middle knowledge states logically exhaustive alternatives for an omniscient deity and so must be true: Counterfactuals of creaturely freedom are known by God either prior to his decree or only after his decree.

Finally, (4) must be true because if counterfactuals of creaturely freedom were known only after the divine decree, then it is God who determined what every creature would do in every circumstance. Augustinian-Calvinist thinkers bear witness to the truth of this premise in their affirmation of compatibilist theories of creaturely freedom. They thereby testify that God's all-determining decree precludes libertarian freedom, which is the sort of freedom with which we are here concerned. Thus, if God knows counterfactual truths about us only posterior to his decree, then there really are no counterfactuals of creaturely freedom. If there are such counterfactuals, they must be true logically prior to the divine decree.

Given the truth of the premises, the conclusion follows that prior to his creative decree God knows all true counterfactuals of creaturely freedom, which is to say that he has middle knowledge, Q.E.D.

Conclusion

In conclusion, while not explicitly taught by the biblical text, the doctrine of divine middle knowledge is certainly compatible with it, which cannot be said of at least some of its competitors. Middle knowledge redounds to the glory of God and illuminates biblical truth in a dazzling way. Moreover, we have good theological and philosophical grounds for affirming middle knowledge. Theologically, middle knowledge enables us to explain both the compatibility of divine foreknowledge with future contingents as well as the basis of divine foreknowledge and, more importantly, to provide an intelligible account of God's providence over a world of free creatures. Philosophically, omniscience by definition entails knowledge of all truth and, since counterfactuals of creaturely freedom are true logically prior to God's creative decree, they must therefore by known by God at that logical moment. Therefore, we should affirm that God has middle knowledge.

AN OPEN-THEISM RESPONSE

Gregory A. Boyd

*R*eading William Lane Craig's fine essay reminded me of just how close Molinism is to the open view. Indeed, I shall argue that the view that has come to be labeled *open theism* could perhaps more accurately be labeled *neo-Molinism*. In essence it differs from the classical Molinist position only in that it expands the content of God's middle knowledge to include "might-counterfactuals." In this response I hope to show that this modification allows the open view to avoid problems which attend to the classical Molinist view while preserving its explanatory power.

The Scope of God's Middle Knowledge

As Craig made clear, defenders of middle knowledge hold that between (viz., "in the middle of") God's knowledge of all logical possibilities, on the one hand, and God's knowledge of what will come to pass, on the other, is God's knowledge of counterfactuals of creaturely freedom: namely, what free agents would do if they were created in other possible worlds. Since God is omniscient, it is argued, he must know the truth value of all propositions. Hence he must know the truth value of all counterfactual propositions, including counterfactuals of creaturely freedom. As Craig argues, the chief value of this position is that it allows God to have significant sovereign control of the world while yet accepting libertarian freedom.

Despite its theological advantages, there are several problems with the classical Molinist position, three of which may be mentioned presently. First, while there is some scriptural warrant for holding that God knows counterfactuals of creaturely freedom, classical Molinism is no better at explaining the "open motif" in Scripture than is any other version of classical theism. It has to take as anthropomorphic all passages in which God changes his mind, expresses regret, experiences surprise or disappointment, speaks and thinks of the future in terms of what may or may not happen, and so on. As I argued in my essay, while Scripture certainly contains anthropomorphisms, there are no good grounds for concluding that all passages which constitute the motif of future openness belong in this category.

Second, classical Molinism is philosophically problematic. In this view, every possible decision any possible free agent might ever make in any possible world is an eternal fact. Every future free decision and every possible future free decision is exhaustively settled in eternity before it takes place. How do we account for this eternal settledness? Craig concedes that it cannot exist because *God* wills it to exist, for that would constitute determinism. But neither can this eternal settledness exist because agents other than God will it to exist, for created agents are not eternal, and Craig rightly denies retroactive causation. Moreover, agents never will the counterfactuals that are supposedly true about them. They are what the agents *would have* willed *had they* been created in a different possible world.

We are left then with the unappealing alternative of denying that *anything* grounds the eternal settledness of future free acts and of counterfactuals of creaturely freedom. From all eternity the fact of what free agents would do in every possible situation was simply there—without any sufficient reason to account for it. It is simply a metaphysical surd. This position, I submit, is at best strongly counterintuitive. It could also be charged with being dualistic, for the settledness of the world, and of every possible world, is depicted as an uncreated reality that eternally coexists alongside God. Like an attribute of God, it has no explanation outside of itself.

Because of this, it's not at all clear that the middle-knowledge position is consistent with libertarian freedom, and this is the third problem with this position. An agent can be said to possess libertarian freedom if it lies within his or her power to do otherwise, given the exact same set of antecedent conditions. But how can we meaningfully say that agents could have done otherwise if all they shall ever do, and all they would have ever done in any possible world, is an unalterable fact an eternity before they even exist? Stated otherwise, how can agents be said to be self-determining when *they* don't ground the definiteness of what they shall do and ever would have done in different circumstances? The definiteness unexplainably eternally precedes them, created by nothing. If agents possess self-determining or libertarian freedom, I argue, *they* must be the ones who ultimately resolve indefinite possibilities into settled facts.

Would-Counterfactuals and Might-Counterfactuals

I am persuaded that Craig is correct in claiming that propositions expressing counterfactuals of creaturely freedom have an eternal truth value and thus that God knows them as true or false. Where Craig and other classical Molinists err, I believe, is in assuming that counterfactuals are exclusively about what agents *would* or *would not* do. These do not exhaust the logical possibilities of counterfactual propositions. The logical antithesis of the statement "agent X would do *y* in situation *z*" is not the statement "agent X would not do *y* in situation *z*." This is a contrary proposition, not a contradictory proposition. The logical antithesis of "agent X would do *y* in situation *z*" is rather the statement "agent X *might not* do *y* in situation *z*." This latter statement also has an eternal truth value and hence must be known by God.

If we include might-counterfactuals among God's middle knowledge, we arrive at the following neo-Molinist position: Between God's pre-creational knowledge of all logical possibilities and God's pre-creational knowledge of what will come to pass is God's "middle knowledge" of what free agents *might or might not do* in certain situations as well as of what free agents *would do* in other situations. If it is true that agent X might or might not do *y* in situation *z*, it is false that agent X would do *y* in situation *z*, and vice versa. On the basis of this knowledge, God chooses to have actualized the possible world that best suits his sovereign purpose. The world God chooses to be actualized, however, is more precisely described as a delimited set of possible worlds, any one of which *might be* actualized, depending on the choices free agents make. Yet because God is infinitely intelligent, he is as perfectly prepared for whatever possible world gets actualized *as if* it were the only possible world that could be actualized. It's just that precisely because we accept that God is infinitely intelligent, a neo-Molinist doesn't suppose that God must choose to falsify all might-counterfactuals in order to acquire this providential advantage.

The Advantages of Neo-Molinism

As with the classical Molinist view, and over against the simple-foreknowledge and Calvinist views, the neo-Molinist view can ascribe to God significant providential control while affirming libertarian freedom. God's knowledge of "would-counterfactuals" and "might-counterfactuals" allows him to providentially bring about the best possible world, given the reality of libertarian freedom. But the neo-Molinist view can accomplish this while avoiding the three problems mentioned above that attend to the classical Molinist position.

First, the neo-Molinist account does not have to dismiss the entire open motif of Scripture as anthropomorphic. We can now accept at face value Scripture's teaching that God sometimes thinks and speaks of the future in terms of what might or might not come to pass (e.g., Ex 4:7-9; 13:17; Jer 26:3; Ezek 12:3). Moreover, we now have no difficulty accounting for how God can sometimes experience regret (e.g., Gen 6:6; 1 Sam 15:11, 35), disappointment and frustration (e.g., Ezek 22:29-31), for people could have, and should have, made different decisions than they did. We have no difficulty accounting for how an omniscient God can change his mind (e.g., Jer 18:7-11; 26:2-3, 13, 19; Jon 3:10), for a world in which some might-counterfactuals are true is a world in which flexibility on the part of God would be an asset, not a liability. We have no difficulty explaining why God tests people "to know" what they will do (e.g., Gen 22:12; Ex 16:4), for some of their future behavior is only describable by might-counterfactuals. And we can even account for why the Bible sometimes depicts God as experiencing surprise (e.g., Is 5:1-5; Jer 3:6-7, 19-20), for while God perfectly anticipates all possible outcomes, when the improbable occurs, it is by definition not what an omniscient God would expect to occur. He is perfectly prepared for it, to be sure. But this doesn't negate the fact that it was improbable.

Second, if we accept that some might-counterfactuals are eternally true, we no longer have the problem of an ungrounded eternal settledness to possible worlds that include libertarian freedom, and there is no longer any problem accounting for libertarian freedom itself. On the one hand, the determinate aspects of any possible world, including worlds that include true might-counterfactuals, are grounded in God's will. For any possible world God might create, there are things that he decides would come to pass if he were to create them and, thus, things that shall come to pass in the world God decides to create. On the other hand, if some might-counterfactuals are true (viz., the world is not *exhaustively* definite from all eternity), there is no longer any problem trying to render intelligible the supposed eternal settledness of future free actions or free actions in other possible worlds. In the neo-Molinist view, there simply is no eternal settledness to libertarian free actions. There are only eternal possibilities of what they might or might not do.

To the extent that would-counterfactuals apply to future free agents, they do so because the actions of these agents flow either from the character God has given them (*habitus infusus,* in classical terminology) or from the character they will acquire if they pursue a certain possible course of action (*habitus acquisitus,* in classical terminology). In either case the would-counterfactuals are not ungrounded, as in classical Molinism. From all eternity God knows that if he chooses to create free agent X, she will have the basic characteristics of *a, b* and *c.* And from all eternity God knows that if agent X freely follows a certain possible life trajectory, she will become the kind of person who would do *x* in situation *z.* The would-counterfactuals for which agent X is morally responsible are contingent on the might-counterfactuals for which she is morally responsible.

A SIMPLE-FOREKNOWLEDGE RESPONSE

David Hunt

*W*illiam Lane Craig's overall position is closest to my own, though we disagree philosophically on some of the details. Let's look first at his response to the classic problem of divine foreknowledge versus human freedom and then at his proposal for augmenting divine foreknowledge with middle knowledge.

Foreknowledge and Fatalism

Craig and I stake out middle positions on the foreknowledge-freewill problem, inasmuch as we both believe that the problem is resolvable without abandoning either exhaustive foreknowledge (Gregory Boyd) or libertarian freedom (Paul Helm). We even share some key intuitions about the problem—for example, that it constitutes a philosophical *puzzle* (like Zeno's Achilles paradox) rather than a serious challenge to Christian belief, and so requires a philosophical rather than theological solution. But we disagree about the *kind* of philosophical solution that is required. Craig is convinced that theological fatalism is just a needlessly complex version of what he calls "Greek fatalism": the view that fatalistic consequences follow from the truth of future-tense statements alone, without any appeal to God. Since the two fatalisms are logically equivalent, Craig avers, they fail for essentially the same reason. I disagree: theological fatalism is much more formidable than Greek fatalism, and its solution involves more than correcting a simple logical fallacy.

The fatalistic thesis, as Craig renders it, is that for any future event x,

(3)   Necessarily, x will happen.

The fatalist endeavors to convince us of this conclusion by (1) citing some other fact to which it is necessarily connected, and (2) noting that this fact is itself necessary. *Greek* fatalism cites as the relevant fact a prior *truth* about the future, such that

(1**)   Necessarily, if it was true that x will happen, then x will happen.

(2**)   Necessarily, it was true that x will happen.

Theological fatalism appeals to a prior *divine cognition* about the future, such that

(1#)   Necessarily, if God believed that x will happen, then x will happen.

(2#)   Necessarily, God believed that x will happen.[1]

Both arguments validly imply (3), and the first premise of each is true. How about the second?

Assuming (for the sake of argument) that x will happen, it follows both that *it was true that x will happen* and also that *God believed that x will happen.* The only question is whether these are true *necessarily,* as (2**) and (2#) assert. Now the sole ground for thinking that they *are* necessary is that the facts they set forth are referenced to the *past.* In the case of (2**), however, this reference rests on nothing more than grammatical artifice. In virtue of *what,* was it (at some time in the past) a fact that x will happen? It was a fact simply in virtue of

---

[1] I deviate at this point from Craig's own formulation, which is couched in terms of fore*knowledge* rather than fore*belief.* As I noted in my chapter, *knowing* some proposition P involves (at least) *believing* P *and* P's being *true.* So the thesis that divine foreknowledge precludes creaturely freedom can be argued in terms of the foreknower's *beliefs,* and it can be argued in terms of the *truths* that are foreknown. The latter is indeed equivalent to Greek fatalism; but to suppose that this is *the* argument for theological fatalism (a red herring that Craig spends too long encouraging) is to ignore the argument based on divine belief. I substitute (1#) and (2#) for Craig's (1) and (2') in order to focus attention on what is distinctive about theological fatalism.

its then being the case that *x will happen*. This "fact about the past" is wholly parasitic on the future. Contrast this with (2#), the fact appealed to by the theological fatalist. In virtue of *what,* was it a fact that God believed that *x* will happen? This was *not* a fact in virtue of anything that *will* happen (though it is possible to infer something about the future *from* this fact about the past); it was a fact simply in virtue of *what God was then thinking.* This "hard" fact about the past, unlike the "soft" fact cited in (2**), is now accidentally (or, to use Craig's terminology, *temporally*) necessary.

Rather than concede this point, Craig prefers to challenge the very notion of temporal necessity. But this is an unpromising stratagem. The idea that the past is over and done with is a *datum,* not something that must (or even could) be argued. Nor is it reducible to considerations of causal closedness, as Craig suggests. A past event whose cause has not yet occurred, as in my tachyonic doorbell example (pp. 85-86), would still be temporally necessary: nothing can now happen such that the buzzer did not sound (given that it did sound). Because the undoing of what is done is "more impossible than the raising of the dead to life, which implies no contradiction, and is called impossible only according to natural power."[2] Aquinas argues that temporal necessity is binding even on God, who can make and unmake merely *causal* necessities at will.

Craig is undoubtedly right that we lack an adequate account of this "peculiar modality," but this is true of many of our most fundamental concepts. We lack, for example, a philosophically adequate theory of *causation.* This does not mean that there are no causes or effects; it just means that we don't really understand what is going on when one thing causes another. Likewise our failure to articulate a philosophically rigorous account of temporal necessity does not mean that it isn't real—our sense of its reality is too basic and deep to require validation by a philosophical theory.

There is, then, an important difference between the argument for Greek fatalism and the argument for theological fatalism: the second premise of the former is false, while the second premise of the latter is true! Instead of resisting the truth of (2#), the antifatalist should welcome it as an opportunity to discover the *real* flaw in the argument—which, to my mind, is the uncritical assumption (based on the Principle of Alternate Possibilities) that (3) is indeed inconsistent with free agency.

Middle Knowledge

So much for Craig's handling of the problem of divine foreknowledge. I turn

---

[2]Thomas Aquinas *Summa Theologica* 1.25.4.

152 —————————————————————————— DIVINE FOREKNOWLEDGE

now to middle knowledge, where there are both theoretical and practical issues to consider.

The practical question concerns Molinism's usefulness for Christian belief. Craig pronounces it "the single most fruitful theological concept I have ever encountered" (p. 125). If we look just at the vexed issue of divine providence, Craig's enthusiasm is understandable. The key questions to ask of any theory of providence are these: how much control does it offer God without jeopardizing human freedom, and how much freedom does it offer human beings without jeopardizing divine control? I do not know of any remotely plausible account of providence that scores as well by this standard as the doctrine of divine middle knowledge. I'm squarely in Craig's camp on this one.

There are other areas, however, in which middle knowledge may be more a hindrance than a help. One such area is the problem of evil. If Zeus were the supreme being, this problem would hardly arise. (We might instead be baffled by why there is so much excess *good* in the world!) Evil is a problem for the God of the Bible only because he is understood to be all-good, all-powerful and all-knowing. So wouldn't conceptualizing God so that he is even *more* knowledgeable (by endowing him with middle knowledge) make the problem even worse?

It's hard to answer this question in the abstract, so let's give it a more concrete form.[3] Consider what might be called the "postmortem problem of evil." The Bible appears to teach that some (many? most?) human beings will spend eternity in hell. Whatever "eternity in hell" amounts to, it is certainly not the purpose for which God created the world—God does not *desire* this for anyone (2 Pet 3:9). But if he is equipped with middle knowledge, he knew exactly who *would* reject him prior to creating anyone; knowing this, he could easily have refrained from creating these people. Why didn't he do so? This is a more difficult question to answer for the Molinist than it is for the open theist (whose God lacks this knowledge) or the defender of simple foreknowledge (whose God knows the actual future but cannot use that knowledge to change the very thing he foreknows). This does not show that there *are* no reasons why God might create people he "middle-knows" would reject him, but the need to posit and defend such reasons is a cost not borne by the non-Molinist.[4]

---

[3] I formulate the abstract version of the argument, and then expose three mistakes that it makes, in my "Evil and Theistic Minimalism," *International Journal for Philosophy of Religion* 49 (June 2001): 133-54.

[4] Making such reasons plausible is harder than one might think. See my "Middle Knowledge and the Soteriological Problem of Evil," *Religious Studies* 27 (March 1991): 3-26; reprinted in *Middle Knowledge: Theory and Applications,* ed. William Hasker, David Basinger and Eef Dekker (Frankfurt: Peter Lang, 2000), pp. 244-68.

Despite difficulties like this one, there are enough advantages to Molinism that I would welcome it *if it were true*. But is it true? This is the theoretical question, which seems to me on balance to go *against* the Molinist.

If there *are* any true counterfactuals of freedom, an omniscient deity will of course know them. But whether there really are such truths is controversial. Craig defends Molinism from one version of the "grounding objection," but he overlooks objections that seem to me more compelling. Owing to space limitations, I can present only one of these here.

What exactly are we claiming when we say something like the following?

If this water had remained on the burner a full five minutes, it would have boiled.

The first part (or *antecedent*) of the counterfactual posits a contrary-to-fact scenario in which the water remained on the burner longer than it actually did. The second part (or *consequent*) then states what would happen in that scenario. Counterfactuals thus have a foot in both the actual and nonactual worlds: the antecedent gives us license to ignore reality (in the stipulated respect); but the consequent, by committing itself to one outcome rather than another, lets us know that not just anything goes. Why is it true that the water would boil under those conditions, rather than true that the water would *not* boil? The reason is that the *actual* world works that way. If this quantity of water did *not* come to a boil after being subjected to this degree of heat for five minutes, physical laws that are true in the actual world would instead be false.

Counterfactuals, in sum, ask us to take the world as it actually is, modifying reality only to the extent that this is required by the contrary-to-fact scenario stipulated in the antecedent. A counterfactual of the form

If *P* were the case, *Q* would be the case.

is not about just any world in which *P* is the case; it's about the *closest-or-most-similar-world-to-the-actual-world* in which *P* is the case, and what it says about that world is that *Q* is also the case.

Consider now a counterfactual of freedom, such as the following:

(J) If Jones were offered the job, he would freely accept it.

Given the above analysis, what makes (J) true rather than (J~)?

(J~) If Jones were offered the job, he would freely reject it.

The answer is simply that there is a nonactual world *W* that meets certain conditions, and in *W* Jones freely accepts the job. What are these conditions? Simply that Jones is offered the job, and everything else is as much like the actual world as possible. Let *C* stand for all those features of *W* in virtue of which it satisfies these conditions. So *W* is a world in which *C* obtains *and* Jones accepts the job, or

W: *C* + *A*.

And it's because of what happens in *W* that (J), and not (J~), is true.

Unfortunately, this is incompatible with the putative freedom of Jones's decision. If Jones accepts the job *freely* in *W,* then *C* must leave it causally open for him to reject the job. (This is an assumption that Craig and I share.) So there is a possible world *W~* that is just like *W* with respect to *C,* except that in *W~* Jones rejects the job; or

W~: *C* + not-*A*.

But then (J) cannot be true. Because *W* and *W~* both include *C,* they are *equally similar* (in the relevant respects) to the actual world. So (J~) has just as much title to being true as (J). Rather, neither is true; what is true is that

> If Jones were offered the job, he *might* accept it and he *might not* accept it.

So much for the impressive resources of Molinism.

Does the above argument "refute" Molinism? That's doubtful. My analysis relies on the standard Lewis-Stalnaker semantics for subjunctive conditionals,[5] which Craig (following Alvin Plantinga's response to the "grounding objection") can always dismiss this way: "It seems to me much clearer that some counterfactuals of freedom are at least possibly true than that the Lewis-Stalnaker theory of counterfactuals is correct."[6] The problem with this line is that the Lewis-Stalnaker semantics seems generally *right:* if this theory were false, the result wouldn't be that (J) now had a chance of being true; rather, I wouldn't even know what I was saying in asserting (J). Until a semantics is developed that can make sense out of counterfactuals of libertarian freedom while retaining what is otherwise plausible about the Lewis-Stalnaker theory, it seems prudent to proceed as though middle knowledge is not available as a theological resource.

---

[5]The most important philosophical treatment of subjunctive conditionals is David Lewis's *Counterfactuals* (Cambridge, Mass.: Harvard University Press, 1973). Robert Stalnaker, in *Inquiry* (Cambridge, Mass.: MIT Press, 1984), offers an account sufficiently close to Lewis's that the general approach they share is often referred to as the "Lewis-Stalnaker" semantics.
[6]This is not a quotation from either Craig or Plantinga but my *adaptation* of Plantinga to the threat posed by Lewis-Stalnaker. Craig quotes Plantinga's original words on p. 140.

AN AUGUSTINIAN-CALVINIST RESPONSE

Paul Helm

*A*s is clear from my comments on Gregory Boyd's contribution, I largely agree with what William Lane Craig says about the open view, particularly its relation to philosophy. And what he has to say about the nature of God's knowledge, his "conceptualist" approach, seems plausible, as do his strictures on "revisionary" concepts of omniscience. Here I shall make some more reflective and critical remarks on his discussion of counterfactuals, then on fatalism, and then on God's being the author of sin.

Counterfactuals

Craig has an interesting discussion of counterfactuals and, as he implies, the Augustinian view (which is roughly equivalent to the Dominican position) has no difficulty ascribing counterfactual knowledge to God. But Craig's discussion needs a bit of clarification. It is only in respect of the true counterfactuals *of the actual world* that God's knowledge of them needs to be (for those whom he calls the Dominicans) logically subsequent to his decree to create that world. There are hosts of true counterfactuals of nonactual worlds that God may know logically prior to his decree to create some world. These are, so to speak, double-barreled counterfactuals, of the following form: If God were to decree some world containing Jones and Smith, then God knows (say) that if in that world Jones were to have met Smith, they would have become fast friends.

It's not clear to me how middle knowledge of the Jesuit variety—according to which God's counterfactual knowledge of the actual world is logically prior to his decree to create that world—helps resolve the question of freedom and foreknowledge. Craig supposes that there is a possible world in which Peter affirmed Christ in precisely the same circumstances in which he denied him. But God wants the possible world in which Peter denies Christ to be actual. So what does he do? Can he decree that possible world? How can God be assured that when he decrees that possible world in which, in circumstances *C*, Peter freely denies Christ, it is that world that is actualized? In addition, simply calling some of what God knows "middle knowledge" does not show us how God can know what Peter would freely do given the actual presence of Peter in circumstances *C*. For it appears (to me at least) that God cannot, by employing his middle knowledge, decree the world in which Peter denies Christ without ensuring that Peter denies Christ, thus compromising Peter's indeterministic freedom so vital to the Molinist and Arminian scheme of things.

In his philosophical defense of Molinism toward the end of his paper, Craig claims, without argument, that there are true counterfactuals of creaturely freedom; he makes this claim on the grounds that this seems plausible, and that if there are true counterfactuals of creaturely freedom, then God knows them in virtue of his omniscience (p. 139). But it only seems plausible if divine foreknowledge and indeterministic human freedom are compatible. And isn't this the question at issue? It seems to me that either the Molinist scheme begs that question or the problem remains to be faced. Luis de Molina himself sought refuge at this point in the idea that God (alone) "supercomprehends" the propositions that form the content of his middle knowledge—that he alone knows infallibly that, for example, in the actual world in circumstances *C*, Peter will freely deny Christ.[1] But how "supercomprehension" works, how it successfully

---

[1]For discussion of the meaning of *supercomprehension* and its place in Molina's thought, see Alfred J. Freddoso's introduction to Luis de Molina's *On Divine Knowledge* (Ithaca, N.Y.: Cornell University Press, 1988), pp. 51-53.

effects the reconciliation between divine foreknowledge and human freedom, remains to this day a well-kept secret.

The biblical evidence for counterfactuals of freedom that Craig offers is, to say the least, ambiguous, just as such evidence is ambiguous in relation to many refined philosophical ideas. The existence in the Bible of counterfactual forms does not provide evidence for those forms being counterfactuals of freedom, as Craig recognizes (p. 125). Nor is the alleged fecundity of the idea of middle knowledge with respect to certain theological issues an argument in its favor. The fruit borne on the tree of Molinism is in any case fruit that the Augustinian-Calvinist perspective does not find to its taste, since its root premise is that the exercise of indeterministic human free choice is necessary to receive God's grace and to profit from it. It is this theological position—which those of the Augustinian-Calvinist persuasion hold cannot be found in Scripture—that motivated Jesuit Molinism and why, historically speaking, it proved so attractive to Arminius as a way of retaining both unattenuated divine omniscience and human indeterministic freedom.[2]

Fatalism

Craig does not define *fatalism,* so at the start of his piece it is not at all clear what he has in mind. However, later on "fatalism" becomes something called "theological fatalism," and later on still the "Augustinian-Calvinist perspective." But it is pretty clear that it is inaccurate to tar the Augustinian or Calvinist with this particular brush. For they hold that the divine decree by which all things come to pass is logically contingent. God might have decreed otherwise. Moreover, in bringing his decrees to pass, God employs means—means of which he himself is the primary cause.[3] So, to take a standard case, when Paul receives divine assurance that both he and his companions onboard ship will be saved (Acts 27:24), they are saved only in virtue of the fact that they did not take to the lifeboats (Acts 27:31). We are entitled to draw the inference that had they

[2]On the connection between Arminius and Molina, see Richard Muller, "The Divine Knowledge," in *God, Creation and Providence in the Thought of Jacob Arminius* (Grand Rapids, Mich.: Baker, 1991), chap. 9.

[3]"We hold not that all things, but rather nothing follows fate: and whereas fate is wont to be taken for a position of the stars in nativities and conceptions, we hold this a vain and frivolous assumption: we neither deny an order of causes wherein the will of God is all in all, neither do we call it by the name of fate. . . . But it does not follow that nothing should be left free to our will, because God knows the certain and set order of all events. For our very wills are in that order of causes, which God knows so surely and hath in His prescience; human wills being the cause of human actions: so that He that keeps a knowledge of the causes of all things, cannot leave men's wills out of that knowledge, knowing them to be the causes of their actions." Augustine *The City of God* 5.9 (trans. John Healey [London: Dent, 1945]).

taken to the lifeboats, they would not have been saved. So the parallel with ancient Greek fatalists that Craig attempts to draw is far from exact (p. 128). In any case, one of the things shown by the tortuous debates on accidental necessity, the alleged distinction between hard and soft facts, and so on is that the issue of divine foreknowledge and freedom is not equivalent to the ancient problem of fatalism. So even if fatalism is refuted along the lines that Craig suggests, there would still be a problem raised by the existence of an infallible foreknower of the future.

Craig suggests that there is an air of mystery about the prima facie incompatibility of divine foreknowledge and human indeterministic freedom. If there is this incompatibility, then there is "some sort of logical constraint . . . my actions are mysteriously constrained" (p. 130). But there is nothing in the least mysterious about this. If God's foreknowledge is consistent with indeterministic freedom, then we may be indeterministically free. If it is not consistent with indeterministic freedom, then we may be free in some other sense or perhaps not free at all. What is needed at this point are arguments for the compatibility of divine foreknowledge and indeterministic freedom—arguments that, oddly, Craig does not provide, nor does he attempt to refute their incompatibility. Occasionally he suggests the beginnings of an argument, as in his question of whether mixing temporal and logical necessity is valid, or of whether a future event could be temporally necessary, or of whether an action's being temporally necessary is compatible with an action's being temporally free (p. 130). If he thinks that none of these claims is valid, then he should suggest some solid reasons why he thinks this.

At length Craig does offer an argument, one about the causal closedness of the past, which he says is what temporal necessity is or implies (p. 131). Suppose it is. Of course the mere causal closedness of the past does not imply that our actions are determined, but the causal closedness of a knowledge claim or a divine belief about the future might well. And that's what the argument is (or should be) about.

God as the Author of Evil

Craig says that the Augustinian-Calvinist perspective (which, as I said earlier, I think he takes to be equivalent to theological fatalism and to fatalism simpliciter) holds that "foreknowledge is based upon foreordination: God knows what will happen because he makes it happen" (p. 135). Three things on this. First, taking this claim at face value, it is not a doctrine that the ancient Greek fatalists would have recognized. Second, these expressions are inaccurate. God's foreordaining x is not equivalent to God's making x happen. For according to the Augustinian-Calvinist perspective, God ordains evil by willingly permitting it. Third, on the question of the authorship of evil, there's not a hairsbreadth between the Augustinian-Calvinist perspective and Craig's Molinism. According to Craig's description of Molinism, "God decreed to create just those circumstances and just those people who would freely do what God willed to happen" (p. 134). While this description does not entail that God is the author of sin (any more than the Augustinian-Calvinist perspective does), it does entail that God decreed all sinful acts to happen and decreed them precisely as they have happened. If this is so, the God of Molina and Arminius seems to be as implicated in the fact of evil as much (or as little) as the God of the Augustinian-Calvinist perspective.

4

THE AUGUSTINIAN-CALVINIST VIEW

Paul Helm

I have been invited to contribute to this volume an essay on divine fore-knowledge and human freedom as viewed from the tradition of Augustine of Hippo and John Calvin. The issue, as classically stated, is whether divine omni-science, as far as it is concerned with the future, is logically consistent with human freedom, where this is understood in an incompatibilist sense.[1] The endless discussions of this issue have been motivated by the underlying assumption that a person can be held responsible only for those actions that are incompatibilistically free. So if divine omniscience is inconsistent with such freedom, then two unappetizing alternatives stare us in the face. Either we

---

[1]*Compatibilist* and *libertarian* are of course terms of art. Thomas P. Flint defines *libertarian-ism* as follows: "Necessarily, for any human agent S, action A and time *t*, if S performs A freely at *t*, then the history of the world prior to *t*, the laws of nature, and the actions of any other agent (including God) prior to and at *t* are jointly compatible with S's refraining from performing A freely" (Thomas P. Flint, "Two Accounts of Providence," in *Divine and Human Action,* ed. T. V. Morris [Ithaca, N.Y.: Cornell University Press, 1988], p. 175). I am happy to accept this definition.

shall have to accept a modified, reduced account of divine omniscience or we shall have to accept that human agents are never responsible for what they do since they are never incompatibilistically free. Some have indeed taken the first of these alternatives;[2] I know of no one who has opted for the other.

On the view to be expounded in this chapter these alternatives do not confront us, for according to this view there is no need to claim that divine foreknowledge is logically consistent with human indeterministic freedom, and there is good reason for not doing so.[3] I will present three broad arguments for the conclusion that a Christian theist may accept a different sense of "free," a compatibilist sense, and that indeed there are good reasons to think that Christianity requires such a view. The arguments are broad in the sense that it is not possible, in a piece such as this, to dot every *i* and to answer or anticipate every objection. Of these three arguments, the first has a more theological character to it than the others in that it depends crucially upon a particular view of God's grace. It offers an argument that should, other things being equal, motivate a Christian to accept a compatibilist account of human action. The second and third arguments are more strictly philosophical. One is an argument for the consistency of divine foreknowledge and human compatibilist freedom from the idea of divine perfection and the principle of simplicity; and the other is an argument for the logical inconsistency of divine foreknowl-

---

[2]Richard Swinburne, *The Coherence of Theism* (Oxford: Clarendon, 1977); William Hasker, *God, Time and Knowledge* (Ithaca, N.Y.: Cornell University Press, 1989).

[3]I shall assume that the overall interpretation of Augustine commits him to some form of compatibilism. Scholars refer to the "later" Augustine in contradistinction to the earlier, seeing a shift away from indeterminism that they think can be found in his early work on free will. Judging by his "Retractions" Augustine himself may have thought the same. Whether one thinks of the later Augustine as a degeneration or an improvement or simply as an "all things considered" position, it is hard to dissent from the view of G. O'Daly that there is little to distinguish the later Augustine's view of the will from that of the compatibilist Jonathan Edwards (G. O'Daly, "Predestination and Freedom in Augustine's Ethics," in *The Philosophy in Christianity*, ed. G. Vesey [Cambridge: Cambridge University Press, 1989]). While John Calvin may never have espoused compatibilism in so many words, a number of pieces of evidence make it reasonable to assume he was committed to compatibilism. One is the distinction he draws in the *Institutes of the Christian Religion* between necessity and compulsion (e.g., *Institutes* 2.3.5). Two significant pieces of external evidence suggest that compatibilism would be congenial to his view. One is that some Calvinist thinkers, such as J. L. Girardeau (*The Will in Its Theological Relations* [Columbia, S.C.: W. J. Duffie, 1891]), have labored to show that Calvin was not a compatibilist; clearly the consensus view is that he was. The second piece of evidence is that Calvin's successors, such as Francis Turretin (1623-87), certainly took such a view, calling it the liberty of rational spontaneity and denying the liberty of indifference (Francis Turretin, *Institutes of Elenctic Theology*, trans. G. M. Giger, ed. James T. Dennison Jr., 3 vols. [Philipsburg, N.J.: P & R, 1992-97], 1.665-68). So I believe that it is reasonable to interpret the Augustinian position, a position that clearly embraces the views of Calvin, as compatibilist.

edge and incompatibilism.

These arguments are consistent with each other, and therefore they may, taken together, be said to present a cumulative case for the Augustinian view. But I do not claim that together they make the Augustinian view compelling; my only claim is that together they make a defensible and reasonable case for the view that divine foreknowledge is consistent with human freedom when this freedom is properly understood. If this case is accepted, then there is no need for, and no advantage in, either trying to provide an understanding of human freedom that is indeterministic or trying to argue that such freedom is logically consistent with divine foreknowledge.

Divine Foreknowledge

I shall begin by saying something about the meaning of "divine foreknowledge." It is possible to distinguish at least three different concepts of divine foreknowledge—at least three different senses in which God may be said to foreknow. One is the straight causal sense: God's knowledge is the cause of things, as Thomas Aquinas famously put it. On this view there would appear to be no distinction between what God causes and what he permits, because, on Aquinas's view, since God foreknows all events, he must cause them all. (Aquinas does in fact allow a sense of divine permission: since God cannot cause evil, since evil is not anything that is positive, God may be said to know it without causing it. We shall have more to say on divine permission later.) A second sense is that in which the foreknowledge of God is logically subsequent to his decree. On this view God's decree is all embracing, and his foreknowledge is simply his knowledge of what he has decreed before that decree takes effect in time. Thus while on this view divine foreknowledge and divine foreordination are necessarily coextensive, they differ in meaning. The third and weakest sense is a sense of divine foreknowledge that is logically prior to God's decree; it is in the light of what he foreknows that God decrees this or that; what he decrees is conditioned by what he foreknows.

My arguments entail, as a conclusion, an understanding of divine foreknowledge according to which at least some instances of divine foreknowledge, as far as they concern human free acts, are to be understood in one or other of the first two senses; these instances are inconsistent with the third sense of foreknowledge. None of the arguments requires one particular account of divine foreknowledge as a premise. Before setting out these arguments and defending them, since this chapter is offered as a contribution to a debate among Christians, I wish to say something further about what I take to be the Christian parameters within which this whole debate, and particularly the Augustinian contribution to it, is set forth.

The Fixed Points

In setting out to reflect, as Christians, upon the relation between God's knowledge and power on the one hand and human responsibility on the other, it is important that we understand what sort of task we face. Christians do not reflect on these concepts in a purely abstract way and then try, in a wholly a priori fashion, to establish the concepts' consistency. For we are constrained by the biblical witness insofar as it refers to and makes use of these ideas. Christians must hold this witness as a set of fixed points, and then we must reflect upon the cogency or coherence of the several parts of that witness. It is perfectly possible that at the end of these reflections we shall reluctantly have to draw the conclusion that we cannot at present see how these parts cohere, that we cannot demonstrate their consistency. Perhaps we shall have to be content with showing that the ideas are not inconsistent. (Think of similar difficulties that may be encountered in trying to understand the doctrine of the Trinity or the incarnation.) But it is not open to us to amend or modify that witness in any way in the interests of greater comprehensibility. Faith seeks understanding, but the understanding gained must not be at the expense of the faith.

What then are these fixed points? In brief, the scriptural worldview is one in which all things are created by God and ordered and governed by him; he numbers the hairs of our head, directs the fall of a sparrow and the flight of an arrow; he turns the hearts of humans as he wishes; like a potter, he has power over human clay. It is true that God is said to forget, to be surprised and to act and react toward his people in blessing and chastisement. These may appear to be the actions of someone with limited knowledge and power, but the scriptural language in such cases is usually recognized as metaphorical or symbolic, language "accommodated" to some human situation or need. I shall not at this point consider further the justification for regarding such language in this way nor the implications of such language for our understanding of God. I will try to say something about these matters in my rejoinders to the other views.

We may think, on purely a priori grounds, that the exact arrangement of molecules in a jar of sugar or of flecks of dust dancing in the sunlight is beneath God's notice. And it may seem that as far as God is concerned nothing turns on there being one arrangement of sugar molecules in the jar instead of another. But no scriptural statements about the nature and character of God suggest that his divine ordering and control of his creation are qualified or attenuated in even such marginal ways; nor, indeed, does any passage of Scripture say that they are not. Perhaps these matters are literally beneath his notice.

But suppose that they are. Then Scripture appears to affirm that everything that is worth God's notice is governed by him. So God's universal and yet particular providence is one fixed point that our theorizing about divine knowledge and freedom should not attempt to overturn.[4]

On the other hand, Scripture teaches that although God ordains everything which comes to pass—even the evil actions and omissions of human beings—men and women are nevertheless accountable to God for their actions and omissions, though they are not accountable for all of these, because a distinction may be drawn between matters that are outside a person's control and cancel responsibility and those matters that are under a person's control. Scripture also has a place for degrees of responsibility or accountability. A person may be more or less accountable for an action, as Scripture also teaches; responsibility may be partly canceled, for example, by partial ignorance.

We need, also, to make a distinction between two kinds of the responsibility. The first is the responsibility we each have before God: an accountability that depends upon God's knowledge of all circumstances, including the thoughts and intentions of our hearts, and that is exercised in accordance with God's loving, wise and righteous character. (I shall call this GR for "responsibility before God.") The second is the responsibility we have as judged by human agencies; by other human beings, such as parents and friends; and by the police and other law-enforcement agencies. (I shall call this HR for "responsibility toward humans.") Ascribing responsibility to oneself or to others is a human, social activity having serious limitations but an activity necessary for carrying out certain social functions and achieving certain ends. Ascribing responsibility under these conditions performs a different function than accountability before God does, a function that has as one of its primary aims the well-ordering of society.

It is important to stress that the basic biblical emphasis, certainly in the New Testament, is upon our accountability to God. Because the moral accountability of one person to another, or legal accountability to the state (HR), depends upon fallible human knowledge of the motivations and circumstances of ourselves and others; each can only be pale and imperfect reflections of GR, the accountability each of us has to God. Human justice and injustice are, when compared to divine justice, necessarily rough and ready.

So when Christians are exploring the relationship between divine knowledge and human responsibility, they might be doing one of two different

---

[4]For a contrasting view, see Peter Van Inwagen, "The Place of Chance in a World Sustained by God," in *Divine and Human Action,* ed. T. V. Morris (Ithaca, N.Y.: Cornell University Press, 1988).

things. First, they might be exploring the implications of divine knowledge for HR as it is exercised, say, in families or between friends and colleagues. This idea of moral responsibility is a familiar one and needs to be distinguished from legal responsibility, to which it is related. But both moral and legal responsibility need in turn to be distinguished from human responsibility before God.

Second, Christians might be exploring the implications of divine knowledge and GR. I take it that when philosophers and theologians, motivated in part by a desire to preserve human responsibility, have attempted to show that divine foreknowledge and human incompatibilism are consistent, it is GR that they have primarily in mind. A sense of responsibility that is not responsibility before God is not the sort of responsibility we ought to want to have.

Why may GR and HR differ? For the following reason: in order to hold others responsible for their actions, it is necessary that one know their state of mind and the circumstances of their actions (as we shall note later). Social and family imperatives may require the ascription of responsibility when full knowledge is unobtainable; perhaps full knowledge is never attainable by us. In such cases what we may have is an ascription of HR and not GR. In some particular case perhaps human and divine verdicts coincide, perhaps not. Thus certain kinds of HR may require strict liability, a responsibility for a particular action X that stands even though a person did not want X to happen and took all reasonable steps not to let X happen. But it is hard to see that there is any case of GR based upon strict liability in this sense.

In the case of GR it must be presumed that God himself has perfect knowledge of the state of mind and the circumstances of every agent and every action. Not only does he have knowledge of the facts, of course, but he also carries out his judgment in an immaculate fashion, not in the warped and biased way that human justice is often meted out. Part of the "righteous judgment of God" is, thus, that it is "according to truth," based upon all and only the relevant facts, and is founded upon perfect justice.

It would be perfectly possible to maintain the importance of GR while being skeptical about the basis on which judgments of HR are made. Indeed, when the apostle Paul urges his readers to "not pronounce judgment before the time" (1 Cor 4:5), he appears to be adopting such a skeptical position; this is not to say that HR bears no relation to GR but to say that the judgments of HR, because of our imperfect knowledge of ourselves and others, are only partial and provisional, open to revision at "the time." Perhaps this should be the general Christian attitude to HR.

Divine sovereignty and human accountability before God—these are two of the fixed points. When we are faced with problems about the consistency of these concepts, it is tempting to modify one or both of them. But we must make every effort to avoid such a course of action. Scripture holds them together, it even speaks of them in the same breath, and so must we. For if Scripture teaches them in this way, they must each be true and so together be consistent, even though it may be difficult for us to grasp this now.

Nowhere is this more noteworthy and striking than when Peter tells his listeners, "This man [Jesus], handed over to you according to the definite plan and foreknowledge of God, you crucified and killed by the hands of those outside the law" (Acts 2:23). Here a divine verdict is passed on the actions of the crucifiers. Whether or not the culpability of those responsible for the crucifixion was a case of HR, it was certainly a case of GR. From this text it is possible to draw the conclusion that there are at least some occasions when the action of a wicked person (in the sense of GR) is the result of the set purpose and foreknowledge of God, for one such occasion was the crucifixion of Christ, the focal event of the Christian faith.

It is tempting to say about the crucifixion of Christ that if the men who crucified Christ were wicked (in the GR sense), then they cannot have acted as a result of God's set purpose. It is equally tempting to say that if the crucifixion of Christ came about as a result of the set purpose of God, then the men who crucified him cannot have been wickedly responsible (in the GR sense) for what they did. But we must resist the temptation to reason either of these ways.

There is a third fixed point, one that perhaps we reflect upon less frequently: God's relation to the universe that he has created and that he sustains and directs is a relation without parallel. It is unique, incomparable, sui generis. This is not surprising, or it ought not to be; after all, there can only be one God, and if by "the universe" we mean the totality of whatever exists apart from God, there can only be one universe. We cannot have experience of more than one God nor of more than one universe.

Those critics of the "argument from design," such as Philo in David Hume's *Dialogues Concerning Natural Religion,* make an important point when they argue that we do not, in the nature of things, have experience of more than one world. Cleanthes claims that the universe reveals such marks of intelligent design as to make it likely that it has a designer, to which Philo replies:

Having found in so many other subjects much more familiar the imperfections and even contradictions of human reason, I never should expect any success from its feeble conjectures and in a subject so sublime and so remote from the sphere of our observations. When two species of objects have always been observed or conjoined together, I can infer, by custom, the existence of one wherever I see the existence of the other; and this I call an argument from experience. But how this argument can have place where the objects, as in the present case, are single, individual, without parallel or specific resemblance, may be difficult to explain. And will any man tell me with a serious countenance that an orderly universe must arise from some thought and art like the human because we have experience of it? To ascertain this reasoning it were requisite that we have experience of the origin of worlds; and it is not sufficient, surely, that we have seen ships and cities arise from human art and contrivance. . . .

Can you pretend to show any such resemblance between the fabric of a house and the generation of a universe? Have you ever seen nature in any such situation as resembles the first arrangement of the elements? Have worlds ever been formed under your eye, and have you had leisure to observe the whole progress of the phenomenon, from the first appearance of order to its final consummation? If you have, then cite your experience and deliver your theory.[5]

This argument reminds us of the general danger of modeling the divine-human relation either on the relations between human beings or on relations between human beings and artifacts. For just as none of us has had experience of many universes but yet we recognize the singularity of this universe, so the relations between God and the universe are singular and cannot be closely modeled on the relationship between intramundane agents.

In our remarks about responsibility we have already seen a need to distinguish between the conditions under which a person may be held responsible for an action within a human society, such as the state or a family, and the conditions that obtain in the case of responsibility before God. When faced with the scriptural claim that the actions leading up to and including the crucifixion were in accordance with the determinate counsel and foreknowledge of God, it is tempting to infer that in the crucifixion God "manipulated" the crucifiers or that they were his "puppets." To say such a thing would be to apply to God concepts derived from (let us say) the behavior of a magician or an entertainer. And this is to forget that those factors which distinguish God from humanity are at least as great as those factors which they have in common. We must therefore resist the temptation to say that in all cases in which one person acts as a result of the set purpose of another intelligent agent, that person is thereby being tricked or made into a puppet.

Emphasizing the sui generis character of the relation between God and his

---

[5]David Hume, *Dialogues Concerning Natural Religion,* ed. Nelson Pike (Indianapolis: Bobbs Merrill, 1970), pp. 30, 32.

creation is simply another way of saying that God's relations with his creation are incomprehensible. We cannot get our minds around them so as to fully understand them because they are unparalleled in human experience. The divine activities are not subsumable under laws, and the creative and interactive activities between human beings only provide a faint reflection of the profundity of the relation between the eternal Creator and his creation. But in saying that God's relations with his creation are incomprehensible, it needs to be borne in mind that comprehensibility is a matter of degree; for a state of affairs to be incomprehensible is not necessary for it to be fully or totally incomprehensible gibberish, but rather for it to be not fully comprehended.

We are mistaken in reasoning that because God's relations with his creation are sui generis—and that because, therefore, we cannot fully comprehend them—we must inevitably fall into paradox, self-contradiction or other kinds of nonsense whenever we attempt to think or speak about them clearly. In what follows we shall try to comprehend aspects of the relation of divine sovereignty and human responsibility while recognizing that we can never, in the nature of things, fully comprehend that relation.

Let us now turn to the arguments.

Argument 1: Foreknowledge, Freedom and Divine Grace

What motivates the Augustinian view at the most fundamental level, I shall argue, is a particular understanding of God's saving grace, an understanding that, this view holds, is the biblical view. I shall briefly elaborate this view of grace and try to show that it is reasonable to think it is consistent with compatibilism, the idea that human actions are free in a sense that is consistent with determinism.[6] Basic to the difference of view between those who think that divine omniscience is consistent with human incompatibilism and those who think that it isn't, is not principally a different understanding of the nature of God or of human freedom, nor even a difference of interpretation of this or that passage of Scripture, but a profoundly different appreciation of the plight of humankind and the power of God.

One can take for granted on the incompatibilist view of human freedom that however divine saving grace is understood and defined, it is this action of God that is causally necessary, but never causally sufficient, for human salva-

---

[6]In speaking of "determinism" we should remember that it refers to a family of views. One member of that family is physical determinism, another is psychological determinism, and so on. As separate argument would be required to specify a more precise sense of determinism I shall continue to use the family name.

tion. Let us suppose, with all evangelical Protestants, that faith in Christ is the instrumental cause of a person's salvation. Then on an incompatibilist view of freedom, God's grace can only ever be causally necessary, not causally sufficient, for the production of such faith. For otherwise faith in Christ would not be a free act. For on the incompatibilist view of freedom what must, in addition, be causally necessary for receiving God's grace is a free, incompatibilist choice on the part of the would-be Christian. Divine grace and such a choice are then together causally sufficient for faith in Christ, for the personal appropriation of Christ. Without such grace no human being would come into a right relationship with God. But on the incompatibilist view by itself, such grace is never sufficient. For even when such divine grace is exercised, given that humankind has a libertarian or incompatibilist will, such a will has the power to resist or frustrate such grace from God. And given that humankind has a nature that is antipathetic to the rule of God, we might expect such power to be exercised in the rejection of the overtures of grace. With such freedom, God's saving grace is always resistible, and so saving grace can never ensure its intended effect.

That is the first point. The second point is that according to Scripture such irresistible grace—the grace that alone is causally sufficient for faith and for a faithful appropriation of Christ—when it is received, is liberating. By receiving it a person is freed from his or her slavery to sin and granted spiritual freedom: the freedom to willingly and gladly serve the living and true God. This sense of "freedom" is, of course, rather different but nonetheless related to the sense of "freedom" that is at issue in the controversy between compatibilists and incompatibilists. It is freedom with a spiritual and moral dimension, freedom necessary to be remade as a person. So not only is the receiving of such grace inconsistent with a libertarian conception of freedom, but there is a further sense of freedom, a moral and spiritual sense, according to which one is free only when one has received such grace. Now if such grace alone ensures true human freedom, as the Augustinian maintains, and if the operation of such grace is inconsistent with incompatibilism, then such incompatibilism cannot itself be necessary for the maintenance of, or the achieving of, true human freedom.

How are we to understand such efficacious grace? Here is a typical expression of the way in which Augustine understands it:

> Unless, therefore, we obtain not simply determination of will, which is freely turned in this direction and that, and has its place amongst those natural goods which a bad man may use badly; but also a good will, which has its place among

those goods of which it is impossible to make a bad use—unless the impossibility is given to us from God, I know not how to defend what is said: "What hast thou that thou didst not receive?" For if we have from God a certain free will, which may still be either good or bad; but the good will comes from ourselves; then that which comes from ourselves is better than that which comes from Him. But inasmuch as it is the height of absurdity to say this, they ought to acknowledge that we attain from God even a good will.[7]

So if God's saving grace is efficacious in renewing the human will, then it is sufficient to attain the end for which it is given: the salvation of the individual to whom it is granted. It is reasonable to suppose that in bringing his saving grace to men and women, God has certain purposes, salvific purposes. And if these purposes are salvific and if grace is efficacious, then the provision of grace is sufficient for attaining that salvific end.

The incompatibilist holds that because the plight of humans is not so great (for they retain inalienable freedom to choose for or against Christ in an incompatibilist sense), the power of God need not be so great either. There is no need of a covenant of sovereign grace to which God is immutably faithful or of divine promises on which the sinner can utterly rely. More particularly, there is no need to receive efficacious saving grace from God. This is, ultimately, why the insistence upon incompatibilism in connection with the issue of divine foreknowledge and human freedom is so superficial. For the Augustinian account of the plight of humankind is such that people cannot want to want God, and his grace is needed not only to help them to want to want him, but also to ensure that they do so. So the claim that such incompatibilistic freedom is consistent with divine omniscience, even if it were convincing, would not get to what, for the Christian, should be the heart of the issue; for only the efficacious grace of God can ensure the salvation of a person in slavery to sin.

What of the objection that some human partners do resist God's grace— apparently successfully? The point about efficacious grace is, in a manner of speaking, a grammatical one. By definition, efficacious saving grace succeeds in the way indicated. Those who successfully resist the grace of God do so because in such cases that grace is not efficacious. For not all God's actions are efficacious in the sense that they bring the person on whom they act to true human freedom. Some of God's actions are resistible and are resisted. What does this imply? Not that there are no irresistible gracious divine energies but

---

[7]Augustine *A Treatise on the Merits and Forgiveness of Sins, and on the Baptism of Infants* 2.30 (in *Augustine, The Anti-Pelagian Writings*, trans. Peter Holmes; vol. V of *Select Library of the Nicene and Post-Nicene Fathers*, ed. Philip Schaff [Grand Rapids, Mich.: Eerdmans, 1971], p. 56).

simply that those which are resisted are not among them.

Those discussing the idea of divine grace sometimes stress its personal character and, in particular, the view that because grace is personal it is therefore relational. This may be helpful, for grace is relational; it relates the divine persons and human persons. But saying this by itself does not help us forward. The question is, what sort of relationship is a personal relationship? Is it a relationship in which the human partner can always resist the divine partner or not?

The chief difficulty over stressing the idea of saving grace as being basically relational concerns the idea often associated with it: that parity between the partners and the ensuing reciprocity are necessary for any genuine personal relationship to be established. Of course it is possible to define a personal relationship in this way, in terms of the parity of those in the relationship, but the result is that whoever insists upon such a definition will simply misdescribe many genuine human relations in the process. For such a definition is surely unconvincing as a claim about ordinary human relations and unequally unconvincing about relations between human beings and God. You may have a relationship with another human being who cannot reciprocate: for instance, with a baby, or with someone of very low intelligence or with someone who is in a coma because she or he has fallen through the ice and is stuck beneath it. Someone in a coma has to be brought back to consciousness and, essentially, to life; but this process is itself a case of exercising a personal relationship. In a parallel way, all that is implied in divine rescuing and bringing to life *is* the establishing of a relationship, the key to which is not incompatibilistic human freedom but the unilateral establishing of a loving relationship that will not let go until it has secured reciprocal love by recreating it. According to Augustinianism, God in grace establishes a genuinely personal relationship with people who are incapable of establishing it for themselves. And God does this by an act of condescension and power—condescension because he is the infinite Creator and has no obligation to do what he does, and power because our plight is such that without that power the relationship could be neither established nor continued. This is a different sort of divine-human relationship than the one usually envisaged by those who claim that God's relations with humankind are personal relations. But isn't it the biblical sort?

I think we can now dismiss the theological argument for the consistency of divine foreknowledge and human incompatibilistic freedom. Divine efficacious saving grace is inconsistent with such freedom; and as (on the Augustinian view) such an account of divine grace is a fundamental feature of the Christian way of salvation, the Christian faith does not need to posit incompatibilism; in fact it needs to posit compatibilism.

Argument 2: Divine Perfection and Providence

My second argument, one that is more strictly philosophical, is derived from the ideas of divine omnipotence and omniscience. We may distinguish between the connotation and denotation (or between the sense and reference) of expressions such as "an omniscient being" or "an omnipotent being." For obvious reasons, let us chiefly consider omniscience, while not ignoring omnipotence altogether. And let us assume, fairly uncontroversially in present circumstances, that the denotation of "an omniscient being" is God alone.

The connotation of *omniscience,* "knowing all things" *(Shorter Oxford Dictionary),* may also seem uncontroversial. If God is omniscient, then he has unlimited knowledge. But (as is well known) matters become more difficult when we inquire more precisely into the connotation of omniscience; what exactly are the "all things" that omniscience knows? For example, is what God can know "limited" by powers possessed by beings other than God, particularly the power of incompatibilistic free choice? Can an omniscient God know what time it is now? Can he know what it is like to be a bat? Two people may each agree that God alone is omniscient but disagree on the connotation of the term. Thus while Aquinas believed that God knows all future free human actions, others, such as Richard Swinburne, believe that he does not. So there is disagreement among philosophers about the connotation of omniscience as this applies to God.

Omniscience might be defined as the knowledge of all truths. But omniscience is limited by what it is possible for the omniscient knower to know. Some have argued that it is not possible for God to know the entire future since there are parts of the future that are unknowable, and that it is not possible for him to know what it is like to be a bat, or what I am doing now, and so on.

So there is scope for disagreement about the precise connotation of omniscience. However, it seems a reasonable principle, in reflecting upon the concept of God in philosophical fashion, that *the connotation of "omni-" terms— such as "omnipotent" and "omniscient"—should, when applied to God, be as wide in their connotation as possible.* (Let us call this principle *A.*) Thus the term *omniscient* is more appropriately applied to God when it connotes knowledge of more types of actions and events than when it connotes knowledge of fewer types of actions and events. Further, the term is more appropriately applied to God when it connotes knowledge of more tokens of each type of action than knowledge of fewer such tokens. After all, the rationale for applying such "omni-" terms to God is to convey the idea of maximality; so it must be reasonable not to limit their application unnecessarily, otherwise the danger is that such terms, when applied to God, come to possess only rhetorical or hyperbolical value. The presumption must be, therefore, with respect to any type of event and to any token of that type, that an omniscient being has knowledge of them, knowing the truths that are the correct descriptions of all such actions, or that he is directly acquainted with all the relevant states of affairs. Of course omniscience may be said to extend further than knowledge over what is the case; it extends to what might possibly be or have been the case. An omniscient being knows not only all actualities but the contents of all possible worlds. This point will become relevant when we shall shortly consider Molinism.

I am claiming, then, that wherever possible one should interpret the term *omniscience* when applied to God as generously as possible, pushing its connotation as far as one can, unless there are overriding reasons not to do so. But it is at this very point that controversy begins. It seems clear to many that there is such an overriding reason in the case of human incompatibilistic freedom, for as we have seen in their view such freedom is necessary for human responsibility and (in some theological systems) necessary for the achieving of merit.

Given the common Christian view that God is omniscient and given principle *A,* it is a priori desirable that divine omniscience should extend to as many facets of creation as possible. It is undesirable that God knows about only some of the things that he has created, presiding over a creation in which some things happen that he does not know about before they occur. For an omniscient being who does not know the future course of free human actions is "less" omniscient than an omniscient being who knows the entire future.

Let us call the degree of knowledge that encompasses all events past, present and future "strong" omniscience and call anything less "weak" omniscience. My argument is that the ascription to God of strong omniscience, as part of ascribing perfection to God's nature, is most at home with compatibilist views of human freedom. It is best to think of a perfect God as one who is essentially strongly omniscient.

But is not essential strong omniscience inconsistent with other essential features of God's character, notably his goodness as expressed in his perfectly righteous and holy moral character? If God is essentially strongly omniscient, and so knows about all events before they occur, then surely he is implicated in the fact of evil and his essential goodness or righteousness is compromised.

At this point many argue that it is possible to preserve the divine righteousness only by postulating a class of actions—indeterministically free actions—

that God cannot actualize but only weakly actualize[8] and that therefore he cannot govern in a positive sense, a sense required by universal and particular providence. Currently many who opt for this position—the compatibility of divine omniscience and human freedom—opt for Molinism, some version of the idea of middle knowledge.

If one accepts the distinction between God's free knowledge, natural knowledge and middle knowledge, then there are, in my view, two principal areas of concern with Molinism. The first is whether the idea of divine middle knowledge of free human actions is possible (a doubt raised by Robert Adams, among others); the second is how God performs the feat of actualizing possible worlds that include libertarian actions without thereby infringing such freedom. Let us suppose God knows that "if A were to be placed in circumstances C, he would freely do X." Then since God has no control over the truth of such counterfactuals, how exactly does God actualize this item of his middle knowledge, should he wish to? What exactly is it to actualize, even to "weakly" actualize, such a possible state of affairs?

The picture one gets from this is of God's knowing all possible worlds, including those that allegedly contain counterfactuals of freedom. These worlds have, so to speak, already run their courses, for they are complete, filled out in every detail. They are, we may suppose, exhaustively describable by a set of unconditional propositions. So the counterfactuals of freedom such worlds may initially be thought to contain are not really counterfactual; what is conditional is the possible world, not bits of it. It is as if God is in his video library, viewing all the videos. For reasons best known to himself, he is attracted to one particular video, the video with you and me in it, just as we are in fact. It is as if he says, by a decision fraught with enormous consequences for us all, "Let it be in fact as this video depicts it to be," knowing (by his omniscience) its most intimate detail. It is as if the videos are accounts of what already has happened in innumerable possible worlds. (How could it be otherwise, if God has full descriptions of them all?) God decides to actualize one such world—to run it, so to speak, or perhaps to rerun it. The problem is how, if each video is a complete description of a possible world, does thinking of God's relation to possible worlds in this way help us to preserve both providence and libertarian freedom? And how does it help with providence and evil? I conclude that Molinism is not a viable way of preserving divine righteousness in the face of evil but that God's righteousness can be preserved in another way.

---

[8]In Alvin Plantinga's terminology, God weakly actualizes what he cannot cause to be actual. See Alvin Plantinga, *The Nature of Necessity* (Oxford: Clarendon, 1974), p. 173.

Let us suppose what is not too difficult: that some human acts are evil. Could such evil actions as these be foreknown by an essentially righteous God? According to both Augustinians and Molinists, they could be. But I have offered a reason to reject Molinism. Yet does not invoking compatibilism (and not middle knowledge) as the reason why God knows all future free actions mean that God is the author of evil? No, the occurrence of evil is consistent with essential strong omniscience, even aside from the Molinist option, because while God could not positively govern evil acts he nevertheless can infallibly know of their occurrence. Although God is not the cause of evil actions, nevertheless evil actions have causes that God can know of and, if he is strongly omniscient, does know of. So God is essentially strongly omniscient with respect both to those acts that he brings about and to all other events the bringing about of which is inconsistent with his essential righteousness.

But how does God know of the causes of evil actions if he himself is not the cause of them? Augustine's answer is that God foreknows future evil by knowingly and willingly permitting particular evil actions. For God to permit some event to occur does not entail that he brings that event about, but it is consistent with his foreknowledge of such events. God does not and can not will evil actions, but he may nevertheless know that they will occur and be willing for them to occur. In permitting evil in this way God acts for the highest and holiest reasons even though the detail of such reasons may be at present hidden from us. But is not one who is willing for an evil action to occur the cause of that action, or at least an accessory, and so himself evil, despite his good intentions? Shortly I wish to present two alternative arguments for thinking not. But first, before we look at these arguments, it is necessary to get clearer on the meaning of willing permission.

The nature of such permission is well expressed by Augustine:

> In a way unspeakably strange and wonderful, even what is done in opposition to His will does not defeat His will. For it would not be done did he not permit it (and of course His permission is not unwilling but willing); nor would a Good Being permit evil to be done only that in his omnipotence He can turn evil into good.[9]

So for X willingly to permit an action *A* is at least this: for *A* to be the action of someone other than X; for X to foreknow the occurrence of *A* and to have

---

[9] Augustine *Enchiridion on Faith, Hope and Love*, trans. J. F. Shaw (Chicago: Henry Regnery, 1961), p. 117; cf. pp. 33, 110.

been able to prevent *A;* and for *A* not to be against X's overall plan. So on this conception God foreknows everything and unconditionally governs everything, but he does not causally determine everything in the sense that he is the efficient cause of everything, though everything that happens has sets of efficient or deficient causes in a way consistent with compatibilist accounts of human actions. Nevertheless, nothing happens that God is unwilling should happen.

How can such willing permission be consistent with both compatibilism and the occurrence of evil actions of which God is not the author? Let us consider an illustration. Suppose that my young daughter is learning to ride a bicycle and that in order to help her retain her balance I hold onto the bicycle seat from behind. Her action on the bicycle and my steadying hand are together causally sufficient for her to maintain her course. But suppose that, in a moment of inadvertence, I take my hand from the seat, and as a result of this she crashes into the wall. There is a causally sufficient story that can be told of the crash in terms of her action together with my omission. In the case of evil actions God may be said, in a similar fashion, to withhold his steadying hand. He does not do so inadvertently but for ends that are entirely consistent with his character but most of which are presently hidden from us. Human nature being what it is, evil results. If one asks how human nature can come to have an inclination to evil in a world created by a wholly good God, then Augustinianism, in common with all other views that are faced with such a question, does not have a satisfactory answer.

For the incompatibilist has no satisfactory explanation of how it is that individuals created by a good God, with moral and spiritual characters of an appropriate kind, can nevertheless, by acts of their free will, choose evil. Invoking incompatibilism at this point does not explain the occurrence of evil in a world created by a good God any more than does the Augustinian account of God's willingly permitting evil in a world created very good. Accounting for the arrival of evil in a world created good by God is a problem faced by all Christians who take the idea of a fall seriously. In contrast to the incompatibilist, the Augustinian says that the removal of God's hand led to the encroachment of evil—to the operation of a causal force arising from a deficiency—that God is not and could not himself be the author of, though he willingly permits it. Such an account, though perfectly consistent, is not an explanation of how evil came to be desired by people created in God's image.

One might supplement this argument with an appeal to the principle of simplicity or economy of explanation. By appealing to simplicity in explanation, one is led to posit as few entities as possible. I believe that a Christian theism that accounts for the onset of evil in terms of an omniscient, omnipotent God and a compatibilist account of human action—even as it recognizes the unresolved problem of the entry of evil into a universe created good and its attractiveness to men and women made good—is preferable (on the grounds of simplicity) to a system of thought that grants God lesser omniscience and omnipotence and that invokes the mysterious faculty of incompatibilistic freedom while leaving the problems of evil's entry and its attractiveness unresolved. A compatibilist account of human action is simpler than an account that invokes incompatibilism because it extends the idea of causal explanations of events, which all recognize is fundamental to natural science, into the realm of human action. One should prefer a simpler hypothesis that provides an explanation equivalent to the explanation given by the more complex hypothesis even if the simpler hypothesis has the same problems as those found in the more complex hypothesis.[10]

One might also invoke simplicity in explanation as an argument against Molinism. If an account that requires God to have only two kinds of knowledge can explain the question of God, human freedom and evil as well as an account that requires God to have three kinds of knowledge, then, other things being equal, the simpler hypothesis is to be preferred.

God knows all future actions and positively governs all acts that are not evil.[11] How exactly he does this raises other questions that we cannot address in detail (though I will make some brief comments later). He governs all other acts, evil acts, by permitting them, since he cannot positively govern them. However, if such permission is to be consistent with God's knowledge of the future, then it has to be a particular kind of permission: it has to be knowingly and willingly given, and it has to be permission of particular actions.[12] The willing permission governs particular action tokens.

So a God who is essentially strongly omniscient positively governs all acts

---

[10]There might be a counterargument to this appeal to simplicity arising from the existence of physical randomness: objective single-case chances such as quantum mechanical probabilities that seem to be inherent to very small-scale processes. But indeterminists usually think of human free choice not as a case of such randomness but as a different kind of happening susceptible to explanation of a distinctive, noncausal kind. Such microindeterminism, if true, does of course mean that our universe is not totally physically deterministic, though it does not necessarily mean that physically uncaused events are causeless *tout court*.

[11]I suspect that such a position requires a distinction between actions which are obligatory, forbidden and permissible, and so would be inconsistent with forms of consequentialism in ethics.

[12]There are problems about the individuation of actions, and the relation of an action's description to its identity is important. I shall assume that these difficulties can be overcome and that it is possible for an act to have more than one individuating description.

that occur except those which are evil, and he negatively governs evil acts by knowingly and willingly permitting them.

One may, therefore, make sense of the idea of divine permission in a way that is consistent with both upholding the divine righteousness and recognizing the existence of evil if one is prepared to maintain that there are types of actions which God can prevent but which he nevertheless cannot cause, even though he may be willing for them to occur and even though those actions have causes that are sufficient for their occurrence in the compatibilist sense. Then God can only control an evil action by knowingly and willingly permitting it, by deciding not to prevent it; and the evil action occurs because it is caused by the natures and circumstances of those who perpetrate it, not by God (because God cannot cause it), though God willingly permits it. (For though God cannot cause it, he can willingly permit it, and he does so, we might presume, as a necessary component part of some broader overall will.) As already noted, one is still left with the questions of exactly why God willingly permitted evil and exactly how evil comes about in a world created by an all-good God. But these questions, surely among the most fundamental of all theological questions, have to be faced by other accounts of God's relation to evil.

So God may knowingly and willingly permit an evil act. Indeed, for an evil act to occur—since God cannot perform an evil act—he must have willingly permitted it to do so; and if he is omniscient, he must have knowingly and willingly permitted it.[13]

Objections to Argument 2

But one still may insist—somewhat implausibly, it seems to me—that if God knowingly and willingly permits action *A*, then God is the cause of *A*. So let us now consider a number of arguments against this claim.[14]

(i) Divine determinism? First, we will address the claim that an appeal to divine willing in the sense defined is a case of divine determinism. Here it is important to have in mind a point made earlier: that the relation between God and his universe is sui generis. This relation has a character that is basically incomprehensible, that our human models and analogies cannot fully capture.

---

[13]It may be said that God suffers loss in the case of any action that is evil (e.g., he suffers the loss of being disobeyed) but that he does not suffer loss as a result of being taken by surprise.

[14]God is, of course, an accessory to the evil. But as God is an accessory to evil in many other accounts of God's relation to evil (e.g., the free-will defense) and as being an accessory is (in any case) a legal term of art, this hardly amounts to a serious objection.

It is tempting, but I believe crude and misleading, to assimilate the working of such knowing and willing permission to intramundane models of causation, and particularly to general physical determinism. Such knowing and willing permission has this in common with determinism: that what is physically determined and what is willingly permitted will each, in virtue of the determinism and the willing permission, come to pass. However, to knowingly and willingly permit an action is not to cause that action; it is to provide a necessary but not sufficient causal condition for the action. Whereas physical determinism has a strong tendency to be reductionistic and has difficulty in finding a place for a range of objects having their own causal powers, the divine willing permission is most certainly not reductionist in this sense.

Hence it is a serious mistake to suppose that classical Christian theism claims that God monopolizes power. According to Augustine, "As He is the Creator of all natures, so is He of all powers: but not the giver of all wills; for wicked wills are not of Him, being against that nature which is of Him."[15] God is the source of all creaturely power, but the powers of creatures, even when efficaciously empowered by God, are really their own and so are distinct from his. If God efficaciously empowers me to type this paper, the typing of this paper is still my action, not God's. The wicked men who crucified Jesus were the cause of his death, even though he was crucified by the determinate counsel and foreknowledge of God (Acts 2:23).

One way of expressing this difference might be as follows. While it seems clear that intramundane causation is transitive—given events A, B and C, if A causes B, and B causes C, then A causes C—there is no necessary transitivity in the case of any causal aspects or features of the divine knowing and willing permission.[16] It is thus not necessarily the case that if God governs by knowingly and willingly permitting some event B, and B causes C, then God causes C; rather God may will by permitting that B causes C and so knowingly and willingly permit C. God's willing permission is thus not a straightforward case of intramundane causation, and those who seek to assimilate God's knowing and willing permission of evil to the actions of someone manipulating a puppet, or to hypnotism, or to brainwashing or programming, have not recognized the truly unique character of such permission.

Alternatively, one may allow that while God is the primary cause of all events that occur, even of all evil acts, he is not and cannot be the secondary

---

[15]Augustine *The City of God* 5.9, trans. John Healey (London: Dent, 1945).
[16]There are presumably some causal features if wicked people are upheld and conserved in their being by God.

cause of any evil act because he is not the secondary cause of any act. But this requirement as it stands is almost certainly too strong; it seems to have the deistic consequence that God cannot directly act in the world that he has created. One may modify this requirement to allow that God is the secondary cause of some acts, which is consistent with his being the secondary cause of morally indifferent acts and of morally good acts. The exact scope of what God causes and what he permits does not matter here, provided that we are clear that he cannot cause evil.

Those who hold that God knowingly and willingly governs whatever comes to pass may nevertheless make a distinction, within that overall government, between what God causes and what he permits. William Hasker says that the central idea of Calvinism is quite simple: "Everything that happens, with no exceptions, is efficaciously determined by God in accordance with his eternal decrees."[17] But we have seen, I hope, there is reason to doubt that the central idea of Calvinism need be as Hasker says it is, without surrendering God's universal and particular providence. To say that each particular action is providentially governed by God is not to say that everything is efficaciously determined by God, though it may be to say that everything that occurs is endorsed by God.

So there are ways of preserving the integrity of the divine righteousness in the case of human acts that are morally evil, namely the idea that God willingly permits particular evil actions, in the sense understood. It is possible that God knowingly governs whatever comes to pass, and it is plausible (if God is omnipotent and omniscient) to suppose that he does so. If, for any event E, E occurs, then God knowingly governs E either by knowingly bringing it about or being knowingly willing for it to occur. Whatever occurs, occurs because God knowingly governs it in this sense; whatever is true in virtue of what occurs is true because God so governs it. So saying that all events are knowingly governed by God, while it entails that all events are intended by God, is not equivalent to asserting that, for any event E, if E occurs, then God has caused it.

Just as many argue in developing a freewill defense that not even God can ensure that a free agent only does what is morally right, so the Augustinian argues that there is no possible world in which the righteous God can be the author of evil. He may, however, willingly permit evil; that is, he may actualize that possible world in which he foreknows that Jones will do a particular evil

---

[17] Clark Pinnock et al., *The Openness of God* (Downers Grove, Ill.: InterVarsity Press, 1994), p. 141.

act.[18] This is an instance of *particular* permission—God permits particular acts—which is distinct from *general* permission, as when a teacher permits a class to write an essay on any topic they choose. And God may give such particular permission willingly, not because he is willing for the evil act to occur per se but because he ordains some wider good of which that act is a necessary part. God's willing permission of evil may in many cases be like the willingness of a parent to allow one of her children to undergo some extremely painful but necessary course of treatment, say the removal of a vital organ, to ensure the survival of another of her children, say by transplanting the removed organ into that child. So also God may willingly permit some particular evil action for some further good, though of course he does so without any of the feelings of psychological pressure or tension that accompany such human permittings.

So does it follow from such knowing and willing permission of evil that the universe is in every detail as God intends it to be?[19] This is an interesting question, but it is unclear as it stands. There is no reason to think that God intends the details of the universe separately; there is one divine will, which encompasses all events. It would be fallacious to suppose that the divine attitude is the same with respect to every detail of what God wills; for one thing, as we have already seen, God is the efficacious cause of some events and willingly permits others.

As Aquinas put it, "God, and nature, and indeed every causal agent, does what is best overall, but not what is best in every part, except when the part is regarded in its relationship to the whole."[20] We may suppose that when God knowingly and willingly permits certain events he does so in furtherance of some wider consideration wholly consistent with his character with respect to which they are a logically necessary condition. And likewise some of those things which he causes are means to some further end. It is a fallacy to think that because some arrangement is wise, every detail of that arrangement, considered in isolation, is wise. It does not follow that every thread of my tartan tie is tartan.

(ii) Fatalism? A second objection is that this view is a species of fatalism. But it is certainly not logical fatalism, since the universe is the outcome not of some principle of logic alone but of the divine creative and providential will,

---

[18]Such foreknowledge cannot be a case of middle knowledge, since I have rejected the appeal to middle knowledge.
[19]This issue is raised by Keith Ward, *Religion and Creation* (Oxford: Clarendon, 1996), p. 219.
[20]Thomas Aquinas *Summa Theologica* 1.48.2, reply 3.

which, we may assume, is logically contingent and either causal or willingly permissive in its operation.

(iii) God cannot respond. A third objection is that on such a view God cannot be responsive to what occurs in the universe, and hence the position entails some version of deism.

Within the one creative and providential will of God it is possible to distinguish those aspects that are unconditional or unilateral from those that are conditional and bilateral. Unconditional aspects are of the form "Let X be," whereas conditional aspects are of the form "Given W, let X be" (where W is brought about by someone other than the one uttering the statement). An example of the first might be "Let the planet Earth be"; an example of the second "If A sins, let him be forgiven." However, we must interpret these conditional expressions in the light of the place of conditions in the overall will of God.

We find an element of conditionality about God's willing permission of such evil, since necessarily he is not the author of it. Nonetheless as Creator he upholds the perpetrator of the evil and knowingly and willingly permits the occurrence of the evil. So the way to understand such conditional aspects of God's overall willing is not as God's response to what he has merely foreseen will happen, but as his response to what he has both foreseen and been willing to permit: for instance, that A will sin. That is, God wills to permit the evil and wills the consequence. He wills evil by willing to permit it, willing it in such a way that he is not himself the author of the evil, which he could not be, while he may will what is not evil by being the author of it, by bringing it about. There is a crucial distinction between a willing of conditionals and a conditional will. God may infallibly know all truths, including all conditional truths, and he may know what his response to the antecedents of some of these conditional truths is. But it does not follow from this that his knowledge is conditional knowledge. God's knowledge that C will happen if A does B need not depend upon his first knowing the conditional "If A does B, then C will happen" and then deciding that because person A does B, God will bring about C.

Argument 3: The Incompatibility of Divine Foreknowledge and Human Freedom

So far I have argued for the Augustinian view that divine foreknowledge and human free action are consistent, understanding human freedom in a compatibilist sense, on the grounds that it is required by the Christian idea of efficacious grace and that it does better justice to the idea of divine omniscience than do some rival accounts. Its main rival, Molinism, has a fundamental difficulty. In presenting these arguments I acknowledge that all accounts of divine and human action face the common problem of accounting for how evil could first occur in a universe created good by a good God.

I turn now to my third argument for the view that human libertarian freedom is unnecessary for a Christian understanding of the relation between divine and human activity. As far as I am aware, although this is not an argument to be found in Augustine's own writings,[21] the conclusion is consistent with a broadly Augustinian position.[22] This is an argument to the conclusion that divine omniscience and human incompatibilist freedom are logically inconsistent. If this is a sound argument and if divine omniscience (in the strong sense in which we have been advocating it) is essential to God's nature, and therefore nonnegotiable for the Christian, then libertarian freedom is inconsistent with it. And if libertarian freedom is inconsistent with divine omniscience and if human sin occurs, then libertarian freedom cannot be necessary for an account of the Christian view of sin and salvation. Once I have offered this argument, I shall end my contribution by considering a couple of objections to it.

Here is the argument: Let us suppose that statement *p*, "Jones will freely eat a tuna sandwich tomorrow," is true and that "freely eat" means "freely eat in accordance with the tenets of human libertarian or incompatibilist freedom." Let us assume that it follows from this that if God were strongly omniscient in the sense that we have been advocating earlier, then God would foreknow that Jones will freely eat a tuna sandwich tomorrow.

Let us suppose, to be more precise, that God foreknew yesterday that Jones will freely eat a tuna sandwich tomorrow. (For the present we are waiving consideration of issues relating to God and time and for the moment are supposing that God is in time.) God's foreknowledge of what Jones will do tomorrow is something that is now past, for he foreknew yesterday what Jones will do. And if that foreknowledge is now past, then it is necessary. It is not logically necessary, since God need never have known about Jones since Jones himself need not have existed. But it is what is sometimes called accidentally or historically necessary. Given that God knew yesterday what Jones will do tomorrow, then God cannot not know. This is because, and on the assumption that, time

---

[21]Note also that Calvin explicitly allows that divine foreknowledge, considered in the abstract, may be consistent with human freedom. "I will freely admit that foreknowledge alone imposes no necessity upon creatures, yet not all assent to this" (Calvin *Institutes* 3.23.6).

[22]Though if Aquinas is regarded as an Augustinian, he can be found rejecting this particular argument. But Aquinas's Augustinianism is decidedly wobbly in places, in my view.

is linear and what has happened cannot now not have happened. We shall return to this crucial point in a moment.

Let us turn our attention to the idea of knowledge. We may say this about the concept of knowledge, that it is necessarily the case that if B knows that q (whatever q is, and whoever B is), then q is true. If someone, anyone, knows that q, then q is true. This is a definitional point, setting out a part of the definition, or a necessary consequence of the definition, of knowledge. (As such it is open to anyone to reject this definition and to use one's own. But this is a widespread and common definition of knowledge and is certainly a definition that accords with basic theological accounts of God's knowledge.) Note that this claim—that if it is necessarily the case that if B knows that q, then q is true—must be distinguished from this claim: If B knows that q, then q is necessarily true. This latter claim certainly does not follow from the concept of knowledge that we are employing here. It does not follow that because I know I am typing at my word processor, then I am necessarily typing at my processor, for I could have chosen not to word-process but, say, to go for a swim instead. So we may say, "Necessarily, if B knows that q, then q" (but not "If B knows that q, then necessarily q.")

So, returning to the argument, we have God's knowledge yesterday that Jones will eat a tuna sandwich tomorrow, knowledge that is accidentally or historically necessary, and we have it being the case that necessarily, what God knows is true. Now it is a well-known theorem in modal logic that if it is necessarily the case that s (necessarily the case now that God knew yesterday that Jones will eat the tuna sandwich tomorrow) and if it is necessarily the case that s entails t (as it is necessarily the case that God's knowledge yesterday that Jones will eat a tuna sandwich tomorrow entails that Jones will eat the sandwich), then it is necessarily the case that Jones will eat the tuna sandwich tomorrow.

This argument may seem slightly complicated, but the basic thought behind it is easy to grasp. The argument is this: if there is something in the past that entails something in the future and if what is past is necessary—accidentally or historically necessary—then what is entailed is similarly accidentally or historically necessary. The necessity of the past is transferred to or transmitted to whatever the past itself entails. In the case under consideration, what the past (God's knowledge yesterday) entails is that Jones will eat his sandwich tomorrow. And since the past is necessary, accidentally necessary, then what it entails (Jones's eating the tuna sandwich tomorrow) is similarly necessary. Therefore, given that God's foreknowledge of p is past and so necessary and given that necessarily if God knows that p then p is true, it follows that what is known, *p,* is itself necessary.

If this is so, then Jones's putative free act of choosing the sandwich must necessarily occur and therefore cannot be free. But if this is so, then divine omniscience is inconsistent with human incompatibilist freedom.

Arguments of this type have been subject to considerable philosophical scrutiny over the years, and objections have been raised to them. So I shall now consider three sorts of objection to this type of argument, objections frequently made but ones that seem to me to be unconvincing.

Objections to Argument 3

(i) Divine timeless eternity. One standard objection to this argument is based upon an appeal to divine timeless eternity:[23] timelessly eternal God does not, strictly speaking, foreknow anything. His knowledge is never, strictly speaking, necessary in virtue of being past, since it is never past.

So on this view of God's relation to time, if God is timelessly strongly omniscient, then there timelessly exists in the divine mind a specification of all events, including all free actions at present future to us, but none of these items is foreknown by God. And this, it is said, rules out the argument from foreknowledge that we have just deployed.

However, let us suppose that God has already publicly inscripted (on a rock or piece of parchment in a cave in the Middle East) one specification in his mind of an action that is future to us now, namely, "Jones will freely eat a tuna sandwich tomorrow."[24] (Think of the idea of biblical prophecy in this connection.) Let's call the inscription "A." It is composed of the proposition "Jones will freely eat a tuna sandwich *x* days after this inscription is made," and the

---

[23]Boethius *The Consolation of Philosophy* 5.6: "His knowledge, too, transcends all temporal change and abides in the immediacy of His presence. It embraces all the infinite recesses of past and future and views them in the immediacy of its knowing as though they are happening in the present. If you wish to consider, then, the foreknowledge or prevision by which He discovers all things, it will be more correct to think of it not as a kind of foreknowledge of the future, but as the knowledge of a never ending presence." Aquinas *Summa Theologica* 1A.14.13: "Now although contingent events come into actual existence successively, God does not, as we do, know them in their actual existence successively, but all at once; because his knowledge is measured by eternity, as is also his existence; and eternity, which exists as a simultaneous whole, takes in the whole of time, as we have said above. Hence all that takes place in time is eternally present to God. . . . It is clear, then, that contingent events are known infallibly by God because they are the objects of the divine gaze in their presence to him; while on the other hand they are future contingent events in relation to their proximate causes."

[24]Aquinas would allow the general principle that a timelessly eternal God could will a change; see, e.g., *Summa Theologica* 1A.19.7: "The conclusion to this argument is not that God's will changes, but that he wills change."

inscription is suitably dated. It is certainly possible for there to be such an inscription, and since we do not know that such an inscription has not in fact been made, then for all we know "A" has been inscribed.

But now let us consider the character of such an inscription. It is the result of some divine action. And if we suppose it has occurred, then that inscription, if it has occurred, will now be past and therefore necessary, accidentally necessary—necessary in the sense that it is in the past and, so, over and done with. It cannot now be the case that the inscription has not been made if in fact it has been made. But now the dated inscription consists of a certain proposition "Jones will eat a tuna sandwich so many days after this inscription has been made." This inscription is made by an omniscient and infallible God (we are supposing), and the content of that inscription—the truth that it asserts, namely that Jones will eat a tuna sandwich at such and such a date—is also accidentally necessary. For the proposition expressed in the inscription cannot now be false. Hence it is necessary, accidentally necessary, that Jones eat the tuna sandwich on such and such a day, and hence Jones cannot be incompatibilistically free not to eat the sandwich on that day. So the cognitive content of the inscription cannot be that Jones incompatibilistically freely eats a tuna sandwich tomorrow. Therefore, Jones is not now free not to eat a tuna sandwich tomorrow. So if, for all we know, timeless omniscience is not consistent with human freedom, then we cannot know that timeless omniscience and human freedom are consistent. Therefore the appeal to timelessness is not sufficient to establish the consistency of divine omniscience and human freedom. This is my reply to the first objection.

(ii) Hard and soft facts. Another current objection to this argument is based upon the claim that some facts about the past are not wholly about the past (these are called "soft" facts). These facts carry implications for the future and so are not accidentally necessary; for in order for such facts to be true, certain claims about the future must also be true. Only facts that are wholly about the past are "hard" facts. And, it is claimed, a fact such as our fact about the past inscription "Jones will eat a tuna sandwich so many days after this inscription has been made" is not wholly about the past, since it is partly, at least, about the future, namely about the time when, according to the inscription, Jones will eat a tuna sandwich. Accordingly, whether or not it is true depends upon whether Jones will in fact eat the tuna sandwich.

One problem with the objection is that the distinction between hard and soft facts is itself not a very clear one, for it would seem that any fact entails some fact or other about the future.[25] The fact that Caesar is now dead implies that Caesar will not be eating breakfast tomorrow. However, we may let this point pass and assume that there are soft facts. Is God's knowledge about Jones such a soft fact? There are at least two reasons to think not. In the first place, God's belief about Jones is one of innumerable beliefs that he holds infallibly, being part of his essential omniscience. So if any of his beliefs were falsified, then he would cease to be God; and so Jones, by his freedom, would have power to bring it about that God did not exist. And this seems to be implausible.

In the second place, we may suppose that God's believing that Jones will eat a tuna sandwich tomorrow involves his mind's being in a certain state akin to the states our minds are in when we believe that Jones will eat a tuna sandwich tomorrow.

Surely nothing can now bring it about that God did not believe that Jones will eat a tuna sandwich tomorrow (if in fact God did believe this). So although this belief of God's has certain features that may make it a soft fact (if indeed there are such facts)—chiefly the feature that it is a belief about the future—it has other features that suggest it is a hard fact. It may be, as John Martin Fischer puts it, a soft fact that is nevertheless fixed by the fixity of the past. It is a hard-core soft fact. To deprive God of such a belief, Jones would have to bring it about that some hard fact about the past was not such a fact, which he manifestly cannot do.[26] The idea of God actually inscribing his belief is intended to make this point vivid.

Perhaps the objection from the hard-fact-soft-fact distinction is sound against divine foreknowledge, but it is not sound against divine forebelief, since (as we saw) for something to be a case of knowledge what is known has to be true. But this is not so in the case of a belief. A belief is still a belief even if it is false. But in the case of God it is necessarily the case that his beliefs are

---

[25]For example, "Christopher Columbus discovered America in 1492" is cited as a hard fact about the past, whereas "Christopher Columbus discovered America 507 years before the writing of this paper" is a soft fact. Philosophers have found it difficult to give a satisfactory distinction between hard and soft facts. Plantinga proposes the following criterion: "No proposition that entails that Paul will mow his lawn in 1999 is a hard fact about the past." John Martin Fischer distinguishes between temporal relationality and nonrelationality (hardness and softness) and fixity and nonfixity (being out of one's control and being in one's control). See John Martin Fischer, *The Metaphysics of Free Will* (Cambridge, Mass.: Blackwell, 1994), p. 115. Given this distinction, perhaps I am arguing that in the example from the argument, God's belief about what Jones will do in the future is soft (for it is relational) and yet fixed for Jones, because for all we know, it has a cognitive content that is true, because all God's beliefs must be true. The hard-fact-soft-fact distinction has been the subject of detailed and sometimes tortuous debate.

[26]For further details, see Fischer, *Metaphysics of Free Will,* chap. 6. I am indebted to Fischer for providing a way of handling the hard-fact-soft-fact objection.

all true. So Jones cannot by any act bring it about that God did not have the belief that he had and that God's beliefs are (in virtue of his omniscience and infallibility) necessarily true.

(iii) Molinism again. It might be said that God could, by his middle knowledge, know what Jones would freely do when Jones was placed in certain circumstances and that God choose to instantiate a world in which Jones is placed in these circumstances. This would mean that God's foreknowledge of what Jones will do was a logical consequence of his knowing what Jones will freely do and, hence, that Jones's freedom is preserved. On this account what God's foreknowledge records is his knowledge of what Jones will freely do. But we have already found reason to reject Molinism. If this reason is cogent, or if others are, then this objection loses its force.

Conclusion

This concludes my exposition of the broadly Augustinian case for holding that it is reasonable to believe that divine foreknowledge and human freedom are consistent, where this freedom is understood in a compatibilist sense, in a sense that is consistent with causal determinism. The argument that I have presented is a cumulative one, consisting of three strands. Firstly, that only such an account of human freedom is logically consistent with divine efficacious grace; causal indeterminism therefore has serious adverse theological consequences. Secondly, that this account does full justice to divine omniscience and is simpler than its closest rivals. And finally, that there is reason to think that in any case divine foreknowledge and human incompatibilism are logically inconsistent. I realize that I have not answered all objections that may be made to these arguments any more than I have made all the serious objections to the rival views. But it is hoped that the dialogue with the various other contributors to this book will afford some opportunity to make good some, at least, of these deficiencies.

AN OPEN-THEISM RESPONSE

Gregory A. Boyd

I shall begin with a significant point on which Paul Helm and I are in agreement, over and against William Lane Craig and David Hunt, and then I will discuss two points on which Helm and I disagree.

God's Infallible Beliefs and the Necessity of the Past

Craig spent a good portion of his essay attempting to establish the compatibility of libertarian freedom and exhaustively definite foreknowledge[1] by exposing the fallacy of the following argument:

  (1) Necessarily, if God foreknows x, then x will happen.
  (2) God foreknows x.
  (3) Therefore, x will necessarily happen.

---

[1] I say "exhaustively *definite* foreknowledge" because this view holds that the total content of God's exhaustive knowledge of the future is definite. The open view holds that God's knowledge of the future is exhaustive but not *exhaustively definite*, because in our view the future consists not only of definite facts but also of indefinite possibilities.

Craig is correct in concluding that this argument is fallacious, for it transfers the logical necessity of the knower (God) to the known *(x)*. What Helm establishes, however, is that exposing the fallacy of this argument doesn't go far in proving that libertarian freedom is compatible with exhaustively definite foreknowledge. For the "necessity" that renders Craig's (and Hunt's) position problematic is not a logical necessity, but an "accidental" or "historical" necessity. This is the kind of necessity possessed by past events. Though past events are *logically* contingent, they are *historically* necessary, for they cannot *now* be other than they are.

The problem with Craig and Hunt's position is that if God eternally foreknows future free acts, then future free acts are "accidentally" or "historically" necessary. Among all the unalterable facts of the past is the content of what God infallibly believes *shall come to pass in the future*. The definiteness of the future is part of the (now necessary) definiteness of the past. Hence, I agree with Helm that if God possesses exhaustively definite foreknowledge, we can exercise no more libertarian freedom with regard to our future acts than we can with regard to any past fact. Both are "accidentally necessary."

Of course, Helm and I differ sharply on how we apply this argument. Helm grants that God possesses exhaustively definite foreknowledge and so denies we have libertarian freedom. I rather affirm that we have libertarian freedom but deny that God possesses exhaustively definite foreknowledge (more on this below). But we agree that this argument exposes a logical difficulty in views such as Craig's and Hunt's, arguments that wish to affirm both exhaustively definite foreknowledge and libertarian freedom.

On the "Anthropomorphic" Nature of "Openness" Passages

The first disagreement I have with Helm's essay concerns his "metaphorical" interpretation of certain passages of Scripture. Helm begins his essay by arguing that "the scriptural worldview is one in which all things are created by God and ordered and governed by him. . . . He turns the hearts of humans as he wishes; like a potter, he has power over human clay" (p. 164). Helm acknowledges that some Scripture seems to stand in tension with this conclusion, for sometimes God is said to be "surprised and to act and react toward his people in blessing and chastisement" (p. 164). In such cases, Helm argues, we are to recognize that Scripture is using "metaphorical or symbolic language, language 'accommodated' to some human situation or need" (p. 164).

The passages Helm has in mind are precisely the passages on which I build much of my case for a partly open future, and the way he explains them (viz., as metaphorical) is precisely the way most classical theists explain them. This hermeneutic is not unproblematic, however. I touched on this issue in my opening essay, but since this constitutes the central biblical objection to my position, it seems expedient to briefly expand on my response to this objection here.

First, as I mentioned in my opening essay, there is nothing in these texts themselves that suggest the authors intended their statements to be read anthropomorphically. Passages that say or depict God as changing his mind, as regretting decisions, as searching hearts "to know" what is in them, and so on, are written as straightforward reports—no different from (say) passages that say that God declares the end from the beginning (Is 46:10) or that God so loved the world that he sent his Son (Jn 3:16). The two passages that are most frequently cited in support of the classical view that God cannot change his mind (Num 23:19; 1 Sam 15:29) do not suggest that God *cannot* recant or change his mind, only that in certain cases he *will not* do so (cf. Jer 15:6; Ezek 24:14; Zech 8:14).

Second, reinterpreting the passages that constitute the motif of future openness as "metaphorical" does not *clarify* these passages: it *undermines* them. We may grant that all God's revelatory language is "accommodated" to our human condition, and we may grant that God sometimes uses metaphors, symbols and anthropomorphisms to accomplish this task. But this nonliteral language accomplishes this task because *it communicates something truthful about God.* But what does saying that God regrets decisions he makes or that he changes his mind truthfully communicate about God if in fact God never regrets his decisions or changes his mind? What does God's reporting to us that he thinks of the future in terms of what might or might not happen (e.g., Ex 13:17; Jer 3:7, 19-20) truly reveal to us if in fact God never really thinks about the future in terms of what might or might not happen? If God in truth doesn't ever change his mind, regret decisions or think in subjunctive terms, then saying he does so doesn't reveal anything true about God at all. It only misrepresents him.

Third, some have argued that advocates of a partly open future are guilty of naive literalism, which they inconsistently apply to the biblical text.[2] We wrongly interpret some but not all anthropomorphisms in a literal fashion. If we were consistent, it is argued, we would believe not only that God literally changes his mind, but also that God literally lacks present knowledge; literally has eyes, arms and a mouth; and literally travels to and from earth—for some

---

passages speak of God in these ways.

If this argument is valid, it can be used against all evangelicals, for all evangelicals take *some* things in Scripture literally (e.g., Jesus is the Savior of all who believe) and *other* things nonliterally (e.g., God has eyes or wings). The issue is not whether some of Scripture is literal and some nonliteral: all agree on this. The issue is why many evangelicals assume that the entire openness motif of Scripture is in the latter category rather than the former. Open theists simply find no exegetical, philosophical or theological warrant for this assumption.

The Difference Between a "Condition" and a "Cause"

A second major disagreement I have with Helm's essay concerns his view of salvation. Helm wagers a good deal of his case for the Calvinistic view of God on his argument that only Calvinism can consistently affirm that people are saved by grace alone. If we must exercise libertarian freedom in order to be saved, he argues, then we contribute something to our salvation. Hence we cannot say that we are saved totally by grace. Two points may be made in response to this argument.

First, if Helm is correct that God is the necessary and sufficient ground of salvation, then the ultimate reason why some are saved and some are not is because God himself chose to save some and not others. Unfortunately, this conclusion stands in tension with the uniform scriptural teaching that God's love is universal and impartial (Acts 10:34; cf. Deut 10:17-19; 2 Chron 19:7; Job 34:19; Is 55:4-5; Mk 12:14; Jn 3:16; Rom 2:10-11; Eph 6:9; 1 Pet 1:17). The Lord does not desire any one to perish, but rather he wants all people to repent and be saved (Ezek 18:23, 32; 33:11; 1 Tim 2:4; 4:10; 2 Pet 3:9). Hence Jesus died as "the atoning sacrifice for our sins, and not for ours only but also for the sins of the whole world" (1 Jn 2:2). If it was only up to God to choose who would be saved, we have every reason to believe *he would choose everyone.*

Second, there is simply no need to deny that humans can and must choose to accept God's offer of salvation in order to affirm that salvation is completely a matter of God's grace. Helm confuses a *condition* of salvation with a *cause* of salvation. If we in any sense *caused* God to save us by exercising faith, that would imply that we merit something from God and thus are not saved solely by grace. But this is not what freewill theists generally affirm or what Scripture teaches. Rather, we hold that salvation is graciously given *on the condition* that one places their trust in the one giving it. This no more makes salvation a merited reward than does my freely accepting a birthday gift makes this gift a reward.

Not only this, but most freewill theists believe that we fallen human beings would not even meet the condition of faith were it not for the gracious work of the Holy Spirit in our lives (see, e.g., Jn 6:44, 65; 1 Cor 12:3; Eph 2:8). We agree with Calvinists that we cannot have faith on our own. We simply reject the Calvinist view that the work of the Holy Spirit is irresistible. People can and do resist the Holy Spirit and thereby thwart the will of God for their lives (see, e.g., Is 63:10; Lk 7:30; Acts 7:51; Eph 4:30; Heb 3:8, 15; 4:7). Hence we affirm that if a person is saved, it is all to the glory of God, whereas if a person is damned, they have only themselves to blame.

A SIMPLE-FOREKNOWLEDGE RESPONSE

David Hunt

*P*aul Helm's principal concern is to argue that Christians should embrace a *compatibilist* account of human freedom. (Roughly, the compatibilist affirms, while the incompatibilist denies, that human freedom is *compatible with determinism.*) Helm offers three arguments for compatibilism, which I consider in reverse order.

Argument 3
The third argument is simply that divine foreknowledge, which Helm rightly regards as a "given," excludes the possibility of human agents' being free in anything other than a compatibilist sense. Since I have already argued against this conclusion at length in my defense of simple foreknowledge, I will not repeat the argument here.

I should, however, note the irony that Helm and I, while taking very different positions on this issue, nevertheless both claim the mantle of St. Augustine! Helm admits that he departs from the master at this point, inasmuch as neither Augustine *nor* Calvin thinks that divine foreknowledge (on its own, apart from considerations of divine grace and sovereignty) excludes incompatibilistic freedom. Since Jonathan Edwards *does* argue in his *Freedom of the Will* that divine foreknowledge by itself rules out incompatibilistic freedom, Helm's position is better labeled "Edwardsian." I naturally commend to Helm the genuinely Augustinian position I defend in my chapter!

Helm and I do share some common ground. We have very similar intuitions about the "Ockhamist" solution,[1] which we both reject. We also eschew the "Boethian" solution, though here our reasons differ. I do so because I want a solution that *also* solves the philosophical puzzle raised by infallible foreknowledge, and the Boethian denial of divine foreknowledge (because God knows things from an atemporal vantage point) simply exempts God from involvement in the puzzle without doing anything to solve it. Helm, however, thinks that Boethianism can't even do this much. I'm not so sure. A committed Boethian might resist Helm's "inscription argument" on the grounds that inscribed rocks and parchments aren't infallible—only God is infallible. (Ditto for cases in which God reveals the future to prophets.) But I won't press the point, since nothing I've argued gives me a stake in this controversy.

Argument 2

I found it very difficult to untangle the main thread of this argument; but I think now that its essential structure is this:

(1) It is theologically desirable that God foreknow his creatures' freely willed actions.

(2) If compatibilism is true, God can foreknow his creatures' freely willed actions.

∴ Compatibilism is true.

The first premise follows from Helm's principle *A,* according to which it is theologically desirable to maximize the scope of divine omniscience. Since I accept this principle, and (1) does follow from principle *A,* let's turn to (2). This premise also seems true, though the situation is complicated a bit by considerations of divine responsibility. When God foreknows a *good* exercise of

---

[1]What I refer to as "the Ockhamist solution" is the position Helm discusses and rejects (without reference to William Ockham) in the section "Hard and Soft Facts" of his main essay.

creaturely freedom, he does so by knowing his present intention to cause a good will in that creature; for God (as Helm sees it) is the source of all good, endowing us not only with *wills* but also with *good wills* (insofar as we have them). But God cannot foreknow *evil* actions by knowing his present intentions, since he is not the cause of evil. He must know future evils in some other way.

Helm suggests two such ways. First, he endorses universal causal determinism. For some things God is the sufficient cause; for everything else there are sufficient causes in the natural workings of this fallen world. It's the latter that must be causally sufficient for evil actions, since God cannot be their cause. So God can know future evil actions by knowing their natural (nondivine) causes. Second, Helm proposes that "God foreknows future evil by knowingly and willingly permitting particular evil actions" (p. 176). God doesn't cause evil actions and so is not responsible for them, but he permits them for reasons of his own.

Neither of these, by itself, can do the job. (The second, which presupposes foreknowledge in its explanation of foreknowledge, is circular.) But they appear to be *jointly* sufficient. In a deterministic universe in which only God is *causa sui,* God's knowledge of present causes tells him what will happen in the future *if he doesn't intervene,* while knowledge of what he has decided to "knowingly and willingly permit" tells him *whether* he will intervene (and if so, how). On this twin basis, God can predict absolutely everything. So premise (2) is true.

The problem with the argument is not the truth of its premises but the fact that the conclusion does not follow from the premises. (It commits the "fallacy of affirming the consequent.") To derive the conclusion validly, Helm needs a premise like this:

(2') If compatibilism *isn't* true, God *can't* foreknow his creatures' freely willed actions.

But Helm nowhere argues for anything like (2'). Indeed, Helm is the last of my coauthors one would expect to limit God's power without adequate explanation!

Not only does Helm fail to explain why other routes to divine foreknowledge are unavailable, but his assumption of universal causal determinism (without which Helm's God could not know future evils) is deeply problematic. The problem of how we can be genuinely responsible for our sins if determinism is true is best postponed until the next section. But two other problems bear brief mention here.

First, Helm invokes "the principle of simplicity or economy of explanation," which favors (he believes) a "compatibilist account of human action" on the grounds that it "extends the idea of causal explanations of events, which all recognize is fundamental to natural science, into the realm of human action" (pp. 177-78). But why should we, as Christians, want to do this? Explanatory economy is enhanced when the number of fundamental explanatory-types is reduced—say, by abandoning animistic explanation or by reducing biological explanation to chemical explanation. Now presumably *divine* action is not to be explained in terms of mechanistic event-causation (God isn't a cog in the universal clockwork); so bringing human action under the explanatory umbrella of natural science does not eliminate the need for a second fundamental explanatory-type—call it "teleological agent-causation"—to cover divine acts like creation, the incarnation or the covenant with Israel. Since our creation "in the image of God" provides some prima facie justification for thinking that God endowed *us* with (limited) powers of teleological agent-causation—and denying ourselves such powers does nothing to advance the cause of explanatory economy (since divine actions would still require non-mechanistic explanation)—this argument for compatibilism fails. Indeed, the interests of simplicity and economy might be better served by going in the opposite direction. The causal laws that are so fundamental to natural science are, after all, decreed by God; they express his (uncaused) will that the created order should operate in this way. This suggests, contrary to Helm, that mechanistic explanation is ultimately reducible to teleological explanation.[2]

Second, if we *were* subject to universal causal determinism, why wouldn't God then be the ultimate cause of *all* our actions (and not just of our good actions)? After all, he created the initial state of the universe and the causal rules by which one state is succeeded by another state, and he foreknew just what would result from his setting things up this way. Unless he created *something* with the power to make an undetermined contribution to reality, God is the sufficient cause of absolutely everything—including our sins.

Argument 1

Helm's first argument against the libertarian conception of human freedom has nothing essentially to do with foreknowledge. It derives instead from an "appreciation of the plight of humankind and the power of God" (p. 169), an

---

[2]This idea is developed in different but complementary ways by Richard Swinburne, *The Existence of God* (Oxford: Oxford University Press, 1979), chap. 8, and by Del Ratzsch, "Nomo(theo)logical Necessity," *Faith and Philosophy* 4 (1987): 383-402.

appreciation that I share to a considerable degree.

This Augustinian view of God and humanity rests (in good Augustinian fashion) on three supports. One is biblical authority: all the passages (far too many even to begin to cite) that speak of divine sovereignty, the corrupting and even incapacitating effects of sin, our need for *salvation* rather than an ethical self-help program, and so on. There are also metaphysical considerations. Whereas God is a self-existent being, *I* am a wholly contingent being, formed of the dust of the ground, summoned out of nonexistence into a borrowed existence; when asked, "What do you have that you did not receive?" (1 Cor 4:7), I can only reply, "Nothing." Finally, this view has the support of honest self-examination. When tracing my actions back to their source, it's hard to arrive at my own "self" as the ultimate cause—especially when endeavoring to *credit* myself with some good deed! "There but for the grace of God go I" expresses a rueful and salutary recognition that I am not the self-dependent captain of my own soul.

If this Augustinian view is also *my* view, then why am I not in Helm's camp? For the simple reason that it constitutes only *part* of the picture. Given just an Augustinian "appreciation of the plight of humankind and the power of God," it might be possible to think that all my actions are the result of external (divine or natural) causes. But this overlooks another important part of the biblical picture, namely, *personal responsibility* for the choices we make in life.

If universal causal determinism is true, then before I was even born there were already in place conditions causally sufficient (barring divine intervention) for all my sinful deeds. But I can't do anything about conditions prior to my birth; hence I can't do anything about the causal consequences of those conditions, among which are my sins.[3] Augustine himself concludes the syllogism this way: "There is no blame involved when nature and necessity determine an action."[4] Causal determinism, in short, is incompatible with moral responsibility.

Helm, of course, thinks they *are* compatible. (That's his thesis, after all.) But nothing he says helps me see *how* they can be compatible. Helm's distinction between GR (responsibility before God) and HR (responsibility toward humans) is particularly unhelpful. These diverge principally because the latter "depends upon fallible human knowledge of the motivations and circum-

---

[3]For an influential development and defense of this argument, see Peter Van Inwagen, *An Essay on Free Will* (Oxford: Clarendon Press, 1983).
[4]Augustine *On Free Choice of the Will* 3.1. All quotations from this work are taken from the translation by Thomas Williams (Indianapolis: Hackett, 1993).

stances of ourselves and others" and is therefore "necessarily rough and ready" (p. 165). The problem is that additional knowledge typically leads to *diminished* responsibility.[5] If causal determinism is true, God's perfect knowledge of the "circumstances of ourselves and others" is knowledge of the very factors that undermine human responsibility. It is therefore puzzling how GR is supposed to vindicate human culpability in the face of universal determinism.

Helm's focus on one part of the larger picture leads him to endorse positions that strike me as extreme. Consider, for example, his claim that "the Augustinian account of the plight of human kind is such that people cannot want to want God" (p. 171). Is this a *biblical* as well as Augustinian position? That's hard to say, since Helm does not cite any scriptures. Romans 7 speaks of someone who cannot *do* the good but nevertheless *wants* to do it, while Philippians 2:13 concerns God's gracious work in the person who can neither will *nor* do the good on his own (but might, like Augustine himself in book 7 of the *Confessions,* desperately *want* to will the good). But I see no scriptural evidence that an inability even to *want* to want God is the universal human condition.

Indeed, there is a sense in which people cannot *help but* want to want God. After all, God made us by nature to want and find our fulfillment in him. Of course Helm would not deny this; his claim is presumably restricted to the postlapsarian human condition. But why does Helm think that the Fall *completely* effaced this orientation toward the divine? Classic theism (Augustine, Aquinas, et al.) consistently treats this orientation as *distorted* rather than *lost—* there's still that "God-shaped vacuum in every human heart," but instead of filling it with God we chase restlessly after various God-substitutes. (Even when pridefully rebelling against God, Augustine asserts, we are engaging "in a perverse imitation of God.")[6] Contrary to Helm, there is reason to believe that at some level even postlapsarian human beings may "want to want to . . . want God."

While it is obvious that I am unpersuaded by Helm's arguments, I should add that free will is one of the most enigmatic issues in all philosophy, and I am prepared to acknowledge the possibility (however small!) that compatibilism might be true after all. I also have a good deal of respect for the theological tradition Helm is representing, and I regard the Calvinist position as

---

[5]Helm himself offers an example: "Thus certain kinds of HR may require strict liability, a responsibility for a particular action X that stands even though a person did not want X to happen and took all reasonable steps not to let X happen. But it is hard to see that there is any case of GR based upon strict liability in this sense" (p. 166).

[6]Augustine *On Free Choice of the Will* 3.25.

very much of a "live option" as I wrestle with the issues covered in this book. Indeed, none of my three interlocutors seems to me to be proposing anything absolutely outrageous, from which one ought to recoil as from a serious heresy. All are responding to very real themes in the biblical witness, and doing so in a responsible way. The problem is that it's just *very difficult* to weave all these themes together into a single coherent story. That's what keeps theologians in business!

This is a problem for my coauthors, and it's a problem for me as well. My account of simple foreknowledge cannot in the end support an understanding of divine and human freedom that comes quite as close to our ordinary intuitions about free agency as Boyd's "open view," or a notion of divine providence that is quite as powerful as the one provided by Craig's Molinism, or a concept of divine grace quite so robust as the one offered by Helm's Augustinianism. I don't know how to get *everything* we want to get in just the way we want to get it—and neither do my coauthors. The most I can responsibly claim is that I can get *more* of it (at least with respect to the issues that lie at the heart of this book). The reader must judge whether this claim is borne out by the arguments.

A MIDDLE-KNOWLEDGE RESPONSE

William Lane Craig

*P*aul Helm begins his essay by specifying several scriptural "fixed points" which any adequate account of divine foreknowledge and human freedom must recognize.[1] He rightly emphasizes, against open views, God's universal foreordination (Eph 1:11). But Helm's formulation of the second point is an understatement: the *reason* people are held accountable is that they have libertarian freedom. Imagine a situation in which one succumbs to temptation. Paul's statement in 1 Corinthians 10:13 implies that in such a situation, God had provided a way of escape that one could have taken but that one failed to do so. In other words, in precisely that situation, one had the power either to succumb or to take the way out—that is to say, one had libertarian freedom. It is precisely because one failed to take the divinely provided way of escape that one is held accountable. With respect to Helm's third point, I see no reason to think that God's relations to creation are unparalleled and incomprehensible.[2]

---

[1]Namely, God's foreordination of everything that comes to pass, human accountability for one's actions and omissions, and God's unique and incomprehensible relation to the world.
[2]I cannot help suspecting that Helm makes this claim because, in the absence of middle

On a Molinist view, God's providential direction is not without parallel. When FBI agents conduct a sting operation to catch a child pornographer or drug trafficker, for example, they put the suspect in circumstances in which they have reason to believe he will freely commit a crime, and on that basis he can be arrested and prosecuted. Thus, there is neither reason nor necessity to cover one's flank by appeals to incomprehensibility of divine relations to the world.

Helm then presents three arguments why Christians ought to accept a compatibilist account of freedom, the goal being to show that divine foreknowledge is consistent with freedom so understood. Unfortunately, this stated project is misconceived. The debate between compatibilism and incompatibilism is quite independent of the problem of divine foreknowledge; and if foreknowledge is, as I think, consistent with incompatibilist freedom, then, of course, it is consistent with compatibilist freedom as well. The question is whether the incompatibilist can consistently affirm divine foreknowledge. Fortunately, some of Helm's subsidiary arguments are relevant to this issue.

His first argument, based upon the efficacy of God's saving grace, is, however, irrelevant. There is just no connection (as Calvin himself, quoted by Helm, recognized) between the question of the intrinsic efficacy of saving grace and divine foreknowledge.[3] Nevertheless, Helm's discussion does raise the question, even if we are bound in things above, what about things below? Are we free to choose among sins? This question will return to haunt Helm's doctrine of divine providence.

Helm's second argument appeals to divine perfection in order to justify the doctrine of foreknowledge. This is a powerful argument, for surely the concept of God is the concept of a greatest conceivable being. Since omniscience is a great-making property, God must be omniscient.[4] If the Principle of Bivalence holds for future contingent propositions (and some are true), then an omni-

---

knowledge, it is, indeed, "tempting to infer that in the crucifixion God 'manipulated' the crucifiers or that they were his 'puppets' " (p. 168), making Helm's position unintelligible.

[3]Someone who thinks foreknowledge and libertarian freedom are clearly consistent could nonetheless be a Calvinist when it comes to the intrinsic efficacy of saving grace, and a theological fatalist could deny that saving grace is intrinsically efficacious.

[4]Unfortunately, Helm misstates the argument, maintaining that "wherever possible one should interpret the term *omniscience* when applied to God as generously as possible" (p. 174). The concept of omniscience is an independently defined notion that does not vary in application to various subjects. *Omniscience* just means knowledge of only and all truths. The question is whether God is omniscient or not. We are not at liberty to change the meaning of *omniscient* just because "God" is the subject of predication, as the revisionist thinks. The point, then, is that God's being the greatest conceivable being gives us good reason for thinking that "God is omniscient" is true, not for massaging the meaning of *omniscient*.

scient deity must possess foreknowledge of future contingents. Helm's further claim that omniscience "is most at home" with compatibilism involves a huge leap in his argument, however. Why is this the case? Does Helm just assume that foreknowledge is based on foreordination? What is wrong with the view of simple foreknowledge?

Rather than address these questions, Helm turns to a potential problem for his view: God's foreknowledge of evil actions. How can God's foreknowledge of such acts be based on his foreordination without God's being the author of evil? Since the Molinist has an answer to this question, Helm turns to a critique of the doctrine of middle knowledge.

Helm mentions two areas of concern. The first involves a passing reference to an objection voiced by Robert Adams. But as this objection has been adequately answered in the literature and Helm does nothing to advance the discussion, we may leave it to the reader to pursue.[5] The second objection consists of merely a question: how does God actualize states of affairs involving libertarian actions, especially sinful actions? Now a question is not an objection, and one is rather surprised by Helm's abruptly terminating the discussion by concluding that Molinism is not a viable solution. In fact, the question is easy to answer, given divine middle knowledge. Imagine, using Helm's analogy, that God has before him via his natural knowledge two videos representing two possible worlds—one in which Adam sins in the Garden of Eden and one in which he does not. Suppose that God knows via his middle knowledge that Adam, if placed in the Garden, would sin. In that case God cannot actualize the video in which Adam does not sin. For if God were to play the video up to the time of Adam's decision, then Adam would freely sin. The video in which Adam does not sin thus represents an infeasible world for God. But as for the other video, that world is easy to actualize. If God knows that Adam would freely sin if placed in the Garden, then in order to actualize that world, all God has to do is place Adam in the Garden! Far from being difficult, we ourselves accomplish this sort of feat all the time. Think of the FBI sting operation. Although the criminals arrested through such operations sometimes complain of "entrapment," the courts have ruled that if the suspect did not have to commit the crime under the circumstances, then he is culpable for his action. So long as the circumstances are freedom-permitting, the person in

---

[5]See literature and discussion in my book *Divine Foreknowledge and Human Freedom,* Brill's Studies in Intellectual History 19 (Leiden: Brill, 1991), pp. 146-67; for a popular-level treatment, see my book *The Only Wise God* (Grand Rapids, Mich.: Baker, 1987; Eugene, Ore.: Wipf & Stock, 2000), pp. 141-44.

them is determined neither by the operative secondary causes nor by God and so acts with libertarian freedom. Of course, since the circumstances themselves may be the result of contingent actions, God will have to weakly actualize them as well. But that is no problem for an omniscient deity.

Contrast Helm's own account of God's foreknowledge of evil acts. Helm wants to help himself to God's permissive will to explain how such acts fit into God's divine plan. Now on a Molinist scheme, divine permission makes sense, for God knows what libertarian agents would do were he to permit them to act freely. But without middle knowledge, how can God know what creatures would do were he to withdraw his steadying hand? Helm's answer must be that, given compatibilism, the creatures' decisions, while not determined by God, are determined by secondary causes, from which God can infer them. I have two worries about this proposed solution. First, it severely compromises the Calvinistic doctrine of divine providence, since there are events in the world not directly determined by God. Indeed, I wonder, does Helm have any doctrine of divine concurrence, according to which everything that happens is caused by God? Second, since free creatures' decisions are indirectly caused by God, he is still implicated in evil. On Helm's view the circumstances in which an evil act is perpetrated are causally sufficient for that act and are themselves directly caused by God (unless they include another evil act). Thus, just as I am responsible for hitting the eight ball into the corner pocket when I strike the cue ball with the intention of hitting the eight ball into the corner pocket, so God is responsible for evil actions of creatures when he sets up causally determining circumstances that make such actions inevitable for the creatures. Helm cannot say that God did not intend for those evil acts to occur, for this would contradict God's universal providence. They are planned by God and, while not directly caused by God, they are indirectly causally determined by God, thereby implicating God in evil. Permission is exonerating only if the immediate cause of the action is a libertarian agent who freely chooses to perform that action.

Finally, Helm's third argument endorses theological fatalism. What strange bedfellows these openness and Reformed theologians be! Together they oppose the compatibility of divine foreknowledge and human freedom. Helm provides no account of temporal necessity; but he offers two reasons for thinking God's past beliefs to be temporally necessary. First, if we could falsify God's beliefs, we should have the power to bring it about that God did not exist. Second, no one can now bring it about that God did not possess a certain belief in the past. Both these objections are based on confusions. Our ability to act otherwise than how God knows we shall implies neither the ability to falsify God's belief nor the ability to bring it about that God did not have that belief.[6] It implies merely that we have the ability to act in ways other than those in which we shall act; and if we were to act in those ways, God's past beliefs would have been different than they were. Helm gives a passing nod to this Ockhamist-Molinist solution and, while finding no fault with it, insists that we have already found reason to reject Molinism. Not only is that not true (Helm merely posed a question), but the solution is independent of middle knowledge, as is evident from William Ockham's espousal of it long before Luis de Molina crafted the doctrine of middle knowledge. God's beliefs about the future, though past, are counterfactually dependent on the occurrence of those foreknown events and so are not temporally necessary, as any adequate account of this modality reveals. Hence, Helm's argument for theological (and logical) fatalism is unsound.

---

[6]The key notion here is the ambiguous idea of "bringing about." For an extensive discussion of the different senses of this expression, see Thomas P. Flint, *Divine Providence,* Cornell Studies in the Philosophy of Religion (Ithaca, N.Y.: Cornell University Press, 1998), pp. 148-58.

GLOSSARY

A-data. Helm's abbreviation for "all things" data, or Scripture references which suggest that God knows and ordains all things. *See also* D-data.

accidental necessity. What must be the case, given some contingent (or "accidental") fact. For example, it is now necessary that Smith will not graduate this year, since he failed all his classes. Because he *could* have passed his classes, and because the impossibility of his graduating on time depends solely on the contingent fact that he did *not* pass his classes, the fact that he can no longer graduate is only *accidentally* necessary. All hard facts about the past are supposed to be accidentally necessary on the grounds that, though it may once have been possible for them not to have been the case (if things had gone differently), since they are now the case, it is no longer possible for them not to be the case. *See also* logical necessity; natural necessity; temporal necessity.

actualization, weak. To bring about something that was previously only "possible" or "potential," but do so indirectly. According to Alvin Plantinga, who coined the term, God can weakly actualize a free choice *C* of a person *P* by creating the state of affairs in which *P* will freely do *C*. Weak actualization is contrasted with strong actualization where God directly actualizes *C*. *See also* actualize.

actualize. To bring about something that was previously only "possible" or "potential." To say that "God actualizes a particular possible world" is just to say that he makes that possible world actual. *See also* actualization, weak.

antecedent. In a conditional statement, the antecedent is the first portion of the statement (the "if" clause). E.g., the antecedent of "If you offer me one million dollars, then I will accept" is "you offer me one million dollars." *See also* consequent.

backtracking counterfactual. A counterfactual statement in which the truth of the antecedent requires that the past be different than it was: e.g., "If I were to pray for my son, he would not have been killed in the wreck."

Boethianism, Boethian solution. The view that God does not exist in time. Most classic theologians, such as Augustine, Anselm and Aquinas, held this position, but the Late Roman philosopher and statesman Boethius (c. 480-528) was particularly influential in its formulation. Boethius applied this conception of God to the problem of divine foreknowledge and human freedom: if God is not in time, he does not *fore*know anything, and the problem dissolves.

causa sui. Latin for "cause of itself" or "self-caused." The term is commonly used to answer the question "Where did God come from?" The answer is that God is *causa sui;* he is self-caused. Some have taken this to mean merely that the existence of God does not need to be causally explained. Others have taken this to mean that literally God causes himself.

compatibilism. The idea that freedom is compatible with necessity, e.g., person *P* is still "free" with respect to choice *C* even though *C* is necessary. This term is most often used to express the idea that freedom is compatible with the kind of necessity entailed by causal determinism (*see* freedom, compatibilist). But this term can also be used to refer to the position of someone who holds that freedom is compatible with divine foreknowledge. Helm is a compatibilist with regard to determinism. Craig and Hunt are compatibilists with regard to foreknowledge. *See also* incompatibilism.

conceptualist model of God's knowledge. A theory of divine knowledge that construes God's knowledge, even his knowledge of future events, as analogous to innate ideas: i.e., God knows future events because he knows all truths and because there are truths about future events.

consequent. In a conditional statement, the consequent is the second portion of the statement (the "then" clause). E.g., the consequent of "If you offer me one million dollars, then I will accept" is "I will accept." *See also* antecedent.

counterfactual knowledge. Knowledge of true counterfactuals. *See also* counterfactuals.

counterfactuals. Hypothetical statements in the subjunctive mood: e.g., "If you were honest, you would confess." *See also* might-counterfactual; would-counterfactual.

counterfactuals of creaturely freedom. Counterfactual propositions in the following form: "If person S were in state of affairs C, S would freely do (or choose) A" where C specifies the whole history of the world prior to the time of the choice. Counterfactual propositions of creaturely freedom therefore express the content of a free choice: e.g., "If you were to offer me one million dollars, I would (freely) accept." *See also* counterfactuals.

D-data. Helm's abbreviation for "dialogue" data, or Scripture references which suggest that God interacts with his creation in very human-like ways. *See also*

A-data.

disquotation principle. The principle that the truth conditions of a statement are just what the statement describes: e.g., the statement "Snow is white" is true if and only if snow is, in fact, white.

efficacious grace. Grace that is sufficiently powerful to achieve its intended, salvific effect.

enthymeme. An argument with one or more unstated but implicit steps, whether in the conclusion or in the premises: e.g., "Socrates lived in Athens; therefore Socrates lived in Greece." This argument is an enthymeme because it involves the unstated premise that Athens is located in Greece.

Evodius's argument. Hunt's label for the argument, as formulated in Augustine's dialogue *On Free Choice of the Will,* that divine foreknowledge is incompatible with human freedom. Augustine puts the argument in the mouth of his dialogue partner, Evodius, hence the term.

fallacy of affirming the consequent. A logical fallacy in which the consequent of a conditional is affirmed and, on the basis of that affirmation, the antecedent is affirmed. For example, "If it rains, the streets will be wet. The streets are wet. Therefore, it has rained."

fatalism. The doctrine that all things happen according to necessity.

Fixed Past Principle. A principle stating that we do not have the power to act in such a way that the past would have been different than if we had acted in that way.

free knowledge. God's knowledge of truths known by him only logically posterior to his creative decree. *See also* middle knowledge; natural knowledge.

freedom, compatibilist. Freedom that is compatible with some version or other of causal determinism.

freedom, Frankfurtian. A conception of freedom that rejects the Principle of Alternate Possibilities. *See also* Principle of Alternate Possibilities.

freedom, incompatibilist. Freedom that is the outcome of an uncaused or self-caused decision or choice. Also often called "libertarian freedom." *See also* libertarian freedom.

future contingents. Future events that do not have to happen.

grounding objection. The claim that there are no true counterfactuals about free decisions because there is nothing to make such statements true.

hard facts. Facts that have been settled or determined by the course of events. Any fact that is genuinely and strictly about the past (e.g., "Yesterday Smith listened to Berg's Violin Concerto") is a hard fact about the past. *See also* soft facts.

incompatibilism. The idea that freedom is incompatible with necessity (e.g., person *P* cannot be "free" with respect to choice *C* if *C* is necessary). This term is most often used to express the idea that freedom is incompatible with the kind of necessity entailed by causal determinism (*see* freedom, incompatibilist). But this term can also be used to refer to the position of someone who holds that freedom is incompatible with divine foreknowledge. Craig, Hunt and Boyd are incompatibilists with regard to determinism. Helm and Boyd are incompatibilists with regard to foreknowledge. *See also* compatibilism.

intramundane models of causation. Accounts of causation that apply only to changes in things which exist in space and time.

Lewis-Stalnaker semantics. The most important theory of subjunctive conditionals/counterfactuals, so named after the contemporary American philosophers David Lewis and Robert Stalnaker, who are responsible for seminal versions of this theory. On their account, a counterfactual of the form "If *P* were the case, *Q* would be the case" is to be understood as asserting that *Q* is the case in some possible world(s), namely, the world(s) in which *P* is the case which is (are) most like (or "closest to") the actual world. *See also* counterfactuals; standard semantics for counterfactuals; subjunctive conditional.

libertarian freedom. A position on the nature and possibility of free agency, under which freedom is incompatible with causal determinism and there exist genuine instances of free agency. Most libertarians (Hunt is an exception) believe this involves commitment to the Principle of Alternate Possibilities. *See also* Principle of Alternate Possibilities; freedom, Frankfurtian.

logical necessity. The strongest form of necessity. If something is logically necessary, there is no possibility at all of it being different than it is. That "nothing is larger than itself" and that "Smith is either a vegetable or a nonvegetable" are both logically necessary. Logical necessities are true no matter how the world happens to be arranged. *See also* accidental necessity; natural necessity; temporal necessity.

mechanistic event-causation. When the cause of an event E_1 is some other event E_0 that, together with the relevant causal laws, necessitates the occurrence of E_1. Such causation is "mechanistic" inasmuch as E_1 follows E_0 automatically, like the workings of a mechanism. *See also* teleological agent-causation.

middle knowledge. God's knowledge of all true counterfactuals about what creatures would freely do under any circumstances logically prior to his creative decree. *See also* free knowledge; natural knowledge.

might-counterfactual. A counterfactual proposition detailing what an agent *might* do in a particular situation: e.g., "If you were to offer me a job at Yale, I *might* take it." *See also* would-counterfactual.

Molinism. The school of thought, taking its name from Luis de Molina (1535-1600), a Spanish Jesuit, that seeks to reconcile divine sovereignty and human freedom by means of the doctrine of middle knowledge.

natural knowledge. God's knowledge of all necessary truths, including all possibilities logically prior to his creative decree. *See also* free knowledge; middle knowledge.

natural necessity. What must be the case, given the nature of things. That an unsupported stone will *fall* is naturally necessary, given the law of gravity; that it will not recite the Gettysburg Address on its way down is also naturally necessary, given that it's a *stone* and not a person. *See also* accidental necessity; logical necessity; temporal necessity.

necessity. *See* accidental necessity; logical necessity; natural necessity; temporal necessity.

Neo-Molinism. Boyd's newly adopted term for his brand of open theism. He uses this term because the open theist, he claims, can embrace God's knowledge of would-counterfactuals *(see)* and might-counterfactuals *(see)*. Of course, this usage of the term *Molinist* is not likely to be embraced by "classical" Molinists (like Craig).

Neo-Platonism. A philosophical movement founded by Plotinus (A.D. 204-270). Based on Platonic principles, Neo-Platonism understands all reality to be dependent on and oriented toward a supreme reality called the "One." Many early Christian theologians, like Augustine, found this the most congenial pagan philosophical system and drew upon it in their own theorizing about God.

nonstandard resolution of vagueness. *See* special resolution for vagueness.

Ockhamism, Ockhamist solution. An approach to the problem of divine foreknowledge versus human freedom, first conceived by William Ockham (c. 1285-1349), a Franciscan theologian and logician. According to Ockham, the fact that God knew one hundred years ago what Smith will do tomorrow is only a "soft" fact about the past; consequently, God's foreknowledge does not render Smith's future action necessary. *See also* hard facts; soft facts; Thomistic Ockhamism.

perceptualist model of God's knowledge. A theory about divine knowledge that construes God's knowledge, even knowledge of future events, as analogous to sense perception; i.e., God knows future events because he "sees" what will happen.

possible worlds. Different ways reality might have been. Each "world" represents a total description of reality, and each of these descriptions differs from one another. When God creates, he makes one possible world "actual."

practical belief. A belief about *what to do*. A practical belief is directed toward an optative proposition of the form "Would that I might do such-and-such." *See also* propositional belief.

Principle of Alternate Possibilities (PAP). The idea that free agency, in the sense presupposed by moral responsibility, entails the agent's ability to do otherwise. One's choosing *A* is "free" in this sense if and only if one *could have* chosen other than *A*. Divine foreknowledge supposedly conflicts with human freedom on the grounds that a divinely foreknown action would not satisfy this principle. This principle is sometimes called the Principle of Alternative Possibilities.

Principle of Bivalence. A principle which states that all declarative utterances (or propositions) are either true or false.

principle of simplicity. Other things being equal, the explanation that invokes the fewest factors is to be preferred.

propositional belief. A belief about *what is true*. A propositional belief is directed toward a declarative proposition asserting that such-and-such is the case (e.g., "London is the capital of England"). *See also* practical belief.

Q.E.D. Abbreviation for *quod erat demonstrandum*, Latin for "which was to be proved."

soft facts. Facts that have not yet been settled or determined by the course of events. Some facts that are grammatically in the past tense are not genuinely about the past (e.g., "Yesterday it was true that Smith will go to church next Sunday"), and some that are genuinely about the past are not strictly about the past (e.g., "Yesterday Smith listened to Berg's Violin Concerto for the last time"). Such facts are merely soft facts about the past. *See also* hard facts.

special resolution for vagueness. A resolution which holds that in the case of backtracking counterfactuals, a nonstandard resolution of vagueness must be used to determine which worlds belong in the sphere of most similar worlds in which the antecedent is true. This resolution of vagueness must be used because such counterfactuals envision some difference in the past if the consequent clause of the counterfactual is true. For example, the truth of the proposition "If the time traveler were not to activate his time machine, he would not have appeared, as he did, in ancient Egypt" requires that the worlds most similar to the actual world in which the antecedent is true are worlds in which the past history of that world differs from that of the actual world.

standard resolution for vagueness. A resolution which holds that in the standard semantics for counterfactual propositions, a counterfactual is true if and only if its consequent clause is true in every possible world in the sphere of worlds most similar to the actual world in which the antecedent clause is true. In determining how worlds are to be ranked in terms of similarity to the actual world, one customarily resolves the vagueness involved in the antecedent by stipulating that the most similar antecedent-permitting worlds will have the same history as the actual world up until the time of the antecedent. So, e.g., the proposition "If Goldwater had been elected, he would have won the Vietnam War" is true if and only if Goldwater wins the Vietnam War in every world in the sphere of possible worlds most similar to the actual world up until the time of the 1964 election where Goldwater wins the election.

standard semantics for counterfactuals. Specifies that counterfactual propositions have the following form: they remain constant with regard to the past, and they inquire as to the changes that occur in possible worlds most similar to our own in which the antecedent is true. *See also* backtracking counterfactual; Lewis-Stalnaker semantics.

subjunctive conditional. A conditional statement in the subjunctive mood. The category of subjunctive conditionals includes the category of counterfactuals. In other words, counterfactuals are a subset of subjunctive conditionals. *See also* counterfactuals.

tachyon. A theoretical particle that is so fast it "moves backward in time," reversing the order of cause and effect. There is no consensus among physicists that tachyons actually exist.

teleological agent-causation. When the cause of an event E_1 is an agent A who brings about E_1 by intentionally doing something. Such causation is "teleological" inasmuch as intentional action aims at an end (or *telos*) that the agent has in mind and that the agent believes would be served by performing the action. *See also* mechanistic event-causation.

temporal necessity. The kind of necessity alleged to characterize events in the past. *See also* accidental necessity; logical necessity; natural necessity.

Thomistic Ockhamism. A version of the Ockhamist solution developed by philosopher Linda Zagzebski, who draws on some of Thomas Aquinas's theories about God and divine omniscience to show how God's knowing one hundred years ago what Smith will do tomorrow might constitute a mere soft fact about the past. *See also* Ockhamism.

truth-maker maximalism. The doctrine that every true statement has a truth-maker.

truth-makers. That by virtue of which a statement is true.

would-counterfactual. A counterfactual proposition detailing what an agent *would* do in a particular situation: e.g., "If you were to offer me one million dollars, I *would* take it." *See also* might-counterfactual.

Zeno's paradoxes. Paradoxes formulated by Zeno, a student of the Greek philosopher Parmenides (fifth century B.C.), to show that motion is only appearance and not reality. Zeno's most famous paradox is that of Achilles and the tortoise, cited in this book as an example of an argument that can be reasonably regarded as fallacious even if it's hard to say what the fallacy is.

Subject Index

Adams, Marilyn McCord, 82n
Adams, Robert, 141n, 175, 204
alternate possibilities, principle of, 86, 88-90, 113, 116, 151, 212
Anselm, St., 69, 74n, 80
Aquinas, Thomas, 11, 69, 74n, 79-80, 89n, 151-52n, 173, 182n, 184n, 200
Arminian(s), 11, 42, 45, 156
Arminianism, 44, 64
Arminius, Jacobus, 11, 70, 157, 159
Augustine, St., 9, 11, 69, 72, 73n, 74, 78-82, 87-91, 157n, 161, 170-71, 176n, 180n, 184, 196, 199-200n
Basinger, David, 100n, 101
Beckwith, Francis, 42n
bivalence, principle of, 56-57, 203, 212
Boethius, 69, 74n, 78-80, 186n
Bonhoeffer, Dietrich, 40n
Brant, Dale Eric, 85n
Brueckner, Anthony, 85n
Boyd, Gregory, 10, 12, 27n, 46-48, 49-52, 54-56, 58-59, 61, 63-64, 149, 155,
Calcidius, 35n
Calvin, John, 11, 37n, 38n, 59, 70, 161-62n, 184n, 196
Calvinism, 60, 193, 205
Calvinist(s), 11, 33, 42, 45, 78-79, 147, 194

Carson, D. A., 126n
Clarke, Adam, 35n
Clement of Alexandria, 37n
counterfactual(s), 111, 153, 155, 208, 213
  backtracking, 111-12, 207
  of creaturely freedom, 111, 139, 142-44, 156-57, 208
  knowledge of, 122, 124-25
  might, 147, 210
Craig, William Lane, 10-12, 67n, 81, 82n, 84n, 85n, 104, 117, 125-26, 144, 149, 150, 155, 156-58, 159, 190-91, 200
data
  all things (A-data), 62-63, 207
  dialogue (D-data), 62-63, 208
design, argument from, 167
determinism, 102, 169n, 179-80, 195, 197
  Calvinistic, 58-59
  causal, 189, 200
  noncausal, 130
  physical, 180
  universal causal, 49, 102, 197, 199-200
disquotation principle, 142, 209
divine cognition, 133
  perceptualist model, 133, 211

  conceptualist model, 133, 155, 208
Edwards, Jonathan, 74n, 162n, 196
evangelical(ism), 10, 12
Evodius, 72-74, 81, 87, 209
fatalism, 113, 117, 126, 128, 130-32, 150, 182, 209
  theological, 205
Fechner, G. T., 35n
Fischer, John Martin, 75n, 83, 83n, 85n, 90n, 116n, 188n
Flint, Thomas P., 66n, 79n, 113n, 125, 140n, 161n, 206n
foreknowledge, 10, 13-14, 37, 48-49, 51, 55, 66, 68-69, 71, 77, 81, 83, 89-91, 96, 98-99, 111, 115, 125, 163, 180, 205
  augmented, 67-68
  Augustinian-Calvinist view, 10-11, 116, 135, 157-59
  classical view, 29-30, 34-35, 37, 39-42, 47-48, 52, 61-64, 104, 192, 200
  diminished, 66-67, 78, 105-6
  exhaustive, 11, 14-17, 20-22, 26, 30-32, 34, 37, 42-43, 48-50, 52-53, 57, 71, 92, 104-5, 107, 190-91n
  Molinist view, 10, 57
  simple, 10-11, 29n, 59,

67-68, 101, 117, 125,
134, 135, 147, 152, 200
Frankfurt, Harry, 89, 89n,
130
Freddoso, Alfred J., 66n,
82n, 110n, 132, 156n
free will, 53, 74, 77, 87-88
defense, 181
freedom, 72, 78, 82, 90-91,
101, 105, 115, 122, 157,
187, 205
compatibilistic, 9, 54, 87,
102, 117, 162n, 169,
172, 176-78, 189, 195,
202, 208-9
incompatibilist, 170, 172,
174, 178, 184, 186,
189, 195-96, 203, 209
indeterministic, 156,
157-58, 162
libertarian, 9, 11, 64, 107,
109, 113, 143, 147,
161, 175, 190-91, 193,
198, 202, 210
Geach, Peter, 66n
Geisler, Norman, 37n
Girardeau, J. L., 162n
grounding objection, 154,
209
Haack, Susan, 128n
Harnack, Adolf, 63
Hasker, William, 67n, 75n,
85n, 96n, 97-100, 117-18,
137n, 141n, 181
Helm, Paul, 11-12, 49, 50,
54, 58, 67n, 104, 149,
190-91, 193, 197-98, 201-6
Hibbard, Billy, 35n
Hoffman, Joshua, 82n
Hume, David, 167, 168n
Hunt, David, 10, 12, 83n,
93n, 97n, 101n, 104,
105-6, 109-10, 114,
116-17, 131, 190
Jaeger, W., 37n
Jones, Major, 35n
Kant, Immanuel, 17

Kapitan, Tomis, 92n, 93n
Kretzmann, Norman, 67n,
89n
Kvanvig, Jonathan, 82n
La Croix, Richard R., 92n
language, 191
anthropomorphic, 23,
37-41, 47, 54, 59, 62,
106, 147, 192,
metaphorical, 191-92
symbolic, 191
Leftow, Brian, 67n
Lequier, Jules, 35n
Lewis, David, 97n, 154
Lewis-Stalnaker semantics,
154, 210
literalism, 58, 63
Luther, Martin, 59, 70, 79
Martyr, Justin, 69
McCabe, Lorenzo, 35n
McLelland, J. C., 37n
middle-knowledge, 10-11,
58, 64, 101, 122-23,
132-35, 143-44, 149, 152,
156, 175, 204-5, 210
Molina, Luis de, 11, 59, 66n,
122, 156n, 159, 206, 211
Molinism, 53-54, 59-60, 144,
152, 159, 178, 184, 189,
203-4
Mormon theology, 58
Morris, Thomas V., 130
Muller, Richard, 157n
Mulligan, Kevin, 140n
naturalism, scientific, 87
Neo-Platonism, 71, 211
Ockham, William, 74n, 82,
84, 85, 90, 196n, 206, 211
Ockhamism, 86, 211
Oden, Thomas, 35n,
omnipotence, 42, 173, 177
omniscience, 25, 42-43, 48,
50, 55-56, 65, 96, 112,
118, 120, 124, 138, 162,
173-75, 177, 183, 186,
187-88
Boethian timeless, 52

open(ness) view (theism),
9-10, 14, 17, 19, 23-24,
27-29, 35, 37, 40-43,
45-46, 53, 58-59, 61-64,
104-6n, 144, 202
Origen, 37n
Pfeiderer, Otto, 35n
Pike, Nelson, 75n, 77n, 82n
Pinnock, Clark, 72n, 94n,
102, 181
Plantinga, Alvin, 66n, 82n,
84n, 85n, 140n, 143, 154,
175n
Platonism, 71, 211
Process thought (theol-
ogy), 43
Purtill, Richard, 66n
Putnam, Hillary, 83
Ratzsch, Del, 125, 198n
Ravizza, Mark, 116n
Reichenbach, Bruce, 82n
Restall, Greg, 142n
Rosenkrantz, Gary, 82n
Russell, Bertrand, 141
science, 18, 47, 49, 198
chaos theory, 18, 49
physics, 18
quantum indeterminacy,
18, 49, 125
Sanders, John, 39n, 97n
Schleiermacher, Friedrich,
120
Scotus, Jon Duns, 74n
Senor, Thomas D., 89n
Simons, Peter, 140n
simplicity, principle of, 162,
198, 212
Smith, Barry, 140n
sola scriptura, 39
Sproul, R. C., 43n
Strimple, Robert, 35n,
Stump, Eleonore, 67n, 89n,
90n
Swinburne, Richard, 66n,
162n, 173, 198n
Talbott, Thomas, 82n
Taylor, Richard, 92n

truth, correspondence theory of, 140
truth makers
    maximalism, 142, 213
    theory of, 140-42, 213
Turretin, Francis, 162n
Van Inwagen, Peter, 165n,

199n
Verbeke, G., 35n
Ward, Keith, 182n
Ware, Bruce, 32, 37n, 192n
Warfield, Ted A., 84n, 85n
Wertheimer, Roger, 111n
Wesley, John, 70

Widerker, David, 83n, 85n
Wierenga, Edward, 66n,
    82n
Wittgenstein, Ludwig, 141
Zagaebski, Linda, 83, 90n
Zemach, Eddy M., 83n
Zeno, 80-81, 114, 213

Scripture Index

Genesis
3:9-11, *58*
6:3, *21*
6:6, *25, 146*
15:13, *16*
15:13-15, *14*
18:21, *58*
22:12, *31, 146*
40, *67*
50:20, *57*

Exodus
3:18, *29*
4:1, *29*
4:5, *29*
4:7-9, *146*
4:8, *29*
4:9, *29*
13:17, *30, 39, 146, 191*
16:4, *146*
32:14, *27, 35, 38*
32:32, *36*

Numbers
11:1-2, *27*
14:12-20, *27*
16:20-35, *27*
16:41-48, *27*
22:38—23:17, *40*
23:19, *39, 40, 191*

Deuteronomy
8:2, *31*
8:21, *31*
9:13-14, *27, 38*

9:18-20, *27, 38*
9:25, *27, 35, 38*
10:17-19, *192*
13:1-3, *31*
18:22, *123*

Judges
3:4, *31*
10:13-15, *27*

1 Samuel
2:27-31, *35*
13:13, *25*
13:13-14, *39*
15, *40*
15:10, *25*
15:11, *40, 146*
15:24-25, *40*
15:29, *39, 191*
15:30, *40*
15:35, *25, 146*
16:18-23, *27*
23:6-10, *122*
31:1-6, *57*

2 Samuel
24:17-25, *27*

1 Kings
13:1-2, *14, 18*
21:21-29, *34*
21:27-29, *26*

2 Kings
13:3-5, *27*
20:1, *35*
20:1-7, *27*

20:6, *35*

1 Chronicles
10:8-12, *57*
10:14, *57*

2 Chronicles
12:5-8, *27, 35*
19:7, *192*
32:31, *31*

Job
34:19, *192*
42:2, *14*

Psalms
44:21, *19*
69:28, *36*
106:23, *35, 38*
139:1-6, *19*
139:4, *68*
139:6, *125*

Proverbs
16:4, *21*

Isaiah
5, *23*
5:1-5, *146*
5:4, *49*
14:27, *14*
38:1-5, *123*
41:22-23, *67*
45:1, *14, 18*
46:9-10, *68*
46:9-11, *14, 15*
46:10, *29, 191*

46:11, *14*
48:3, *14, 24*
48:3-5, *14, 16*
55:4-5, *192*
63:10, *28, 193*

Jeremiah
3, *24, 50*
3:6-7, *23, 24, 146*
3:7, *191*
3:19-20, *24, 146,*
  191
15:6, *40, 191*
18, *32*
18:1-10, *18, 38, 39*
18:4-10, *51*
18:7-11, *146*
19:5, *23, 50*
26, *33*
26:2-3, *33, 38, 146*
26:3, *30, 37, 146*
26:13, *33, 34, 38,*
  156
26:19, *146*
38:17-18, *123*

Ezekiel
4:9-15, *35*
12:3, *30, 146*
18:23, *28, 192*
18:32, *28, 192*
22:29-31, *146*
22:30-31, *27*
24:14, *40, 191*
26:7-21, *14*
33:11, *28, 192*

Hosea
3, *43*
11:1, *21*

Joel
2:12-13, *33*
2:13-14, *38*

Amos
7:1-6, *35, 123*

Jonah
3:1-10, *123*
3:9, *36*
3:10, *36, 146*
4:2, *33, 38*

Zechariah
8:14, *40, 191*

Matthew
2:15, *21*
6:10, *45*
10:30, *41*
12:40, *30*
16:21, *30*
16:21-23, *20*
17:27, *123*
26, *67*
26:24, *28, 123*
26:25, *83*
26:33, *19*
26:34, *14, 19*
26:35, *19*
26:39, *30*
28:20, *45*

Mark
12:14, *192*
14:30, *56*

Luke
1:18-22, *19*
1:59-64, *19*
7:30, *193*
22:24-27, *20, 43*

John
1:18, *39*
2:19, *30*
3:16, *28, 191, 192*
3:16-18, *28*
6:44, *193*
6:64, *14, 20*
6:65, *193*
6:70-71, *14*
13:18-19, *14*
15:22, *123*

15:24, *123*
17:12, *14, 21*
18:36, *123*
19:28-29, *14, 21*
19:34-37, *14, 21*
21:6, *123*
21:15-19, *20*
21:17, *61*

Acts
2:23, *14, 21, 30, 133, 166,*
  179
4:27-28, *14, 21, 30, 133*
7:51, *28, 193*
10:34, *192*
10:38, *45*
17:26, *18*
17:27, *18, 28*
17:30, *28*
27:24, *156*
27:31, *156*

Romans
1:24-27, *21*
2:10-11, *192*
7, *199*
8:17, *45*
8:18, *45*
8:28, *14, 27, 46, 61*
8:35-39, *45*
9:15-21, *53*
9:22, *21*

1 Corinthians
2:8, *56, 57, 134,*
  139
4:5, *165*
4:7, *198*
10:13, *201*
12:3, *193*

Galatians
4:4, *134*

Ephesians
1:11, *14, 46, 60, 201*
2:8, *193*

3:9-11, *134*
4:30, *28, 193*
5:25-27, *20, 43*
6:9, *192*

Philippians
2:5-8, *43*
2:13, *199*
4:7-9, *45*
4:15, *20*

1 Timothy
2:3-4, *28*

2:4, *192*
4:10, *28, 192*

Hebrews
3:8, *28, 193*
3:15, *28, 193*
4:7, *28, 193*
4:13, *60*
6:18, *30*

1 Peter
1:17, *192*
1:20, *14, 134*

2 Peter
1:2, *124*
3:9, *28, 151, 192*

1 John
2:2, *192*
3:8, *45*

Revelation
3:5, *36*
13:8, *30*
22:18-19, *36*